THE MATTER OF THE PAGE

Publication of this volume has been made possible, in part,
through the generous support and enduring vision of
WARREN G. MOON.

The Matter of the Page

ESSAYS IN SEARCH OF ANCIENT
AND MEDIEVAL
AUTHORS

SHANE BUTLER

THE UNIVERSITY OF WISCONSIN PRESS

The University of Wisconsin Press
1930 Monroe Street, 3rd Floor
Madison, Wisconsin 53711-2059
uwpress.wisc.edu

3 Henrietta Street
London WCE 8LU, England
eurospanbookstore.com

1   3   5   4   2

Printed in the United States of America

Library of Congress Cataloging-in-Publication Data
Butler, Shane, 1970–
The matter of the page : essays in search of ancient and
medieval authors / Shane Butler.
p.   cm.—(Wisconsin studies in classics)
Includes bibliographical references and index.
ISBN 978-0-299-24824-6 (pbk.: alk. paper)
ISBN 978-0-299-24823-9 (e-book)
1. Classical literature—Criticism, Textual.
2. Literature, Medieval—Criticism, Textual.
3. Authorship.
I. Title.   II. Series: Wisconsin studies in classics.
PA3521.B88   2011
880.091—dc22
2010011574

For

EMMA

and

LEO

CONTENTS

ACKNOWLEDGMENTS

Versions or portions of this book's individual chapters have been heard by the following audiences, who are thanked collectively for their corrections and suggestions: Seminar on the History of Material Texts, University of Pennsylvania (introduction, chapters 1 and 6); Classics Colloquium, Bryn Mawr College (chapter 3); Department of Classics, UCLA (chapter 3); Classics Colloquium, Columbia University (chapters 3 and 6); "Technologies of Writing from Antiquity to Early Modern Europe," Conference at the University of Pennsylvania, March 28-9, 2003 (chapter 4); Third Penn-Leiden Colloquium on Ancient Values, Leiden University, June 3-6, 2004 (chapter 5); "Invisible Cities," Conference at Stanford University, February 11-12, 2005 (chapter 5); "Forms of Address," Annual Conference of the English Institute, Harvard University, October 20-22, 2006 (chapter 1); special lecture series for the Opera Institute's production of Monteverdi's *Orfeo*, California State University, Long Beach, March 10, 2008 (chapter 1). I would also like to thank, again collectively, my wonderful colleagues at the University of California, Los Angeles, both inside and outside Classics. Many libraries have contributed to the making of this book, but I would like to extend special thanks to those of UCLA and of the American Academy in Rome.

Of this book's many single debts, the ones owed to the following require named thanks here: David Blank, Carmela Vircillo Franklin, Joseph Farrell, Sander Goldberg, Sean Keilen, Kathryn Morgan, Alex Purves, Peter Stallybrass, Mario Telò, James Thacker, and Carolyn Williams. Very special thanks to James I. Porter and to James Tatum for their tireless help and encouragement, without which this book would never have been published. I cannot thank by name the careful and thoughtful anonymous readers of my manuscript, but wherever possible, I have used their comments and queries to make this a better book. I would also like to thank the editors of this series, especially Patricia Rosenmeyer, as well as senior acquisitions editor Raphael Kadushin.

I should note that a shorter version of chapter 1, "The Backward Glance," appeared with the same title in *Arion* 17.2 (Fall 2009). No other part of this book has been published before now.

My dedicatees have shown love and friendship to an author; in the following essays, I shall try to imitate their example.

THE MATTER OF THE PAGE

INTRODUCTION

PRESENTING THE AUTHOR

More than four decades have now passed since Roland Barthes announced "The Death of the Author."[1] Others had anticipated this obituary, and many have repeated it, although precise emphases have varied: authorial intent is unrecoverable or irrelevant; meaning is constituted by readers, or by communities thereof; the literary text is an instantiation of the social text; any of a number of things, some of them conspicuously unauthored, may be read as texts, and even as literature; what we call an "author" is really our projection of the "author-function" we require for the work of interpretation.[2] I shall not rehearse the myriad ways in which these moves have been salutary and liberating, including for this scholar (and author!), born after Barthes's essay and raised to keep his authors safely buried and his attention elsewhere. If, however, this book makes an implicit case for resuscitating the author (or at least of reviving the habit of talking about her as a real person), it does so in the confidence that the author's return, at this point, is scarcely likely to make us forget what we learned during her death.

Why do I feel a need to bring her back, here and now? The germ of this book lies in the many years I spent living with an artist, from whom I learned that making art is a strange and beautiful thing, even as my education as a scholar seemed to leave me with fewer and fewer ways to talk about the strangeness and beauty of that making. Once the cigarette smoke had cleared and the canvas had dried, did those days, weeks, months of effort really no longer exist or matter? It was, perhaps, inevitable that I would be drawn, in my own simultaneous work on ancient literature, to the scenes of material struggle sometimes embedded there, like this one from the Roman poet Persius, whose author-function awakens after a night of hard drinking, needs to vomit but only manages to burp, and then tries to write:

> Iam liber et positis bicolor membrana capillis
> inque manus chartae nodosaque venit harundo.
> Tum querimur crassus calamo quod pendeat umor.
> Nigra sed infusa vanescit sepia lympha;
> dilutas querimur geminet quod fistula guttas.
> O miser inque dies ultra miser, hucine rerum
> venimus?

> Okay, got a book. And parchment (hair side
> yellow, flesh side white). Plus papyrus.
> And a knotted reed-pen. Damn! The ink clogs,
> hangs from the nib. Add a little water: Damn!
> There goes the black, here come thin drops, in twos.
> You pathetic loser, more pathetic every day:
> Has my life really come to this?[3]

I could not ignore my living painter, and increasingly, I felt I should not ignore my ancient poets, who likewise filled my days with such conspicuous evidence that, without their working, there would be no work. "This one was one who was working," as Gertrude Stein says (repeatedly) in her 1909 "Portrait" of Picasso, a copy of which was given to me, incidentally, by an always working, always out-of-work actor-friend.[4]

"[T]he birth of the reader must be ransomed by the death of the Author," concludes Barthes; all we have to lose are "God and his hypostases."[5] On its own terms, this would not be a bad bargain. But the liberating rejection of the author as an authority—indeed, as Authority Himself—seems inadvertently to have cost us something more down-to-earth: the author as "one who was working," like Stein herself, who here as elsewhere is really working on her self-portrait as an artist. It is the latter kind of author rather than the former for whom the present book proposes to search: not the author as God, but the author as *writer*. And to be clear from the outset, I mean this word primarily in its most literal sense, for we shall go looking for the writer first and foremost in those moments in which literature seeks to preserve (some might say, "to stage," and so be it) the scene of its own material creation. I shall endeavor to show that this is something far smaller—and infinitely more important—than a messy desk or studio: it is a sometimes split-second glimpse of what it means to make and therefore, and above all, *to lose*.

The nature of that loss will become clearer once we are in the thick of things, in chapter 1. I want instead to devote the remainder of this introduction to setting the stage with at least one essential prop: the page.

The Matter of the Page

A few years ago, I published a book on the role of the written word in the career of antiquity's most famous orator, Cicero.[6] By attempting to demonstrate that *even Cicero* cannot be understood outside a complex web of written practices, I hoped to suggest the same more generally of Rome's "oral society," a myth, I argued, devised by the Romans themselves, one to which we have succumbed all too willingly. And though this demonstration took aim primarily at a prevalent view of ancient political life, it suggested the utility of a similar inquiry into ancient poetics, since ancient poets, only slightly less than ancient orators, have been subjected to a myth of a primary orality, one that disencumbers them of the accessories of writing and turns them into inspired *vates*— singers, bards, prophets. The recitation of poetry, like the delivery of oratory, does not change the fact that most surviving texts of either kind were composed on tablets and, sooner or later, circulated in books (with occasional material variations on both ends).[7] The lover of ancient poets knows that they were constantly aware of this fact, that in countless self-conscious ways they call attention to their poems as inscribed objects, as we already have seen Persius doing. Any serious effort to make ancient poetry legible, therefore, must reconstruct, at least in part, its material habitat as a written text. And this is true not only for poetry, *stricto sensu*, but also for many kinds of literary prose.

The "material question," however, is always stretched across two tensions. The first may be summarized by Roger Stoddard's now-famous observation, taken as axiomatic by Roger Chartier and Guglielmo Cavallo, that "authors do *not* write books."[8] As a general rule, they instead write and revise drafts. If they are responsible for a first fair copy, then they are, by that point, not authors but, rather, copyists of their own work, and most or all subsequent copies will be the business of other copyists (including printers). The history of the book, in other words, is the history of authors, writing, only if it is the history of all material processes that lead up to a book; otherwise, it is the history of publishing and its aftermath. To insist instead, however, on the history of the draft is not to solve the problem, since authors tend to be aware not only of where they are, materially, but also of where they are going. Thus Catullus can ask, in the poem he appends to the start of his collection, "To whom shall I give my charming new little book," its edges neatly trimmed? But inside, he describes his poetizing as "playing in my tablets."[9] These poems, in other words, ask to be seen both in papyrus and in wax.[10]

This brings us to the second tension. Do such references to the text's own materiality urge us to make historicist claims about these particular writing materials, about the history of the papyrus roll and the history of the waxed tablet, neither of which was exactly like the page on which we read or write? Or do they instead invite us to think broadly about *materiality itself*? (This might, for example, seem to be especially the case for Catullus, where writing materials function, at least in part, as sexual appendages, metaphors for the more pressing materiality of the author's own body[11] — though this, of course, would then lead us into historicist considerations of desire, and so on.) In other words, is the materiality of writing a specific thing, locatable to the technologies of a particular time and place? Or may we speak of a more general "thingness" that has been writing's product across the centuries of its use? The two poles of this question of contingency are often figured, on the one hand, by the written word, common to all systems of writing (and, since Derrida, something like the irreducible emblem of thought itself, of which material writing is only a belated symptom), and, on the other hand, the book, the technological transformations of which are well known and, indeed, are often celebrated as epoch-making: roll to codex, papyrus to parchment to paper, manuscript to print.

The essays in this book look beyond — or better, within — all these polarities (draft and book, book and word, composing and copying, author and reader, contingency and universality), not in search of a resolution or compromise, but in the conviction that the heart of the matter is to be found instead in the middling architectures of the text, home to a more basic form of the tension from which these extremes radiate outward, like compass points. A number of such intermediate forms or platforms of the text will be visible in what follows, but the most conspicuous by far will be the page, attention to which will become representative of what might be called this book's method.

Let us, therefore, sketch a brief history of the page, in reverse, like a palimpsest, starting with what is most recent and moving thence to older forms of writing. It is surely remarkable that outside the "text itself" in the narrowest possible sense, the page is the only major aspect of the printed book to survive, with its name intact, the transition to cyberspace. Gone are dust-jackets, bindings, fly-leaves; for what resembles a table of contents we have borrowed a term from cuisine, "menu"; indices have been replaced by searches. But pages are still everywhere. This is even more remarkable when one considers that even the word "book" has often been left behind, although many sophisticated sites would seem to deserve the name, and indeed, many "electronic resources" have conserved the very titles of the books they have been designed to replace. (E-books offer a kind of exception, though the "book" in the name seems to be there precisely to suggest that these are hybrids which also exist—or, at least, could also exist—in a virtually indistinguishable printed form.) The word "book" lingers partially in the hardware term "notebook" (though most prefer "laptop") and, perhaps, in a Web browser's "bookmarks"—though, of course, bookmarks do not mark books but, rather, pages, which is why, for example, the French somewhat more accurately call a bookmark a *marque-pages*.[12]

The page had already survived the print revolution of a half-millennium ago. This, perhaps, seems less surprising, since the printing press conserved the form of the codex—it only changed the method of copying. Print would, however, over time, appear to stabilize an ambiguity in the meaning of "page" in the era of the handwritten codex, when the term could designate either a leaf, or one side of a leaf. Since the page-breaks in a printed edition are the same across copies, the utility of numbering pages (chiefly for reference) soon became obvious, with printers initially preferring to count leaves but eventually settling on sides of leaves: page one is thus the first side of the first numbered leaf, and so on. In truth, this did not finally settle the matter; even today, if we were to accuse someone of ripping a page out of a book, it would never occur to us to specify that the theft was, in fact, of two pages.

But let us go back more than a millennium earlier, to the page's most remarkable transition of all: that from roll to codex. Applied to the book-roll, the Latin *pagina* (whence our word "page") corresponds to the Greek *selis* and designates a column of writing. In a quality product, this need not have anything to do with the individual sheets (Greek, *kollēmata*, Latin, *schidae* or *scidae*) of papyrus that were carefully glued together to make a roll, since columns crossed these without notice.[13] The codex, of course, could not allow the same—a column could not wrap, left to right, around the edge of a leaf or across the binding without evident discomfort—but some early codices do preserve the column's basic form, fitting two or three onto each side of the leaf.[14] The *pagina*, though, soon stretched to fill its new environs, and by the early Middle Ages, the multicolumned page is the exception, and *pagina* presumably had come to mean only what it has meant ever since: "page."[15]

This shift in the meaning of *pagina* may look, at first, like an important change, but it actually marks a rather astounding continuity. Let us first note that, beyond the designation of a "column" in a book-roll, other ancient uses of *pagina* correspond to what we ourselves would call a "page."[16] The word is cognate with *pango*, which means "to fix by driving in," as in boundary stones or the trees of a planned grove. *Pagina* could depend on the second of these:

Latin uses other agricultural terms, like *exarare*, for writing, and the phrase *pangere versus*, probably "to plant some verses," i.e., to write them (in wax) is common.[17] But it probably suggests instead the first: a *pagina* is a bounded space set out for writing—a leaf in a waxed tablet, a single sheet of papyrus or parchment, or a column in a book-roll.[18] Garden or enclosure, the page is, ironically enough, from its very origin, a plot available for plots (to play on our own not unrelated double sense of the word "plot").[19] More to the point, the column of the book-roll is not the *pagina avant la page*; it is simply a slightly strange episode in the long history of the page as a bounded space. In other words, the roll too has pages.

Nevertheless, let us briefly return to the book's shift from roll to codex, since the page's move from one to the other will help us to see what it is that a page really does. It is fairly clear that Christians, whose preference for the codex was early and strong, were responsible for its rise to preeminence over the roll, even, eventually, for pagan literature, by which time certain practical advantages of the codex were sufficiently evident to ensure the roll's doom.[20] The fraught question of the origins of that Christian preference need not detain us here, except to note that some of the codex's eventual virtues, like a vastly greater capacity than a single roll, were later developments.[21] Let us simply remind ourselves of the strangeness of the place to which the codex would soon take the book. Probably the best examples of this are late-antique biblical codices, which embrace, at a minimum, the four gospels—the same story, told four times—between two covers, prefacing to them the Eusebian canon tables, a system of indices to parallel gospel passages.[22] Around these tables scribes regularly drew colonnaded arcades, perverse echoes of the roll's *paginae*, like columns spoliated from an ancient temple to be put to a very different architectural use. This is most emphatically *not* a book to be read cover-to-cover, at least not in that order. The beginning and the end, the *alpha* and the *omega*, are on every page here, and one must move constantly back and forth in order to know what this book really means.[23]

From this vantage point, it is tempting to look back on the roll as something like the codex's opposite, a space made for stories that unroll from start to finish, in a long, steady, progressive sweep—the perfect material support for antiquity's most exalted literary form, the epic.[24] There is, I think, a grain of truth in this view, but for the most part, it not only grossly oversimplifies classical literature (about which I shall have more to say in the first chapter—for now let it suffice to note that, if epic is a linear journey, then it is one gone horribly awry), but it also seriously misrepresents the book-roll. If humankind had truly wanted to realize materially only the linear trajectory of narrative, it would have set down stories in an unbroken line of writing on long, thin strips (though no sooner would someone have tried to tidy these cumbersome ribbons by, for example, winding them around spools, than this material text too would have hinted at narrative's potential recursiveness). Instead, all books break the line of writing at fairly regular intervals and organize sets of these segments, again at regular intervals, into the roughly quadrilateral space that is the page. The page is thus that physical aspect of the book that most persistently invites our eyes to move in directions other than the forward one, that potentially asserts, visually, the synchronic (and recursive) aspects of a narrative, over and against the diachronic ones. Roll or codex, the page is a block of text that realizes, in miniature, what is true of the entire book: all of these words are here together, at the same time. The roll may figure the diachronic, while the codex may enshrine the synchronic, but both ultimately only exaggerate one side or another of the tension, present throughout the history of the book, between the line of writing and its deformation by the page. Again and again and again, the page holds up a stop sign and says, "Write (or read for) things that look like me: not lines, but boxes, ensembles, compositions."[25]

So far I have been describing the page as a horizontal continuity across the whole long history of the book—roll to codex, manuscript to print, print to computer. But consider the far more obvious fact that the page offers a vertical continuity as well. Earlier we noted that authors do not write books: they write drafts—on tablets, in notebooks, with word processors. But it is immediately clear that these too share with the book what all books share with each other: the page. It is thus the page, and not the book, that is the pervasive material condition of literature, for it names the one space that authors and readers have in common.

Two objections, however, immediately spring to mind. First, the author's page, in terms of where it starts and ends, is almost never the same as the reader's page, just as, over the long history of the book, pagination has generally been consistent among copies of the same text only in the case of the same printed edition.[26] The page, in this sense, would more accurately be described as a private space, which authors do not share with readers and which even readers of the same work may not share with one another. All that remains consistent from author to reader is the page's basic geometry; its coordinates and dimensions, by contrast, inevitably shift. And this brings us to an even more serious objection. Having made the page transcend, horizontally and vertically, all specific materialities of the text, what sense does it make for us to call the page "material" at all?

The page, in fact, has analogs which we would be even less inclined to view as material aspects of the text. Among the largest of these is the chapter, the relative autonomy of which mirrors, in miniature, that of the book itself. Smaller still—but often sharing the same name in Latin, *caput*—is the paragraph.[27] The paragraph, in turn, is at least partially related to the period, that grand, soaring sentence that seems to come back around to where it started (*periodos*, "a road around").[28] Finally, there is the ordinary sentence and, indeed, syntax itself, the synchronic structures of all language, whether written or not. In fact, what we earlier saw as the basic message of both page and book—these words are not merely a sequence but are also all here together, at the same time—is more or less the very definition of syntax, *suntaxis*, the arrangement of single elements in simultaneous relationship to one another.

Perhaps, however, we can distinguish the page by calling it the black sheep of this family, conspicuous for the impertinence and arbitrariness with which it repeatedly barges into the text, chopping up stories, sentences, and even words where it wills. It is not that the page does not have its own rules of decorum (think of one-inch margins, still checked in my students' dissertations by ruler-wielding librarians!), but these are not the same as or necessarily in synch with the rules of language (from syntax to composition). The page intervenes *as if from outside*, seemingly rudely and randomly but actually only with unforgiving discipline. The phrase I have italicized, in fact, would seem to be key to anything we choose to label a "material" constraint on the text. But we should note at once that this apparent exteriority is rife with problems. Consider a different materiality of language: that of speech, which requires an elaborate apparatus of organs and vibrating media that arguably makes it every bit as "material" as writing. Here, breath is the ever-present disciplinarian: we can try to synchronize it with our thoughts, but if we do not, it will intervene all the same, forcing us to stop and regroup. But to conclude from this that breath is, therefore, external to language is to complete a *reductio ad absurdum*. Simply put, there is no language without matter (unless by language we mean *logos* in the suspect sense of truth or God). This is the case even when the matter in question is just the pinkish sponge inside our skulls, from which me may extract "memory" as the name of yet another synchronic constraint on (seemingly) linear language.

If, therefore, this book persists in using the page as an emblem for writing, and writing as an emblem for materiality, and materiality as an emblem for something perhaps as big as language itself, then it does so in full awareness that these are metonymic simplifications. In any case, I am following the lead of my authors, as I hope will be evident by the end. To be clear, I am not advocating here any dogged determinism, a kind of revamped New Criticism with a materialist twist, by which every literary text is condemned to tell, first and foremost, the story of the page. I simply am proposing a temporary shift of focus, not necessarily meant to last any longer than the duration of the present book, which will blur some things to which we normally are very attentive, while it brings some others into sharper view. Each of the following essays, in fact, approaches the page from a different angle and to somewhat different ends. Nevertheless, each tends to follow the same intuition that what may matter most about the material text is that it is the most obvious place where writers become their own first readers. This, in effect, will be our theoretical back door into our long unfashionable subject: we shall follow the lead of Barthes and others in regarding a text's meaning as constituted by readers, but we shall strike out on our own in search of that most peculiar reader of all: the author. And every time we find her, she will be (or will just have been) writing.

I should end by introducing myself as author, as reader, for I am very much the latter as I look over what follows, recently written. For the most part, both the question of the author and the emblem of the page will serve my (other) readers as guiding threads to what I hope is not too much a maze. But I should caution, by way of full disclosure, that these are essays in the truest sense of the word, intended far more as journeys to be enjoyed along the way than as efficient directions to a final destination. Properly speaking, they may be read in any order, and convention is the principal reason for their chronological arrangement. Nevertheless, the first chapter (which comes first because of its place on the mythological timeline that makes Orpheus the first poet), on the backward glance that sent Eurydice to her second doom, offers something of a parable for the work of reading for the writer; readers may well want to begin here. Chapters 2 and 3 are a pair. The first examines Thucydides' first-hand account of the devastating plague at Athens during the Peloponnesian War, focusing on the handful of words by which he intrudes into his history in order to reveal that he was himself sick and saw others suffering the same. We shall see how Thucydides quietly makes the page figure his own skin, where writing does the work of disease. Chapter 3 turns to Lucretius' translation of the Thucydidean plague into Latin poetry as the finale of his monumental *De rerum natura*. We shall read Lucretius, however, through the eyes of Cicero, who knew the work and may even have edited it. Cicero's often articulated theories of composition, which require art to cohere with the elegant efficiency of the human body, will help to reveal the Lucretian achievement of a scene of decomposition that has been arranged as carefully as a fine mosaic. Chapter 4 turns from poetry to Cicero's more natural habitats—oratory, philosophy, and letters—in order to consider some broad implications of erasability for the freedom and fixity of the self, political and otherwise. Chapter 5 tries to answer the question, "Is the page flat?" It first complicates our picture of the story of Narcissus, whose encounter with his own *imago* haunts this entire book, beginning already in chapter 1. We then turn to Seneca (and Nero) to explore Rome's obsession with what lies beneath the surface. Chapter 6, finally, moves to the Middle Ages, and to one of Latin's only major pre-Modern texts by a woman, the *Handbook* of Dhuoda, which she wrote for her son, a noble hostage in the court of Charles the Bald. Bending familiar medieval tropes of the written word to the purposes of her own *écriture féminine*, Dhuoda imagines her pages first as mirrors, which, variously angled, enable her to see her son and him to see her. But by the book's end, the page has become a tomb, and the author imagines her own body lying beneath its words.

As should now be clear from these summaries, the attention of the present book will oscillate between materiality proper and materiality as trope, with a decided emphasis, after this introduction, on the latter. Indeed, from this point on, close literary reading will be our primary mode of approach. I should also note that the authors and texts covered here appear as a result of my own idiosyncratic interests; they are not meant to be representative of anything else. By including a classical Greek and ending with a Carolingian, I hope to give a sense of the *longue durée* of some of the tensions common to all of the texts I examine, but I could have begun even earlier and ended far later. What I have placed between them is all ancient and Roman, simply because that is where this classical Latinist is most at home.

1

THE BACKWARD GLANCE

Of all the turning points in the history of poetry, the most important lies just below the surface of the earth, almost at the end of the steep climb up from Hell. This is the spot where Orpheus ignored the terms imposed upon him and looked over his shoulder at the wife he had just won back from death with a song. Those who tell the story expand the instant in which Eurydice vanishes into a brief chaos of futile grasps and fleeting words, just enough to make this point in time visible to us. And into this vertiginous moment they mix only the rudest beginnings of an answer to the question she and we have only barely time to ask: why? In the intervening eons, which comprise nothing less than the whole of literary history—for Orpheus was the first poet, we are told—that cataclysm has so often been remembered that it has acquired a tragic inevitability: Orpheus must look back; else, this is not his story. So too must his new wife die to begin with, and he himself must finally be dismembered.[1]

But the story of the first poet surely seeks to tell us something about all poets, and indeed, its beginning and end are bound up in familiar if complicated themes about the relationship between poetry and death, body and song, tradition and immortality. Nevertheless, the midpoint of the myth has remained elusive: why must the poet look back? Let us begin with what we are told by poets themselves, specifically Vergil and Ovid, the former in his fourth *Georgic*, the latter in the tenth book of his *Metamorphoses*, our two main sources for the myth.[2] We start with Vergil:

13

Iamque pedem referens casus evaserat omnis,
redditaque Eurydice superas veniebat ad auras,
pone sequens, namque hanc dederat Proserpina legem,
cum subita incautum dementia cepit amantem,
ignoscenda quidem, scirent si ignoscere Manes.
Restitit, Eurydicenque suam, iam luce sub ipsa,
immemor, heu, victusque animi respexit. Ibi omnis
effusus labor atque immitis rupta tyranni
foedera, terque fragor stagnis auditus Avernis.
Illa 'quis et me' inquit 'miseram et te perdidit, Orpheu,
quis tantus furor? En iterum crudelia retro
fata vocant, conditque natantia lumina somnus.
Iamque vale: feror ingenti circumdata nocte
invalidasque tibi tendens, heu non tua, palmas.'
Dixit et ex oculis subito, ceu fumus in auras
commixtus tenuis fugit diversa, neque illum
prensantem nequiquam umbras et multa volentem
dicere praeterea vidit . . .[3]

A sudden *dementia*, the poet writes, "seized [Orpheus], careless even as he loved." He was for a moment *immemor*, "forgetful"—presumably of Proserpina's injunction not to look back until free of the Underworld. Or perhaps he was simply unable to remember Eurydice's face? *Victus animi*, something like "mentally undone," *respexit*, "he looked back." We are as puzzled as Eurydice, who with her last words begins to ask, "Who has ruined you and poor me, Orpheus?" *Quis et me miseram et te perdidit, Orpheu?*—and this last vocative rings like an unfinished answer to her own question, for the same Orpheus who won her release from death now sends her back. But her *quis?* turns out to be not a "who" but a "what": *quis tantus furor*, she continues, "what madness so great . . . ?" And with that, she slips away. Stretching out her arms and crying a last "farewell," she vanishes, "like smoke dissolved in insubstantial air," leaving him still "wanting to say many things."

Any hope for clarification from Ovid finds, instead, only amplified uncertainty:

Carpitur acclivis per muta silentia trames,
arduus, obscurus, caligine densus opaca,
nec procul abfuerunt telluris margine summae.
Hic ne deficeret metuens avidusque videndi
flexit amans oculos, et protinus illa relapsa est,
bracchiaque intendens prendique et prendere certans

nil nisi cedentes infelix adripit auras.
Iamque iterum moriens non est de coniuge quidquam
questa suo (quid enim nisi se quereretur amatam?)
supremumque 'vale', quod iam vix auribus ille
acciperet, dixit, revolutaque rursus eodem est.[4]

Orpheus "fears that strength is failing"—hers? his? The Latin is unclear. He is "anxious to see," *avidus videndi*, but, significantly, Ovid provides no object here, as if that desired vision were an end to itself: Orpheus does not want his wife; he simply wants *to see*. "What complaint could she offer except that she had been loved?" Thus, at the very moment when Orpheus makes Eurydice vanish, Ovid silences her, and so too the reader, to whom the rhetorical question is addressed, and likewise, finally, himself. We are all still quietly wondering, "Why?" even as Eurydice utters, again, the "farewell" (echoed from Vergil but now barely audible) with which she seems to mock us: *Vale*, "goodbye, good luck, have a nice life."

And there Vergil and Ovid leave us, with nothing like a real answer.[5] To do better, we will need to look beyond the passages that purport to tell us the Orpheus story. But where? Orpheus, torn finally to bits by maenads, his head and lyre still sounding as they floated down the Hebrus river, is everywhere and nowhere, an ever-fainter but never-ending echo, all but inaudible beneath the endless lines of verse produced by poets in his wake. To try to hear him, we begin now a detour through a moment of silence, a tear in the very fabric of poetry, a way through, a way back to something almost crudely elemental about the art he is said to have invented. That this will lead us finally back to Orpheus is something I must ask my readers to take, for now, on faith.

In fifty-nine places in the course of almost ten thousand hexameters, the text of Vergil's *Aeneid* breaks off into nothingness, half-lines that yield to the blank page, where this generally fairly noisy poem falls suddenly silent, if only for a second or two.[6] Many of these pauses seem so appropriate to their context, so eloquent in their speechlessness, that some readers have suggested that Vergil meant to leave them empty.[7] But most have connected them instead to assertions by Vergil's ancient biographers that he fell fatally ill before completing his revisions, that, when no one would bring his draft to his deathbed so that he could burn the imperfect poem, he left instructions forbidding its publication, but that his literary executors, under higher orders from Augustus, released the work without attempting to fill its lacunae.[8] It is through one of these gaps, near the middle of book nine, that we must now descend.

Vergil, *Aeneid*, book 9, line 467, offers just two names in the genitive case and then stops: *Euryali et Nisi*, "Of Euryalus and Nisus . . ." This half-line actually ends their story, which had begun almost 300 lines earlier; it thus offers a kind of belated title: this was the tale of Euryalus and Nisus. Indeed, the entire episode, among Vergil's most daring and beautiful, has sometimes been thought to have begun as a separate work, perhaps a youthful *epyllion* later integrated, imperfectly, into the poet's *magnum opus*.[9]

Euryali et Nisi in line 467 modifies *capita* in line 466 — thus, "the heads of Euryalus and Nisus." And since these are, in fact, the severed heads of the two lovers, mounted on pikes and paraded before their horrified Trojan comrades, the genitive may be said to assert, with grim irony, possession of what Nisus and Euryalus most emphatically possess no longer:

> Quin ipsa arrectis, visu miserabile, in hastis
> praefigunt capita et multo clamore sequuntur
> Euryali et Nisi.
>
> Indeed, shouting all the way, they follow the very heads —
> stuck (gruesome sight!) on spears — of Euryalus and Nisus.[10]

Or to put things another way, the story ends by naming two people who no longer exist; this very final genitive is thus that of a Roman epitaph, *Dis Manibus Euryali et Nisi*, "to the sacred shades of Euryalus and Nisus." And the silence that follows is most chillingly that of the tomb.

But we have begun at the end; let us now review the whole story from the top. At the beginning of book 9, Aeneas is still far from the Trojan camp, seeking Italian allies. Turnus, advised of this absence by the goddess Iris, tries to draw the Trojans out of their camp for a fight, and when this fails, he sets fire to their ships, which, however, are transformed into sea-nymphs. Frustrated, Turnus and his troops retire to drink and game late into the night. The Trojans watch all from their ramparts; among them is Nisus, who guards the gate, in the company of his beloved Euryalus, "than whom no other follower of Aeneas was more beautiful" (Vergil, *Aeneid* 9.179–80). Nisus proposes to go in search of Aeneas; Euryalus insists on coming with him. The two present themselves as volunteers to the grateful Trojan commanders, who, showering them with tears and prizes, send them on their way.

Their way, however, will be no simple matter, despite Nisus's assurances that they had learned the lay of the land when they used to hunt there, and that "the correct path will not elude us as we make our way" (*nec nos via fallit euntis*) (*Aeneid* 9.243). As the story of a journey gone awry, the episode resembles the entire poem, to say nothing of other epics.[11] Indeed, epic tends to exploit in a particularly visible way what might well be called the most operative tension of narrative: that between the relentless forward march of the text itself, letter after letter, word after word, and the endless ways in which the story suspends or deforms that motion, through description, digression, detour. Without error, there can be no odyssey, and we are so conditioned to expect such wanderings that we know where this story is going as soon as Nisus promises not to get lost. What we don't expect, however, is just how lost we soon shall be.

Egressi superant fossas, "they left the camp and crossed the ditches" (*Aeneid* 9.314). This margin surrounds the Trojan camp, but it also rings the text that follows, for as we already have seen, the episode will bring Nisus and Euryalus—or, at least, their heads—back to the edge of the very same gap. The pair's prior trajectory is at once bent: "and through the dark of night they seek the enemy camp," i.e., not Aeneas, since they will first wreak some havoc among their adversaries before proceeding on their mission (*Aeneid* 9.314-16).[12] The distraction from their notional object immediately slows the story to a near halt, for just one line later we confront, along with our heroes, as spectators, a scene so static that the poet seems to be claiming for his page a simultaneity proper instead to the visual arts: "Scattered here and there (*passim*) they see bodies dissolved by wine and sleep and poured across the grass, and chariots drawn up on the bank, and men (*viros*) lying prone between reins and wheels, side-by-side (*simul*) with their weapons (*arma*), side-by-side with their wineskins" (*Aeneid* 9.316-18).[13] Everything that should move is still: the chariot and its parts, the wine that has lent its liquidity to the bodies poured across the grass, and, as we can scarcely fail to notice, the prime movers of Vergil's epic—arms and men.[14]

Hac iter est, announces Nisus, something like "this is the way we need to go," and he instructs Euryalus to follow him and carefully guard their back, while he himself lays waste to what we have just seen (*Aeneid* 9.321-23).[15] The pair literally hack their way through what follows, with Vergil describing the carnage they inflict in gruesome detail, until Nisus decides that they should move along, "for a way has been made through the enemy" (*Aeneid* 9.366).[16] Donning their spoils, they resume their mission, but as they cross out of the enemy camp, a glint from the newly won helmet worn by Euryalus attracts the attention of an embassy en route from Latina. Challenged, Nisus and Euryalus plunge into the woods.

The woods, of course, could hardly be lacking from this story—the woods that bewitch all who enter into confusion, error, repetition, recursiveness. No one moves through the woods quickly, or in a straight line; something always happens here.[17] But let us also remember—and the point is not unrelated—that for ancient poets, the woods (*silva* in Latin, *hulē* in Greek) also figured the very stuff of literary production, the timber of which poems were made, including everything from subject "matter" to literary models to rough notes to the waxed wooden tablets on which most poets composed.[18] It is, in this regard, no accident that a wood gathers around Orpheus, product of his song but also source of the stories he tells.[19] Enter the woods and we are in the poet's workshop.[20]

Before allowing us to follow Nisus and Euryalus into the woods, Vergil briefly shifts point-of-view in order to delineate this wood from outside: "The mounted soldiers dash toward the paths they know well, this way, and this way, and they ring (*coronant*) all the exits with guards" (*Aeneid* 9.379–80). This margin makes the wood into a kind of page within the page of the entire expedition (bordered, as we have seen, by the camp's ditches), as if we were zeroing in on something at the center of our focus but not yet legible. In we go!

"The wood was one which bristled far and wide with thickets and black oaks, which dense brambles choked from every direction. Only here and there shone a path through secret byways. The shadowy canopy and hulking animals cause Euryalus to falter; fear leaves him confused about where the paths lie" (*Aeneid* 9.381–85). Nisus, unaware that Euryalus is no longer behind him, keeps going, but three lines later, Vergil halts him too in his tracks: *stetit*, "he came to a complete stop." And then comes the moment we have been waiting for: "and in vain he looked back at his friend, who was gone" (*et frustra absentem respexit amicum*) (*Aeneid* 9.389).[21] A backward glance, a loss—but Nisus will go farther than Orpheus, for he now attempts the impossible: to reverse the story's motion altogether. "'Unlucky Euryalus, where did I leave you behind? Along what path shall I follow (*quave sequar*)—rewinding (*revolvens*) my whole twisted route, again, in reverse (*rursus*), through the deceptive forest?' And at once he searches out his footprints and closely follows them (*legit*), backwards (*retro*), winding his way (*errat*) through the silent thickets" (*Aeneid* 9.390–93). We pause to note just two things about this remarkable reversal. The first is the perversity of Nisus's question, *qua sequar*, "by what path shall I follow?" The object is notionally "you," from the line before, but since Nisus has been the leader, this doesn't properly make sense. In fact, Nisus will follow instead his own footprints—in other words, he will follow himself. And one way or another, following yourself requires going backward. The second peculiarity is the sudden appearance of the vocabulary of reading: *revolvere* (Nisus will "rewind" his journey, like a papyrus roll) and *legere*, the actual verb for reading, a favorite of Vergil's to mean "to follow closely, step-by-step" (Nisus will "read" his own tracks).[22]

Naturally, these will not lead him literally backward through the text. Instead, he finds himself at the edge of a glen, where he at last spies Euryalus, surrounded by enemy soldiers. Still under cover of the woods, Nisus begins to pick off his beloved's assailants with javelins, one by one. The soldiers are thrown into a temporary panic, but they then vow to answer the still unseen menace by unleashing their fury on Euryalus. "Me! Me! The author of this deed is here! Turn your weapons on me!" cries Nisus, emerging at last from the woods, a subject desperate to become an object (*Aeneid* 9.427).[23] But it is too late for Euryalus: "a sword, thrust with violent force, penetrates his ribs and bursts his pale chest. He doubles over in death; gore moves down his handsome limbs; and his collapsed neck reposes on his shoulders, just as a crimson flower, nicked by the plow, droops dying, or poppies bow their heads, their necks weak, under the weight of a random rain-shower" (*Aeneid* 9.431–37). These extraordinary lines, made at once more beautiful and more horrible by a sensuality that edges toward eroticism, seem to embody all we have seen so far: their emphasis on color makes poetry like painting; the oozing gore—blood that does not flow as it should—offers a kind of emblem for this whole clotted narrative; Euryalus's body turns in on itself (*volvitur*), like a book that has wound its way to the end. But if Euryalus's journey is over—as is that of Nisus, who, pierced by swords, hurls his own dying body onto his beloved's corpse—ours suddenly takes a new direction. Not this way, or that way, but back, and then down.

As ancient commentators did not fail to notice, Vergil's image of a flower nicked by the passing plow is borrowed from a very famous poem by Catullus, describing a love that has withered.[24] The poppy, instead, is pilfered from Homer; the episode's center thus reflects its frame, for the nocturnal expedition of Nisus and Euryalus is a very free reworking of similar excursions in the *Iliad*, one by Odysseus and Diomedes and another by the Trojan spy Dolon.[25] Indeed, the entire episode is underpinned by literary precedents, and especially haunted by echoes are its woods.

One of these reverberations, however, sounds some very peculiar notes. Nisus's backward glance and subsequent backtrack through the woods reprise an analogous scene not in another work by another author but, instead, in the very same *Aeneid*'s second book, where Aeneas tells Dido and her court the story of his escape from Troy.[26] Having decided to abandon the burning city, Aeneas places his aged father on his shoulders, takes his son by the hand, and instructs his wife Creusa to follow at some distance. Safely outside the walls, he looks back, but she is missing (*amissam respexi*) (*Aeneid* 2.741). He plunges back into the wreckage, retracing his steps: *et vestigia retro / observata sequor*, almost the same words we have seen used of Nisus, *et vestigia retro / observata legit* (*Aeneid* 2.753–54; 9.392–93).

But if book 9 looks back at book 2, book 2 takes us even farther. Aeneas finds not Creusa but her ghost, who consoles him and commands him to flee. She concludes thus:

"'And now, goodbye (*iamque vale*), and keep the love of the son we share.'
When she had pronounced these words, she left me there, weeping, and wanting to say so much (*multa volentem / dicere*), and receded into the insubstantial
air (*tenuisque recessit in auras*). Thrice I tried there to wrap my arms around her
neck; thrice the phantom, embraced in vain, eluded my grasp, like a gentle
breeze, or a winged dream." (*Aeneid* 2.789–94)[27]

But we have had this dream before, for the passage reproduces, at times word
for word, the language of Eurydice's final parting from Orpheus in the fourth
Georgic:

"And now, goodbye (*iamque vale*)! I am being carried, surrounded by massive
night, stretching—ohhh, no longer yours—my palms toward you . . ." She
spoke thus, and then suddenly scattered and vanished from sight, like smoke
dissolved in insubstantial air (*ceu fumus in auras commixtus tenuis*). Nor did she
see him further, as he snatched at shadows to no avail, wanting to say so much
(*multa volentem dicere*).[28]

And one thing more: Creusa as the name of Aeneas' wife is not attested before
Vergil's own day; an earlier tradition knew her as Eurydice.[29]

   And so, Euryalus is Creusa is Eurydice, and Nisus is Aeneas is Orpheus.
We might be tempted to stop here, with this answer to the question posed at
the beginning of this chapter: the Orphic look back is the backward glance of
poetic imitation. (We might add that, in the later tradition of Latin commen-
taries on classical texts, *respicere* regularly means "to imitate.") But this answer
does not really satisfy. Why, first of all, should imitation mean loss? Is it not
instead a kind of recovery and appropriation?[30] Orpheus had gone to Hell to
rescue Eurydice, but it is precisely his backward glance, let us remember, that
sends her back. Furthermore, what, strictly speaking, did the *first* poet have to
imitate, unless, like Vergil, he imitated himself?

   The detail that much of Vergil's imitation here is directed not toward literary precedent, but toward his own authorial past is not, in fact, irrelevant. It is
sometimes forgotten that imitation belongs not only to the collegial ether of
Helicon or Parnassus but also to the decidedly more terrestrial atmosphere of
the ancient classroom. Here the reworking of one's own writing joined other
exercises of *retractatio* ("rehandling" or "remanagement") of a model, whether
by using the same words to a different effect, or by using different words to tell
the same story: "It is useful not only to paraphrase others' writings but also to re-
manage our own in a variety of ways (*etiam nostra pluribus modis tractare*), carefully choosing certain themes and rendering them in as many ways as possible,

just as shape after shape is modeled, again and again, from the same wax."[31] Quintilian's simile of the sculpting of wax is especially apt—indeed, is itself a kind of example—for it reworks the very material in which such reworkings would take place, i.e., the wax of his student's tablets: "Erase, and rewrite the same story, in a different way." And this almost crude materiality is a reminder that literary imitation is only the tip of the iceberg of a vast array of literal regressions and recursions that writers are taught to pursue. Whether the matter at hand is a reworking of the sort just described or, simply, the revision of an unicum (*retractare* can be used to describe either), the author does not move in a straight line but, rather, is always doubling back. Indeed, Suetonius reports that Vergil was famous for his revisions of the *Georgics*:

> Cum Georgica scriberet, traditur cotidie meditatos mane plurimos versus dictare solitus ac per totum diem retractando ad paucissimos redigere, non absurde carmen se more ursae parere dicens et lambendo demum effingere.

> Tradition has it that, when he was writing the *Georgics*, his daily practice was to dictate a large number of verses he had devised in the morning and then, by going back over them (*retractando*) all day long, to edit them down to just a few, saying, not entirely without reason, that he was giving birth to his poem as a bear does, licking it into shape only afterward.[32]

It is impossible to know how much of this colorful portrait is true, but it does tell us how someone far closer to Vergil's world than we are was able to imagine him working. He rises as a bard, full of the god, as blind to the text as Homer was. But his singing is actually dictation, i.e., already a kind of writing (the one reserved for those writers lucky enough to have a secretary or scribe among their writing materials). And once the text is in the room, it—and not the poet—is the inevitable object of attention. Then *the poet's real work begins*, work imagined as physical, manual labor, described by a simile not unlike, but cruder than, Quintilian's, by which the reviser is like the mother bear who must (it once was widely believed) lick her cub, born almost formless, into shape. This materiality, in fact, seems to have infected the story's beginning, for the poet/bard does not simply exhale inspired verses: these already have been crafted, contemplated (*meditatos*) in the at least temporary fixity of his own mind, his own memory. Simply put, there is no point in the tenses of this sentence in which the text is as yet unborn; its creation has been entirely eclipsed by its *being worked on*.

Again we seem close to an answer: the poet's backward glance is that of revision. But this too falls short, for, from Orpheus to Nisus, we have been presented with scenes of *incalculable* loss. We can imagine revision to be so devastating only either by following Suetonius in his likely hyperbole, exaggerating just how much the author must discard (from *plurimos* to *paucissimos*), or by inflating the author's narcissism to the point that every cut, every cancellation is as excruciating as the sword-thrust that fells Euryalus. There are some poets for whom the latter may well be close to the truth, but it seems hard to believe of the Vergil who was prepared to burn the entire *Aeneid* for want of time to revise it. And more importantly, to see the backward glance as that of revision is to suppose that it always looks to produce change. There is, in fact, another kind of looking back, one which comes, instead, when there is no more work to be done.

We are only a few steps away from this other, more painful backward glance. But to take them, we are going to need some help from elsewhere. It comes to us from Orpheus' *third* look back in Latin literature. The first, as we have seen, is in Vergil, on the way up from Hell; the second is on the same slope, but in Ovid; the third is also in Ovid, but it takes place instead at the very end of the story. After devoting more than an entire book of the *Metamorphoses*—and some of his most daring poetry—to Orpheus, Ovid seems to ruin everything with a fatuous finale in which Orpheus, himself finally dead, at last rejoins his wife in the Underworld:

> Hic modo coniunctis spatiantur passibus ambo;
> nunc praecedentem sequitur, nunc praevius anteit
> **Eurydicen**que suam iam tuto respicit **Orpheus**.[33]

> Here at last the pair takes long walks at a shared pace. Sometimes she goes first and he follows, sometimes, out in front, he precedes, and at last Orpheus looks back, without risk, at his Eurydice.

The sentiment is as schmaltzy as that of Charles Dickens's alternate, happy ending to *Great Expectations*: "I saw no shadow of another parting from her . . ."[34] But equally excruciating is Ovid's word picture. There's Eurydice, on the left, and there's Orpheus, out front, on the right, leading her along, and this time, safely looking back.

Actually, this is cleverer than it first seems, for Ovid has set us up for a play on the meaning of "follow." Eurydice in this last line "follows" Orpheus because she is behind him in the left-to-right movement of the line of writing, although, in a more ordinary sense, it is Orpheus who "follows" Eurydice, since *Orpheus* comes after *Eurydicen*. In fact, the ambiguity of "following" is general to any act of reading. As we move through a text, what follows in the sense of what comes next is what lies farther down the page (or writing-column), deeper into the book. But what follows in the sense of what lies in our wake is what we already have read. So too for the writer: what follows a poet, like a pied piper, or more to the point, like an Orpheus, whose music dragged people, beasts, plants, and rocks in his train, is that which has already been written, that which can now be read. And there it is, I would argue: the backward glance without which poetry cannot exist.

Let us briefly take the poet's point of view. At the end of every line, we are reassured that what we are making is poetry. We look back and say, that works, that's done. Writing, indeed, requires incessant review of what we have written: word by word, page by page, book by book—day by day, in Vergil's case. But it is the poetic line that most pointedly demands this reflection and embodies its resulting loss. The end of the line, the completion of the meter: it all comes together and, click, it's finished, it's gone.[35] These words belong to the page now, and thence to its readers, and thus not to poetry as *poiēsis*, making, but to poetry as the afterlife of that making. To write is to lose; the poem is what is left when the poet looks back—and moves on. "Und er gehorcht, indem er überschreitet."[36]

Orpheus has almost reached the margin—Ovid actually uses this word, *nec procul abfuerunt telluris margine summae*[37]—and is "anxious to see" the verse he has made, step by step, metrical foot by metrical foot. He longs to contemplate what he has taken out of himself and put down in wax. But like all mirrors, this reflection is alienating. Orpheus, like Narcissus, can love what he sees, but it is no longer his, or more accurately, it is no longer he. In other words, the backward glance is the name we should give to all moments, including these most elemental ones, when the poet—call him Orpheus—suddenly becomes a reader of himself. Or to put it another way, it is at the ends of things, including the ends of lines, that poets become one of us, their readers. And it is thus in the unended, like the unfinished line into which we stumbled a little while ago, and which we mistook for a tomb, that we catch a glimpse of the poet who is still a living author, still, after all these centuries, unwilling to look back, to let go, to lose.

Two important implications of all this merit additional comment. A moment ago, in search of a more elemental answer, we rejected our own suggestion that the Orphic turn was that of allusion, i.e., a backward glance at literary precedent. Nevertheless, it can scarcely be a coincidence that Vergil enshrines what he has to say about looking backward in the complex intertextual (and intratextual) nest through which we have just traveled. Nor can it be chance that the myth at the bottom of these explorations is one whose ending, in which the poet is dismembered and his head and lyre thrown into a river, where they still produce music that echoes off the passing banks, has been seen since antiquity as emblematic of the reading that imitative writers must do, dissecting their models, only to reassemble the *disiecti membra poetae* into their own, new compositions.[38] Surely, in fact, we can find in imitation an extension of the backward glance we have found at the end of every line, a lavish and productive metaphor (like the Orpheus story itself) for the incessant retrospection that all writing, imitative or not, makes irresistible. Poets who imitate, in other words, are not writing as readers: rather, they are reading as writers, who always look back. And this realization should, perhaps, shake our confidence that imitation is primarily about the authority of the literary past or the learned play of an eventual readership and lead us to consider it as, first and foremost, a reverie on the very page below the poet's nose.

The second implication, which regards Eurydice, requires a longer note.

The Romance of the Page

It is, of course, no accident that Eurydice is a woman; indeed, the entire myth can be read as a parable of her gender. Orpheus's is the second male gaze to be her undoing: the first was that of Aristaeus, who spies and chases her, until she steps on the snake that fatally bites her.[39] She flees Aristaeus; she follows Orpheus: these are her two places in relation to the men who desire her. The story has her more (often) dead than alive; she is Other both as woman and as death, as womb and as tomb, as whence and as whither. She is not just one woman, but all; she begins the story as a wife but ends it as a mother, as Orpheus, on that narrow passage toward the light, looks back at the woman behind him. "Eurydice is the limit of what art can attain; concealed behind a name and covered by a veil, she is the profoundly dark point towards which art, desire, death, and the night all seem to lead," writes Maurice Blanchot.[40] But at least since H. D.'s angry "Eurydice," some have wondered aloud why the making of art should have to be over a woman's dead body:[41]

> what was it that crossed my face
> with the light from yours
> and your glance?
> what was it you saw in my face?
> the light of your own face,
> the fire of your own presence?[42]

Orpheus's ostensibly loving glance is only narcissism; shade or reflection, Eurydice does not really matter here, or rather, she is only matter: a corpse.

The feminist analysis we have only just begun must eventually replay, paradoxically, the sexism of the myth itself, making Eurydice vanish yet again: first, by revealing that woman is only a device here, and second, by observing that she is not the only one possible. The latter point is already suggested by Eurydice's eventual replacement, in the *Aeneid*, by Euryalus. But it is clearer still in Ovid, who anticipates H. D.'s complaint by basing details of Orpheus's backward glance on his own earlier description of Narcissus, who ignored both girls and boys in preference for a lake. Woman is lucky, Ovid seems to say, when she finds herself the object of such reflection; otherwise she is, like Echo, entirely extraneous to male desire.

Iste ego sum, sighs Narcissus, finally, to his lake: "That's me," to use ungrammatical English to capture the subject-object complexity of the Latin, where a demonstrative pronoun with a second-person force elides (*ist'ego*) with "I" to produce an impossibly ambiguous hybrid we can otherwise only translate as "the one you have there, I."[43] Desire, even heterosexual desire, is always this disorienting in Ovid, already in his first erotic episode, in which Apollo pursues Daphne. God and nymph, male and female: they seem safely different—except that Ovid quietly compares Daphne to Diana, Apollo's twin sister.[44]

Like so many objects of desire in Ovid, Daphne is transformed into a tree, and it is not hard to see such trees as figures for writing, either because of their leaves, or because of their bark (*liber*), which ancient etymologists believed to have been one of the first surfaces on which humans wrote (hence the same word came to mean "book").[45] Daphne, of course, becomes not just any tree, but the laurel, which Apollo, god of poetry, decrees to be, henceforth, poetry's symbol and the poet's crown. Apollo who loves Daphne ends the story (and launches the rest of Ovid's poem) as the poet who loves poetry. To ask whether this latter narcissism is homosexual or heterosexual might seem strange, were the question not to resurface, even more insistently, in the case of Orpheus, poetry's other major patron.

Back on the surface of the earth after his second loss of Eurydice, Orpheus does two things. The first is to reject the love of women, turning instead to that of boys, an art he also teaches to his fellow Thracians.[46] His second response is to sing, filling the rest of Ovid's tenth book with a fugue of stories that echo his own even as they transform it. Like Ovid himself, Orpheus begins with Apollo in love, this time with a boy, Cyparissus, who likewise will become a tree, though one that figures not poetry, but death. (The cypress, in fact, is in Orpheus's audience, for his music uproots a whole forest, flora and fauna, that gathers around him to listen, rapt.) Actually, Ovid leaves us unsure whether it is Orpheus or the poet himself who is narrating here; Orpheus subsequently begins in earnest with a brief mention of the story of Jupiter and Ganymede, then a full telling of Apollo's love for Hyacinthus, whose gore the devastated god transforms into a flower on whose petals he inscribes the sounds of his grief.[47] Terms shift a bit for Pygmalion, who like Orpheus scorns the love of women but loves instead a female statue of his own making (and which subsequently comes to life). Myrrha, next, falls in love with her own father, who is tricked into sleeping with her in the dark, where he gives her the nickname "daughter." Their union produces Adonis, whose androgynous beauty captures Venus, who foregoes her usual femininity in order to woo him. To her lover she herself tells (through Orpheus, who speaks in turn through Ovid) the story of the athletic Atalanta and her lover Hippomenes, who looks back at the woman he has defeated and won in a footrace. Gored by a boar, Adonis too becomes a flower, though the transformation takes "a full hour, but no more,"[48] which is roughly how long Orpheus has been singing. With this, the poem is interrupted by the end of the roll, for the story's ending is deferred to the start of book 11, where Orpheus himself is at once interrupted by the angry maenads who will murder and dismember him for his misogyny.

Woman frames this collection, but her precise place within it is more elusive. It would be safer to say that these are stories of subjects and objects variously trapped in desire; here as elsewhere, Ovid uses gender as a ready marker of difference, but it is not his only tool, nor does he use it in a simple way. And more importantly, all differences and similarities in the Orphic ensemble are called to the service of the overarching question that the stories' emphasis on storytelling, art-making, and writing makes clear: are the stories that I (Ovid, Orpheus, Venus) tell like me or unlike me? Is my poem an *iste* or an *ego*? The seemingly impossible answer is always: both. The bisexual poet writes an androgynous page, but this is only the beginning of the romance, for these desires mingle at once with another: that between writer and reader.

This, in fact, is precisely where we began, on the upward slope from Hell. Vergil has been telling all from Orpheus's point of view, but at the moment of Eurydice's disappearance, he abruptly switches perspective: "and she did not see him after that, as he snatched in vain at shadows and wanted to say so much."[49] Ovid, always ready to amplify and keenly aware that as an imitator he is a reader here long before he is a writer, seems to transfer to Eurydice, at least in part, the grasping that Vergil gives to Orpheus, using a series of genderless participles whose referent is unclear:

> flexit amans oculos, et protinus illa relapsa est,
> bracchiaque intendens prendique et prendere certans
> nil nisi cedentes infelix adripit auras.

> . . . loving, he bent his gaze, and at once she slid backward,
> and with outstretched arms, and struggling to be grasped and to grasp,
> she/he snatches at nothing but breezes that gave way.[50]

At the center of all this, a matched pair of infinitives, "to be grasped and to grasp," links these two figures even as it forever divides them—Ovid's most explicit look back at his own Narcissus, who "while seeking is sought" and "plunged his arms into the waters but did not clasp himself in them."[51] But the Orphic page is not simply a mirror. The story in which we have found a scene of writing ends, in both Vergil and Ovid, from Eurydice's point of view. It is thus the poet, not she, who finally vanishes "like smoke dissolved in insubstantial air," the poet whom we ourselves, in this chapter, have struggled to glimpse (if not to grasp). That Orpheus does not really care about Eurydice is not just a feminist complaint; it is also a readerly one. Our only consolation is that the poet too has known this loss. The Vergil who reads Vergil—whether by this we mean the author of the *Aeneid* who reads the *Georgics*, or the author of *Aeneid* 9 who reads *Aeneid* 2, or the Vergil who, anywhere, reads the line he has just completed—is a Eurydice to his own departed Orpheus. And then, as Ovid puts it, *revolutaque rursus eodem est*, "she turns round back where she started,"[52] and the poet, and the poem, start again.

2

MYSELF SICK

Let us imagine a Byzantine grammarian blessed with a fine classical library, one lined with many works we know, but with just as many now lost to us. From these he draws the citations that fill his learned treatises on ancient language and style. In the course of one such study, he offers a discussion of the Greek word *autos*, explaining that, used intensively, it performs one of two opposing operations, either setting the thing described apart from, or emphasizing its connection to, what surrounds it. He then provides examples: "Thus: Though others lie, I myself (*autos*) tell the truth. Or: Being himself (*autos*) Athenian, he too can attend the Assembly. Or that well-known moment when the writer"—and here he names an author otherwise unknown to us—"tells us that he was himself sick (*autos nosēsas*)." Among the rare readers of such grammatical works, rarer still would be the one who would pause here to wonder who this sick author had been, what sort of affliction he had endured, whether being "himself sick" had made him like or unlike others around him, and finally, whether his illness had in any way shaped the text for which he once, apparently, had been famous.

The true story of the transmission of the phrase *autos nosēsas*—which does, in fact, reach us from antiquity—will seem very different from the one I have just imagined. First of all, it is not a fragment but appears instead in the midst of a monumental work that survives complete. Its author is one of antiquity's most celebrated. The illness in question was no passing indisposition but was instead an epidemic of nightmarish severity and scale. The author's telling us that he himself fell victim is one of only two or three moments in which he

28

connects the events described in his work directly to his own life. And though he could not have known this, he thereby tethers to this real catastrophe a vast and imaginative literary tradition that he unwittingly launched. As it happens, being sick made the author like his contemporaries but unlike the centuries of other writers who would imitate his tale of suffering. All of this should have made *autos nosēsas* into one of antiquity's most remembered phrases, not quite *arma virumque*, perhaps, but something close. Instead, its neglect has been almost as complete as it would have been had it survived alone, as a disembodied grammatical example, buried deep in a volume of Byzantine erudition. But to imagine it thus, shorn of all context, is to begin the work of its recovery. For, as it actually survives, it is woven so deeply into a richly colored narrative that few readers stop to think about it in its own right.

The work I have been avoiding naming begins, "Thucydides, an Athenian, wrote an account of the war between the Peloponnesians and the Athenians." This beginning is remarkable for a number of reasons, but above all for the way in which, just one word in, the author and the text have become indistinguishable. This conflation is not unlike that enacted by a question it would be all too easy to ask: Have you read Thucydides? To answer yes is to acknowledge that one has read the word "Thucydides," as well as the many that follow in the course of the work we commonly call the *History of the Peloponnesian War*. What is the affliction that transforms living, breathing authors into words on the page and their names into the names of their works? Writing, of course: Thucydides is here because he "wrote."[1] The twentieth-century death of the author commemorated in my introduction came only at the end of a very long illness: writers have been succumbing to texts ever since they first learned to write their own names.[2]

This Thucydides who wrote Thucydides resurfaces from time to time as our author and investigator but not as anything more until the work's second book and its account of the devastating Athenian plague of 430 BC.[3] There the *autos* we have been considering points back (in a roundabout way) to the work's very first word, for it is Thucydides who was himself sick: "I shall show these things, having been myself sick" (*egō . . . tauta dēlōsō autos te nosēsas*).[4] Here, as in that opening clause, the author appears *qua* author, though with a change of verb: "he wrote an account" (*xunegrapse*) has become "I shall show" (*dēlōsō*).[5] The *autos* that renames Thucydides is here the subject of a first-person verb: "I, having been *myself* sick, shall show . . ."[6] No less significant than the difference in person is the difference in tense: Thucydides will show . . . when? The future here pretends to look forward in the text: in the following passages, "I shall show." But since this demonstration, as Thucydides will explain, is presented specifically for the benefit of posterity, the verb points just as well to future generations. What is remarkable is that a verb that purports to locate the author in the first person, right here, right now, writing the text as it unfolds, already imagines that work from the point of view of the reader. It thus anticipates the *xunegrapse* of the first sentence, which, of course, can truthfully be written only after the work is done.[7] These complicated temporalities may be summarized thus: texts are always pushing authors as writers into their past, allowing them to linger, like the rest of us, only as readers. Thucydides who will write Thucydides becomes Thucydides who wrote Thucydides and thus Thucydides who reads Thucydides. And though that metamorphosis properly begins long before the author puts pen to page, it is at that point of contact, we suppose, that the shock of it all is most palpably felt.

"I shall show these things, having been myself sick and having myself seen others suffering the same" (*tauta dēlōsō autos te nosēsas kai autos idōn allous paschontas*). My translation reproduces the Greek's linear, additive syntax, but it largely loses the shape of the ideas mapped by these words, which are arranged like a bull's-eye target. In the outer loop, on either side, are positioned "showing" (*dēlōsō*) and "seeing" (*idōn*), practically interchangeable activities—because he has seen, he can show, but once he has shown, we, like he, can see "others suffering." Just inside, *autos*, twice, reflected across the sentence's midpoint. Then, a double conjunction (*te . . . kai*) rings the dead center, *nosēsas*, the sentence's real object of attention.

I myself, I myself shall show. . . . But there is no safety for the subject here. For it was Thucydides' own body, which he and all the others must have pored over day and night, which first "showed" the tell-tale signs of infection.[8] And so, once he has again shown these symptoms by writing them down, he again sees himself in the page of his symptomatology, another one of those "suffering others." "These things," "I shall show," "myself," "being sick," "seeing," "others suffering"—each one of these words actually names Thucydides himself.

Here, finally, is the entire sentence:

Λεγέτω μὲν οὖν περὶ αὐτοῦ ὡς ἕκαστος γιγνώσκει καὶ ἰατρὸς καὶ ἰδιώτης, ἀφ' ὅτου εἰκὸς ἦν γενέσθαι αὐτό, καὶ τὰς αἰτίας ἅστινας νομίζει τοσαύτης μεταβολῆς ἱκανὰς εἶναι δύναμιν ἐς τὸ μεταστῆσαι σχεῖν· ἐγὼ δὲ οἷόν τε ἐγίγνετο λέξω, καὶ ἀφ' ὧν ἄν τις σκοπῶν, εἴ ποτε καὶ αὖθις ἐπιπέσοι, μάλιστ' ἂν ἔχοι τι προειδὼς μὴ ἀγνοεῖν, ταῦτα δηλώσω αὐτός τε νοσήσας καὶ αὐτὸς ἰδὼν ἄλλους πάσχοντας.

Let any individual, whether a doctor or not, speak about the plague as he understands it, its likely origins, the causes he thinks sufficient to produce such extensive change and upheaval, but I, having been myself sick and having myself seen others suffering the same, shall tell how it unfolded, and I shall show those things by which, should it ever strike again, anyone who is observant, having first learned what to look for, may not fail to recognize it.[9]

And this is what Thucydides shows:

It was widely agreed that, with respect to other illnesses, the year was remarkably disease-free. Besides, any prior condition degenerated into this one in the end. Other victims, not from any apparent cause, but unexpectedly, while entirely healthy, were seized by severe head-fevers and redness and swelling in their eyes; internally, both throat and tongue suddenly turned blood-red and made the breath abnormal, foul. Next came sneezing and hoarseness, not long after which the physical ordeal moved down into the chest, with severe coughing. And it violently disturbed the stomach, once it had settled there, followed by every ejection of bile for which the doctors have a name, the pain of which was exhausting. Unsuccessful attempts to vomit that produced violent convulsions befell most sufferers, some just as the above symptoms subsided, others much later. Externally, the body was not particularly warm to the touch, nor was it pale, but reddish, dark, and erupting in ulcers and small blisters. Internally, the body's temperature rose to the point that victims could not bear to be covered by the thinnest clothes, sheets, or anything else, preferring instead to be naked, more than happy to hurl themselves into cold water, if they could have. Indeed, many who had no one to take care of them did precisely that, plunging into the cisterns, gripped by thirst without end. But it made no difference whether they drank much or little. Another torment: rest and sleep constantly eluded them.

During the illness's most acute phase, the body did not waste but, rather, held up to its ordeal better than one would have expected. Most, as a result, were finished off by the internal fever with some of their strength still left, on the ninth (or seventh) day. Alternatively, if they made it through this, then the disease descended into the intestines, causing severe ulceration, even as unmitigated diarrhea fell upon them, and many in this second category perished, in the end, from weakness.

Starting from the top, taking position first in the head, the affliction spread through the entire body, and if a victim made it through the worst, then the disease turned instead to the extremities and left its mark (*epesēmainen*)—crashing down upon the genitals and the fingers and toes. Many escaped with the loss of these; others, with that of their eyes. No sooner had they recovered than survivors were gripped by a total and indiscriminate loss of memory and were unable to recognize either themselves or their friends. (Thucydides, *Peloponnesian War* 2.49)

Our instinct is to look away from such a picture—or if to look, then to do so furtively, compulsively, fascinated by our own disgust. In either case we are consoled to know that others suffer thus, not we. Perhaps this is why scholars have been so ready to follow the lead of Thucydides' third-person verbs and to detect here—and to adopt for themselves—a clinical distance from these horrors. Here is what A. W. Gomme, in his long-standard commentary on Thucydides, has to say about this passage: "[T]hat part of Thucydides' story of the great pestilence which is a detailed account of the *symptoms* is, essentially, a digression in the *History* (for they have little to do with politics or war); it is there primarily because he was interested, scientifically, in the disease."[10] But can anyone witness death on this scale (the question is as applicable to the whole war as to the plague) and even the disintegration and disfigurement of one's own body, and retain for these symptoms a merely "scientific" interest? Bound up in Gomme's bizarre dehumanization of his object of study are notions about the role of the historian that go back, of course, to Thucydides himself, who at the beginning of his work offers a famous description of the importance of plainness and accuracy to his method (*Peloponnesian War* 1.20-22). But the author of this autopsy cannot really have been as bloodless as Gomme—or the fleetingness of *nosēsas*—suggests.

In fact, the canonical view that Thucydides devotes extended attention to the plague as a learned amateur anxious to display his competence at medical description was rejected forty years ago by Adam Parry, who, in a brief but biting article, dismantles the thesis that his language and aims are primarily technical.[11] Parry demonstrates instead the plague's many similarities, in language and form, to the war itself, concluding that the former is an integral part of the latter's pathos: "The attempt . . . to see the description of the Plague as a modern scientific treatise, and to persuade us that Thucydides saw it as a thing subject to rational human control, obscures for us not only the compassionate poetry with which the Plague is in fact described, but also the whole meaning of the History."[12]

Ancient readers went even farther than Parry in finding "poetry" in Thucydides, whom they prized primarily neither for his science nor even for his history but for his literary accomplishment, regarding him as one of Greek literature's greatest prose stylists: "The colors (*chrōmata*) of Thucydides' style are solidity (*striphnon*) and density (*puknon*), incisiveness (*pikron*) and starkness (*austēron*), gravity (*embrithes*) and an ability to incite awe, fear, and most of all, empathy (*deinon, phoberon, pathētikon*). When his overall plan and his verbal talent work together, the results are completely successful and wonderful."[13] These words of high praise come, in fact, from Thucydides' most vociferous ancient critic, Dionysius of Halicarnassus, who, despite the grumbling that fills his treatise on his writing, nevertheless saw him as the leading practitioner of the "grand" style.[14] One very much suspects that the account of the plague, which Dionysius nowhere criticizes, was on his mind here as exemplary of the coincidence of style and substance he celebrates. Indeed, it is remarkable how many of the rhetorical "colors" (*chrōmata*, otherwise used especially of the skin and its "complexion") that Dionysius singles out could be said to be symptomatic of the plague itself. Two of them, in fact, appear in Thucydides' subsequent description of the plague's social effects: he singles out as "the most dreadful thing" (*deinotaton*) the double curse of personal despair and collective contagion—those who became sick were sure they would die, while those not yet sick who tried to help them became ill themselves—and he concludes the entire account with a note on the doubleness of the Athenians' suffering (*pathos*) in this year, with war outside the city, and disease within. These twin doubles reveal again how closely knit this narrative is: the city's exterior looks like its interior; the body politic dissolves as rapidly as the bodies that compose it; a common despair afflicts both soul and world. Study the outside that you may know the inside, the plague seems to teach us, and we are to apply that lesson to the text itself, whose style, even, may be used to diagnose something deeper.

Another ancient reader, known as Demetrius, in his treatise *On Style*, responds directly to Thucydides' symptomatology, singling out its first clause as an example of the "grand" style. He offers this remarkable explanation:

> In a number of instances, cacophony in the arrangement of words produces a grand effect . . . Thucydides almost everywhere avoids a smooth, polished arrangement; instead, he always seems to be tripping over something, like someone going down bumpy roads, such as when he says, "It was widely agreed that, with respect to other illnesses, the year was remarkably disease-free." It would have been simpler and sweeter-sounding to say, "with respect to other illnesses, the year was remarkably free of disease." But this would have robbed the line of its grandeur.[15]

Let us take the deliberate misstep that Demetrius hears in that final monosyllable as a cue for our own closer reading, for it sets in motion the downward tumble that characterizes the whole passage. This movement follows the course of the plague's precipitous spread through the body, literally from head to toe. Actual downward movement (*katebainen, stērixeien, epikationtos, anōthen*) is echoed by the metaphorical description of a symptom "falling upon" (*enepipte, epipiptousēs*) its victim, and it sometimes is hard to say whether actual or metaphorical movement is the primary meaning (*kateskēpte*).[16] The result is a general sinking feeling punctuated by moments of near vertigo, concentrated in the passage's most dramatic image, that of parched victims hurling (*rhiptein*) themselves into cisterns, immediately replayed by the description of others gulping down (*katheistēkei*) water to no avail: the external well that does not quench is thus mirrored by the unquenchable one that is the victim's own esophagus.

This last mirroring is crucial, for here the passage's downward movement meets its opposite but complementary force: the disease's constant bubble upward from the victim's insides, its externalization as observable symptom. Symptoms are what Thucydides has promised us, so that the plague, should it return, may be recognized by "anyone who looks."[17] This looking, of course, must be directed toward two objects: the world, secondarily, but first of all, Thucydides' symptomatology, where we are shown what to watch for. This symptom-riddled text is a picture of those bodily surfaces marked by the same, that insistently naked skin on which pustules and ulcers have "flowered" in a variety of purples and reds, the plague's eerie analogue for the page's ink. Writing does the work of disease, as if they were two versions of the same fall into materiality and rise into readability, concomitant forces that meet on the surface, on the skin, on the page. And thus the Thucydides who wrote Thucydides offers here even more than a self-portrait: he almost literally makes present his own diseased flesh (mingled with that of others) beneath the pressures of his pen. Clinical distance? Thucydides surely reproduces instead the alienation and revulsion every victim must have felt. In that final, grand image of survivors unable, or unwilling, to recognize themselves lies the question he too must ask, now of his page, as once of his body: Is that really me? Did that skin really contain me? And finally (though here we move into a new set of questions): Does that picture of my skin really capture what it was all like?

At a broader level, the plague subjects language itself to something of a crisis: how much simplification of difference is tolerable, even at the superficial level of a description of symptoms? We can decide we know the difference between blisters, pustules, and ulcers, for example, but is every blister like the next, from body to body, or even on the same one? Thucydides nods at this problem in his passing reference to "every ejection of bile for which doctors have a name." Thucydides does not give us these names. What sense would they make to us? Does he even know them himself? And what good does it do that doctors name what they cannot cure? Presumably, furthermore, we are supposed to imagine still other ejections for which no name yet exists. In any case, the phrase is merely a way of speaking, a gesture toward an unnamable horror: no lexicon could ever name every disintegration these bodies endured. But at the same time, even the ordinary words for the body's parts—head, throat, lungs, bowels—seem too numerous, as the plague reduces us all to little more than heaps of flesh and fluid. A description of the plague is, in this respect, eerily like the plague itself: indiscriminate, indifferent, indeed, a demolisher of structures of difference, a leveler. "The distinctiveness of the plague is that it ultimately destroys all forms of distinctiveness," as René Girard neatly puts it.[18]

Immediately following his symptomatology, Thucydides notes that the *eidos* of the plague defies description, that it is literally "stronger than language" (*kreisson logou*), just as the pain it caused exceeded the limits of human endurance. *Eidos* in such a context would ordinarily be, simply, "visible form," but translators usually give it here its extended meaning as "kind," "character," "nature." A recent commentator reveals the problem by preferring "form" but insisting that *kreisson logou* be translated "beyond explanation" — "hardly 'beyond description' since Thucydides has just described it."[19] But has he? Surely we should rather take the author at his word: I simply cannot convey what the plague really looked like. What instead he can do is made clear by the rest of the sentence: "What the plague looked like goes beyond what words can tell; the particulars of each individual case were more than human nature could bear. It showed (*edēlōse*) itself to be especially different from familiar illnesses in the following detail: many bodies lay unburied, but the birds and four-legged animals which feed on human flesh either would not come near them or else, tasting them, shared their death" (*Peloponnesian War* 2.50.1). In other words, Thucydides can offer elements, patterns, symptoms (here it is the plague itself that "shows"). He can show us the plague's skin, trace its outline. But he scarcely can fill this with all the things he saw (to say nothing of the things he felt) in that year of terror.[20] *Eidos* is not so much "kind" as its opposite: the devil was in the details, and few of these were generalizable to the entire epidemic.[21] (This, in fact, is exactly what Thucydides says at the beginning of the next paragraph: "This, then, was the plague, to give a general picture, leaving aside many other matters of detail, for what happened to one victim was never exactly the same as what happened to the next" [*Peloponnesian War* 2.51.1].) To put things crudely, we cannot really "get" the plague from Thucydides, as he himself takes pains to caution (or reassure) us.

What would have been better? We might wish that Thucydides had been more like Daniel Defoe, who in his *Journal of the Plague Year* claims to offer us stories of real people coping, day by day, house by house, with the London plague of 1665. But Thucydides would have every right to reply that Defoe's account seems largely to be a fiction. Surely, though, he could have told us a bit more about himself? What course did the disease follow in his own body? Did he too lose his fingers, or his genitals? And by what miracle did he survive? Is it shame at his disfigurement, or guilt for his survival, or humility at the enormity of what he has undertaken to describe that leads him to intrude into this narrative by no more than a phrase? We would not have been much worse off — we might complain, with a hint of cruelty — had *autos nosēsas* been all that survived of your *History*, Thucydides. But to these questions and provocations, Thucydides simply replies, once again, "myself sick."

Our exasperation, though, tells us something new about authorship. In the last chapter, we made a case for recovering the author, if not as a writer, then at least as the first reader of the text beneath her pen. But the author is not only the text's first reader: she is also a peculiar kind of reader, a peculiarity that persists even after the work is done. We all sometimes identify with the texts we read, but the author is that one reader who can look down and say, unabashedly, like Narcissus, *iste ego sum*, "that's me." Thucydides wrote Thucydides, but significantly, the same convention applies even if what you write is not your own story or even your own history. Thus, to use the subject of the next chapter as an example, Lucretius wrote Lucretius, even though what he wrote as the grand finale of his six-book poem was a Latin translation, often word-for-word, of the Thucydidean plague.

But whose story is Thucydides' in the first place? He tells us, famously, that he wants his history to be a *ktēma es aiei*, "a possession for all time" (*Peloponnesian War* I.22.4). This may seem like a bid for authorial immortality, but it really is something like the opposite, for a possession is a thing, and a thing cannot be immortal, only monumental: here lies Thucydides; i.e., Thucydides is here no longer.[22] Was he ever? Perhaps his absence was the point all along. By telling us of a plague that few victims survived, surely Thucydides asks us (and thus himself) to imagine, briefly, that he too succumbed, that the body he made bleed on the page, as the page, did not escape this story and thus is still here, a corpse. This is my body, he seems to say: take it away from me.

3

❧

LATIN DECOMPOSITION

For the year 94 BC, the *Chronicon* of Jerome offers an enigmatic notice containing precious facts—if they are true—from the obscure life of one of Rome's greatest poets:

> Titus Lucretius poeta nascitur, qui postea amatorio poculo in furorem versus, cum aliquot libros per intervalla insaniae conscripsisset, quos postea Cicero emendavit, propria se manu interfecit anno aetatis XLIIII.

> Birth of Titus Lucretius, poet. Later driven mad by a love-potion, he committed suicide at age forty-four, having written, during breaks in his insanity, several books which Cicero later corrected.[1]

There is much here that could be said to be scandalous: sex, drugs, madness, suicide. And yet it is a seemingly drab bibliographical note—*quos postea Cicero emendavit*—which has caused Lucretian scholars the most unease. Karl Lachmann avoids the nightmarish possibility of philosophical tinkering with the text by the anti-Epicurean Cicero by proposing that *Cicero* here actually designates the orator's brother Quintus, who, "though not unfamiliar with philosophy, was not devoted to any particular school."[2] Others have sought instead to minimize the force of *emendavit*. H. A. J. Munro, for example, supposes that Cicero was "patron more than actual editor" and offered "his name rather than his time," passing the poem along to a team of copyists after "only a few hours in looking over it or hearing it read to him."[3] Cyril Bailey similarly takes the verb to mean only "that Cicero glanced at the poem" and stipulates that any critical interventions can have been only "from the purely poetic point of view."[4] This last limitation is already implicit in the so-called *vita Borgiana*, which imagines the poet reading his books, as he wrote them, to an obliging Cicero, who periodically interrupts him to urge restraint in his metaphors (*inter legendum aliquando admonitus ut in translationibus servaret verecundiam*).[5] But even John Masson, who discovered the *vita* in a Renaissance manuscript and took this vignette to be "genuine, and derived from Suetonius,"[6] pauses to scratch his head: "One cannot help wondering what Cicero thought of Lucretius's poem. Its matter we know that he disapproved. But what of its style? That he could have approved only partially. It is, indeed, the antipodes of his own. What would Boileau have said of Victor Hugo's poetry?"[7] Such squirming is the ultimate culprit for the scholarly blunders we have just rehearsed: Lachmann's suggestion is far-fetched ("Cicero," by itself, can only mean the one and only); Munro and Bailey force onto *emendare* meanings that it cannot bear; the *vita Borgiana* is almost certainly a Renaissance forgery.[8] Indeed, Masson's question lingers as the most honest acknowledgment of what scholars really seem to have been asking themselves all along: what could Ciceronian *bon sens* ever have made of the pyrotechnic genius of the *De rerum natura*? In the end, most have been content largely to ignore this meeting of such seemingly different minds—or, indeed, to dismiss Jerome's entire entry as a clever piece of biographical fiction.[9]

Doubting Jerome, however, does not quite settle the matter, first of all because it suggests that ancient readers found the attribution of an editorial role to Cicero plausible, leaving us again to wonder whether modern readers have been missing something. More importantly, we happen to know that, whatever the meaning or reliability of Jerome's account, Cicero did, in fact, at least *read* the poem, for he himself tells us so, in a letter to his brother Quintus:

> Lucreti poemata ut scribis ita sunt, multis luminibus ingeni, multae tamen artis.

> The poetry of Lucretius has just what you say in your letter: "many flashes of genius." But, at the same time, it shows considerable artistry.[10]

The praise is cryptic and at least partially quoted from Quintus, but it leaves no doubt that Cicero found things to admire in what he read, including—and somewhat to his surprise, in the most likely understanding of his wording—poetic *ars*.[11]

This chapter will try to shed new light on what those artistic qualities might have been and, along the way, on Cicero (including Cicero *poeta*) and Lucretius themselves. To do so, we follow the lead of Masson and of his Renaissance forger, leaving aside questions of scientific and philosophical content in order to imagine the text through the eyes of Cicero the stylist. The following sections, however, offer a slightly uncustomary take on what Ciceronian style really was all about—and, incidentally, why it would continue to matter for centuries of writers (and not just orators). Near the end, we shall try to begin to answer a further question about the remarkable influence that Lucretius' poem—and in particular, its finale—would exert on subsequent Latin poetry, all the way to the Renaissance.

Worms

In the second book of his satires, Lucilius seems to have offered a version in hexameters of the trial for extortion of the elder Quintus Mucius Scaevola, a friend. In the following fragment, Lucilius has Scaevola mercilessly ridicule the rhetorical style of his accuser, Titus Albucius:

> quam lepide lexis compostae ut tesserulae omnes
> arte pavimento atque emblemate vermiculato
>
> How charmingly, like little tiles, are the words composed,
> all artfully, as in a pavement and vermiculate emblem.[12]

What kinds of mosaics did Lucilius have in mind? The syntax of the two lines is a bit unclear, but Lucilius's ultimate reference is to the finest products of the mosaic-setter: "emblems," i.e., studio pieces made of tiny cubes and then "set into" larger pavements worked more crudely (hence, *emblēma*, an "insert," from *emballō*). In such work the *tesserae* minutely trace the contours of the objects represented and thence ripple outward in waves that eventually converge with other undulating contours. From a distance, the best of such mosaics can seem to be paintings; from close by, the array of wriggling lines can indeed (with a little imagination) resemble a bed of worms, whence the adjective *vermiculatus*,[13] as well as the technical term *opus vermiculatum* sometimes seen in modern art-historical scholarship, though the phrase does not survive in any ancient text.

The principal point of the entire Lucilian gibe is usually taken to be the one implicit in Scaevola's use of the Greek words *lexis* and *emblēma*: Albucius, whose exuberant philhellenism went far beyond that of Lucilius and his friends, has pursued a style that is prettily and preciously Greek.[14] But we know these lines from Cicero, who quotes from them in three different works and whose own interest is clearly in the double simile that lies at the heart of Lucilius's image: namely, there exists a rhetorical style (in this case, that of Albucius) that is like mosaic-work that is, in turn, like worms.

There is much at stake here, and in order to get at it we must pursue a somewhat complicated excursus through Cicero's *rhetorica*. Cicero twice cites the Lucilian verses in full, once in the *De oratore* and again in the *Orator*. One might assume that Cicero reports the jest approvingly—that is to say, that Cicero's own views on vermiculate rhetoric coincide with those of the Lucilian Scaevola. But in fact Cicero's precise perspective remains rather elusive. We start with the *De oratore*, where the quotation nominally is made by the orator Lucius Licinius Crassus, principal speaker of the fictitious dialogue. Crassus's banter around the two lines is colloquial to the point of obscurity, but his basic meaning is plain enough: Lucilius, Albucius, and Crassus himself may differ in degree of skill, but all share an interest in *conlocatio verborum*, the proper placement of words. Crassus describes their common technique as follows:

> Conlocationis est componere et struere verba sic ut neve asper eorum concursus neve hiulcus sit, sed quodam modo coagmentatus et levis.

> *Conlocatio* involves arranging and assembling words in such a way that their meeting may be neither rough nor gaping, but in effect well-joined and smooth.[15]

Since there is nothing in this language that could not be applied just as easily to the arranger of vermiculate mosaics, the Ciceronian Crassus seems to be suggesting that, in rhetoric as in mosaic, the vermiculate is a good thing after all.

In the *Orator*, Cicero himself, no longer ventriloquizing but speaking instead in his own voice, offers what first appears to be a different view:

> Let us consider the nature of that first goal (inasmuch as it most especially requires care), namely, the creation of a structure of some sort (*ut fiat quasi structura quaedam*)—not, however, in a belabored way (*nec tamen fiat operose*), for such work would be both endless and infantile (*nam esset cum infinitus tum puerilis labor*), on which count Scaevola, in Lucilius, wittily assails Albucius,
>
> > quam lepide lexis compostae ut tesserulae omnes
> > arte pavimento atque emblemate vermiculato
>
> I do not want this construction to appear (?) so minute (*nolo haec tam minuta*

constructio appareat). But in any case, a practiced pen will make this way of composing easy (*sed tamen stilus exercitatus efficiet facilem hanc viam componendi*).[16]

Under scrutiny, Cicero's advice here is not quite as straightforward as it might at first seem. In the first place, Cicero's rejection of *labor* that is *infinitus* and *puerilis* finds an oddly discordant echo in the *stilus exercitatus* invoked after the verses. Given Cicero's advice to young orators in the *De oratore* that writing is the best training for speaking (*stilus optimus et praestantissimus dicendi effector ac magister*),[17] he seems in the *Orator* to be relying on a common artistic (and pedagogical) paradox: one must work at something precisely so that it may become easy—in this case, one must exercise one's pen (or with one's pen) so that one's future orations need not be constructed *operose*. But even this does not mean that the seasoned orator has no work to do. When Cicero says, *nolo haec tam minuta constructa appareat*, context is everything, for in the pages that precede and follow, Cicero is describing—in what can only be called minute detail—not only the proper placement of words but also that of syllables into the sonorous rhythms of Ciceronian prose. Indeed, the key word here is *appareat*: "I do not want this construction to *appear* so minute"—Cicero does not say that the construction should not *be* so minute. Besides, the Latin does not really mean what we have been saying it means, though the rearrangement of the words into the order *nolo tam minuta haec constructio appareat* in some of the manuscripts (and in editions that follow them) doubtless represents an effort to force this meaning onto the text. In fact, *apparere* is almost never used as a linking verb in classical Latin, and so Cicero plainly means this: "I do not want so minute a construction *to be visible*."[18] The vermiculate vice may have consequences for *constructio*, but the problem itself lies emphatically at the level of perception.

We are now prepared to consider a third passage from Cicero's *rhetorica*. A few months before the *Orator*, Cicero wrote the *Brutus*, and there too he refers to the Lucilian verses, albeit in paraphrase.[19] Warmly praising the oratory of the recently deceased Marcus Calidius, and singling out his skill in constructing periods, Cicero says this:

In comparison to his period (*comprensio verborum*), nothing was as delicate, nothing was as flexible, nothing could have been shaped in greater accord with his intent. In short, no orator matched his ability in this. First of all, his period was so pure that nothing was more limpid (*ita purus erat ut nihil liquidius*), and it flowed so freely that nowhere did it stick (*ita libere fluebat ut nusquam adhaeresceret*). You could discern no word that was not positioned in its place and joined as if, to quote Lucilius, part of a vermiculate emblem (*nullum nisi loco positum et tamquam in vermiculato emblemate, ut ait Lucilius, structum verbum videres*).[20]

Lucilius had used *vermiculatus* to designate a style that was radically and relentlessly tessellated. In the *De oratore* and the *Orator*, Cicero conserves this meaning, however ambiguous the advice he ultimately offers. But in the *Brutus*, where the absence of a full quotation of the Lucilian verses perhaps mitigated the pressure to remain faithful to their original intent, Cicero exactly reverses Lucilius's meaning, making *vermiculatus* a compliment for uninterrupted rhetorical flow.[21]

How can the vermiculate be both virtue and its opposed vice? One begins with a simple answer: all of the persons considered thus far, save perhaps Albucius, would agree that intricacy is not an end to itself but is instead a means to an end. And Cicero, at least, knows that this end is nothing less than the effacement of that very intricacy, since the fully composed work ideally gives no evidence of its composition out of discrete parts. (In a phrase sometimes falsely but plausibly attributed to antiquity, *ars est celare artem*.)[22] In this regard, vermiculate mosaic-work is praiseworthy for its illusionistic ambitions, but ultimately it falls victim to its own crude materiality, since any viewer need only move closer and the illusion dissolves. Not so for the well-composed speech, the joins of which are seamless from any distance to all but the practiced eye of the connoisseur, who, like Cicero in the case of Calidius, can still recognize—and appreciate—the vermiculate underpinnings of rhetorical polish.

Stars

Perusers of the *Oxford Classical Dictionary* whose eyes happen to light on the bottom of the second column of page 136 are probably shocked to learn that "the most widely read poem, after the *Iliad* and *Odyssey*, in the ancient world" was the *Phaenomena* of Aratus, a poem about star-gazing and predicting the weather.[23] C. J. Toomer, a historian of science and writer of the Aratus article, does not tell us how he arrived at such a calculus, but he may well be right. And in any case, even the mere plausibility of Toomer's observation is enough to make us marvel at the poem's oblivion in modern scholarship: the sum total of all works on Aratus in the past century scarcely matches the bibliography on just one of the Homeric epics in a single bad year. The fact that the editors of the *OCD* assigned antiquity's third "most widely read poem" to a historian of science already hints at the problem, as does the fact that, if you go looking for the *Phaenomena* in a university library, you will find editions divided between the sections for Greek literature and general astronomy. Aratus might have hoped for some rehabilitation—or at least some sympathy—from Douglas Kidd's hefty 1997 edition and commentary, result, Kidd tells us in his preface, of three decades of painstaking work on a poem that "has been the victim of many misunderstandings."[24] But in his introduction to the poem, Kidd studiously avoids commenting on the work's literary merit, only once warming to his subject enough to say this: "Aratus relieves the solemnity and repetitive nature of his subject matter with lighter touches of dry humor and verbal wit."[25] This is not exactly the encouragement we need before tackling 1,154 Homericizing hexameters.

But modern scholars—both the few who read Aratus and the many who avoid him—seem to be missing something that must have been readily perceived by the poem's ancient fans. Certainly it is unwise to judge the poem as a straightforward astronomical handbook, since on this score the poem's errors received harsh judgment already in antiquity, suggesting that the poem's enduring popularity was not the result of its accuracy. Cicero himself observes that "learned men agree that Aratus, though ignorant of astronomy, spoke about the heavens and the stars with gorgeous poetry."[26] And, indeed, even the *OCD*, despite its initial decision to treat the poem as monument in the history of science, concedes that it "was read more for its literary charm." But pointing out that a poem is literature—even charming literature—does not quite suffice to explain the success of the *Phaenomena*. Rather, the poem's charms—and probably the secret of its success—lie in a very precise conflation: Aratus presents astronomy as something very much like poetry itself.[27]

The similarity exists at two levels. The first is what we might call a "readerly" level: inasmuch as the stargazer is concerned with the recognition of *sēmeia*—here "constellations" but more generally "signs"—his or her search for meaning in the sky ("reading the stars") is not unlike the search for meaning in the text. But the more important similarity is a "writerly" one: as the poet arranges words into meaningful phrases and sentences, so the stargazer—let us for the sake of argument imagine one of those first stargazers to organize the heavens—arranges stars into constellations. At the most basic level, both activities are *poiēsis* because both are built of acts of composition.

Of course, the composer of the stars is subject to a material constraint not shared by the composer of words: the stars may not be moved to suit his or her purposes; composition is limited to the decision of which stars to associate with which, and how. This simple dilemma is surely responsible for the fact that the sky was found to be full of things that twist and turn. Ask a child to connect a page of randomly placed dots and you will likely receive a picture of a snake, or a caterpillar, or an octopus—no solutions are simpler. And so the starry page of heaven is filled with curved things: a snake, a dragon, a hydra, a dolphin, a scorpion, a wreath, a swan, rivers and other flowing water, and several fish, to name only the most obvious.

But watch what happens when this serpentine sky meets the page of the poet:

> Τὰς δὲ δι' ἀμφοτέρας οἵη ποταμοῖο ἀπορρὼξ
> εἰλεῖται, μέγα θαῦμα, Δράκων, περί τ' ἀμφί τ' ἐαγὼς
> μυρίος· αἱ δ' ἄρα οἱ σπείρης ἑκάτερθε φέρονται
> Ἄρκτοι, κυανέου πεφυλαγμέναι ὠκεανοῖο.
> Αὐτὰρ ὅ γ' ἄλλην μὲν νεάτῃ ἐπιτείνεται οὐρῇ,
> ἄλλην δὲ σπείρῃ περιτέμνεται·

> Between both (the Bears), like a segment of a river, tightly winds a great wonder, the Dragon, its course broken by countless windings around and back; and the Bears are borne along on either side of its coil, keeping clear of the glistening blue Ocean. Over one it stretches with the tip of its tail, while it cuts off the other with its coil.[28]

This slithering dragon, product of the compositional constraints of the sky, slips into those of the written line, gliding left to right and back again as our eyes trace the unfolding of the poet's image. But here and there the monster twists free, in part through the more flexible connections (even more dramatic in the Greek) allowed by pronouns, and encircles two constellations that had been described several lines earlier. This is the Aratean game.[29]

It surely was the poem's marriage of form and content that attracted not only readers but also imitators. Among these imitators were also translators, and among these translators was the young Cicero. A surviving fragment of his *Aratea* preserves part of his Latin version of the lines we have just considered:

> Has inter veluti rapido cum gurgite flumen
> torvu' Draco serpit subter superaque revolvens
> sese conficiensque sinus e corpore flexos.[30]

Cicero seeks to outdo his model in at least two ways. First, in describing the dragon's movement, he takes advantage of a Latin verb, *serpere*, that not only is cognate with "serpent" but which also has as its initial letter, emphasized by the alliteration that follows (*serpit subter superaque*) the *S* that embodies that movement, to say nothing of the snake's hiss. (Cicero uses *serpere* throughout his translation of the poem, not only when describing serpents—and often when there is no justification in the Greek original.) Second, Cicero greatly amplifies his model's brief description of the serpent's winding path, having it turn on itself in order to twist curves from its own body (*sese conficiensque sinus e corpore flexos*), an image perhaps prefigured by the whirlpool (*gurges*), likewise absent in Aratus. Are Cicero's changes effective? On balance, we probably must say that, in his efforts to stitch the serpentine image more tightly together, Cicero has rendered the verses' structure both more intricate and more conspicuous. In other words, he has succumbed to the vicious side of the vermiculate. Alas, it would not be the last time.

Snakes

According to Plutarch, the young Cicero prized poetry above all other intellectual pursuits. The biographer singles out for mention a work composed while Cicero was still a boy, based on the slippery story of Glaucus, the fisherman who was transformed into a half man, half-fish, a poem of which no other trace has survived, unless we unknowingly hear it echoed in Ovid's treatment of the same theme. Perhaps from the same general period was another lost poem, this one on the most magnificent of serpentine subjects, the Nile (subject, likewise, of one of antiquity's most famous surviving vermiculate mosaics, in Palestrina, where the river, lined with vignettes of life in its waters and on its banks, winds left and right across a large pavement[31]). More importantly, the Nilotic theme reminds us that many of the aesthetic currents we have been sampling flowed from, or at least through, Alexandria. But returning to our subject: if Plutarch is to be believed, there came a moment in which Cicero "was looked upon as the best poet, as well as the greatest orator, in Rome."[32]

But whatever heights Cicero the young poet attained, his eventual fall from grace was absolute. It would be cruel to rehearse all of the negative things that have been said about Cicero's poetry; let us content ourselves with the withering quip of Tacitus:

> Fecerunt enim et carmina et in bibliothecas retulerunt, non melius quam Cicero, sed felicius, quia illos fecisse pauciores sciunt.

> [Brutus and Caesar] wrote poems and had them placed in libraries—no better than Cicero, but more luckily, since fewer know that they did so.[33]

In this regard, time has been slightly kinder: only the *Aratea* reaches us by an independent manuscript tradition (and this in mutilated form); the bulk of the remaining fragments survive as quotations in later texts, most of which are Cicero's own philosophical treatises.

Cicero's *De divinatione* preserves one of the longer fragments: thirteen lines from the *Marius*, an encomium of that other famous man from Arpinum, a work of uncertain date. In the passage Marius finds a favorable omen in a deadly struggle he witnesses between an eagle and a snake:

> Hic Iovis altisoni subito **pinnata satelles**
> arboris e trunco *serpentis* **saucia** *morsu*
> **subrigit ipsa feris transfigens unguibus** *anguem*
> *semianimum et varia graviter cervice micantem*
> *quem se intorquentem* **lanians rostroque cruentans**
> **iam satiata animos iam duros ulta dolores**
> **abiecit** *ecflantem et laceratum* **adfligit** in unda
> **seque** obitu a solis nitidos **convertit** ad ortus.

> In a flash the winged herald of thundering Jove, stung by the bite of a snake, rises up from the trunk of a tree with her talons, fierce, trans-fixing the snake, half-alive and twitching heavily from its spangled neck and which, as it twists on itself, she rips and bloodies with her beak. Then, having appeased her rage, having avenged her deep pain, she hurls it away, breathing its last, and casts its torn body on the sea. Then she turns her course from the setting to the bright rising of the sun.[34]

To help us see what Cicero is doing here, I have placed all the words that refer to the eagle in boldface and those that refer to the snake in italics. We first note *unguibus anguem*, which juxtaposes two words that differ by only one letter, *unguis* and *anguis*, to designate the two animals precisely at the moment in the narrative when they fuse into a nearly indistinguishable mass. All around, the phrases describing the eagle and the snake alternate, suggesting the way in which the animals themselves are locked in struggle. At the center of it all lies a long description of the snake, bent around three lines, with *graviter* dead center, like a fulcrum. Elsewhere, the struggle is so intense that sometimes it is momentarily difficult to know which animal is designated by which word. Thus the reflexive pronoun appears twice in the passage but once designates the snake, once the eagle. And indeed in each of those two moments, the indi-vidual animal's body mimics the confusion of the whole struggle by turning back on itself (*se intorquentem; se convertit*).

Not exactly a *technopaignion* (the ancient ancestor of calligrams and other pattern poems),[35] Cicero's verses, nevertheless, are pointedly aware of their appearance as a written text, outstripping the more limited serpentine word-games of Aratus. Here, Cicero comes close to a kind of crude map or even pic-ture of the action, which is concentrated on a single scene, not unlike the frozen moments immortalized by the constellations. Indeed, the visual is doubly assertive here: first, in the ecphrastic mode of the poem's content, and second, in the calligrammic conceits of its form. Both aspects resist any effort by the reader to build meaning incrementally, word by word: we need the whole picture to make sense of this story.

Of course, such a deferral is in the very nature of syntax, which in Latin, in particular, can make us wait very long indeed before the pieces all come together. Indeed, this is part of what makes Cicero's word picture work: the entire eight-line excerpt is a single sentence. Other hexameter poets must occasionally go on for as long as this, but one worries a bit that this fragment may be representative of a rather ponderous whole. That Cicero's sentences are too long has been many a Latin student's lament, struggling, of course, not with his poetry (which no one reads) but with his oratory (which we all have been reading since his own lifetime). In oratory, however, the long sentence is, to the trained ear, not a vice but a high virtue; indeed, Cicero would perfect to the point of making his own that mightiest of sentences: the period. We need not concern ourselves here with the long struggles of ancient theorists to define the period, variously on the basis of its size, structure, or sound.[36] What strikes us instead is the metaphor that gives it its name: this is a sentence that somehow comes back around—hence *periodos*, *peri-hodos*, the "road around." In other words, we have here yet another curve, oddly similar, geometrically, to the strangely persistent poetic snake (seen in Aratus, in Cicero's translation of Aratus, and in his own *Marius*) that doubles back on itself.[37]

The period, in fact, is the most elegant and famous curve of ancient compositional theory, and its curvilinear recursiveness is retained (even as its "road" is somewhat lost) in most of the equivalent Latin terms listed by Cicero in an important discussion in the *Orator*: *ambitus, circuitus, comprehensio, continuatio, circumscriptio*.[38] It is this last suggestion that most stands out: *circumscriptio*, a "contour," an "outline." By this word, Rome's greatest orator, in his treatise on the ideal orator, analogizes the most magnificent achievement of oratory to something produced not orally at all, but by a pen—indeed, not even a pen that produces words but one which, instead, traces the perimeter of the (two-dimensional) space that the orator's words notionally occupy. The visual is once again assertive here, and as before, it stands above all for the simultaneity that is natural to the pictorial arts, for the orator who delivers his periods one word at a time must count on his listeners to hold them all in the temporary fixity of their memories until he comes back around, completing the metaphorical full circle of his meaning. The verbal memory of an ancient Roman raised on harangues in the Forum was doubtless far better than our own, and it was further helped by rhythmical and other rhetorical signposting along the period's path that modern readers tend to hear only faintly, if at all. Nevertheless, it is difficult not to suppose that, just as for the poems considered above, the period's most natural habitats were the wax in which it emerged (in the orator's study) and the papyrus to which it was destined (as a "published" oration).[39] When he calls a period a *circumscriptio*, therefore, Cicero is hinting that it can best be seen and admired (he is speaking, in the *Orator*, as a critic—and largely of orators he knows *only* through books) in written form.

Memory and writing, whether allies or, as Plato famously argues, antagonists,[40] provide the fixity that is impossible in speech alone, which can only offer word after word—indeed, not even this, but rather, sound after sound, linked together into words only in the mind that pronounces or hears them. Language itself, in other words, is impossible without such fixity; composition elevates that most basic need into a high aesthetic principle. Pursuit of that principle, however, was fraught with pitfalls, as we have seen, since the poet or orator who devotes too much attention to composition in the quasi-pictorial sense of "arrangement" risks producing not a painting but a mosaic, i.e., a tessellated, segmented style of the sort for which Lucilius derides Albucius. Indeed, to our analysis of the Lucilian critique above, we may now add this even deeper problem: too much (synchronic) arrangement gets in the way of language's other need: (diachronic) flow. Too much flow, on the other hand, overwhelms the compositional principle with an incongruous stream-of-consciousness, famously analogized by Horace, in the opening verses of the *Ars Poetica*, to a grotesque painting:

> Humano capiti cervicem pictor equinam
> iungere si velit, et varias inducere plumas
> undique collatis membris, ut turpiter atrum
> desinat in piscem mulier formosa superne,
> spectatum admissi risum teneatis, amici?
> Credite, Pisones, isti tabulae fore librum
> persimilem cuius, velut aegri somnia, vanae
> fingenter species, ut nec pes nec caput uni
> reddatur formae.

> If, to a human head, some painter should choose to attach a horse's neck, and to stick colorful feathers onto limbs assembled from all quarters, so that what was a shapely woman above would end, hideously, in a black fish, would you, my friends, let in to admire it, be able to keep from laughing? My dear Romans, suppose

that there were to be a book very like that painting, one whose images, like the dreams of a delirious person, would be fashioned in such an empty way that neither head nor foot would correspond to a single figure.[41]

Both painter and poet here violate a basic imperative to artistic unity (the mostly Aristotelian vein that Horace will mine for lines to come),[42] but scholars tend to miss that the central point of the analogy is the *difference* between the two: bad poets produce such monstrosities—and Roman readers tolerate them—because they lose sight of what no painter or spectator, by contrast, can miss. Indeed, clues that the real target of this parody will be not a painting but a text are there, long before *credite* etc., in the curvy things— a horse's neck, a shapely woman's torso, a fish's tail—that make a disjointed mockery of the self-reflexive flow that poetic or rhetorical composition is supposed to produce.[43] We may contrast Cicero's praise of Calidius, in the passage from the *Brutus* considered earlier, for composition that, instead, was so minutely expert as to produce a period "which flowed so freely that nowhere did it stick" (*ita libere fluebat ut nusquam adhaeresceret*).

Further exploration of Horace's prescriptions would take us far afield. But before leaving the *Ars Poetica*, let us note that its opening image begins *humano capite*, only then to dissolve, through the painter-poet's compositional faults, into zoological monstrosity.[44] The human body, and even humanity itself, for reasons that will become clearer below, have a deep stake in successful composition; failure, by contrast, leads to black fishtails—or, to return whence we began, to beds of worms. Perhaps, in fact, the Lucilian *vermiculatus* is not entirely innocent of an at least subconscious association with that "boneless and bloodless hoard," as Lucretius will unforgettably describe it,[45] against which the life of every human body is hedged, until it succumbs at last to death and to wriggling *de*composition. And with this, we turn to the finale of the poem Cicero read.

Bodies

The *De rerum natura* ends with a lavish description of the plague that devastated Athens in the second year of the Peloponnesian War, closely based (often word-for-word) on the account of Thucydides, who, as we saw in the last chapter, was himself a victim—and rare survivor. Lucretius, however, prefaces the plague with a general description of how such epidemics arise and spread, placing the blame on the movement of air over long distances to places to which it is not native:

Proinde ubi se caelum, quod nobis forte alienum,
commovet atque aer inimicus serpere coepit,
ut nebula ac nubes paulatim repit et omne,
qua graditur conturbat et immutare coactat,
fit quoque ut, in nostrum cum venit denique caelum,
corrumpat reddatque sui simile atque alienum.

Thus, when an atmosphere which happens to be foreign to us
shifts, and harmful air begins to wind its way (*serpere coepit*), then,
just as a mist or fog creeps along, bit by bit, and confuses everything, wherever it spreads, and makes things change form, so it
happens, likewise, that when this air reaches our atmosphere, it
corrupts it and makes it like itself and unlike what we are used to.
(*De rerum natura* 6.1119–24)

Our attention is at once attracted to *serpere*. Here the word is no isolated
conceit but instead sets in motion all that follows. As moves the *aer inimicus*,
so moves disease, and with the disease moves the poem, to say nothing of
the reader, uncomfortably implicated in this pestilential creep. Indeed, several
elements lend Lucretius's final scene what we could almost call a cinematic
feel. There is, first of all, the sense of an aerial view of the devastation: the
reader, a stranger to the suffering below, hovers with the invading *aer*. But
more important is the fact that the myriad actors in this tragic scene by and
large do not themselves move, being paralyzed by disease. As a result, the
movement *of* the scene is not movement *in* the scene but is instead the movement of the poem itself, like the sweep of a camera over a bloody battlefield
after the fighting has ended, and the only the action that remains lies in
countless final struggles with death. There *is* in the account a notional movement through time, since Lucretius describes the disease's progressive effects—
from the onset of symptoms to the almost inevitable end on the eighth or ninth
day. But this progression is not in fact entirely chronological, since Lucretius
does not describe just one victim's decline but instead skips from one diseased
body to another—again, as if a camera were surveying the devastation and
picking out sufferers who, having contracted the disease at different moments,
exhibit different stages of its symptoms. In other words, the Lucretian finale
moves as much through space as through time. This is not unlike Aratus, surveying the stars, and on reflection it was true in Cicero's *Marius* as well, where
the collapse of time almost into a single instant transforms the action (expressed almost entirely by participles) into a question of each animal's location
in space. But Lucretius far outdoes both: his slowdown is longer than any that

Cicero sustains, and unlike Aratus, he tells not the miscellaneous stories of the sky but, rather, through various frozen victims, the single story of the plague itself.

Stopped in their tracks not only by disease but also by the whole synchronic, panoramic narrative in which they have been preserved, the bodies of the victims of the Lucretian plague turn in on themselves, grinding to a halt even internally:

> Principio caput incensum fervore gerebant
> et duplicis oculos suffusa luce rubentes.
> Sudabant etiam fauces intrinsequos atrae
> sanguine et ulceribus vocis via saepta coibat,
> atque animi interpres manabat lingua cruore
> debilitata malis, motu gravis, aspera tactu.

> The first symptoms were a head aflame with fever and both eyes bathed in a pinkish glow. The throat perspired and, within, turned black with blood, while the voice's path, fenced with sores, closed on itself, and the tongue—interpreter of the mind!—weak with pain, slow to move, rough to touch, now oozed with gore. (*De rerum natura* 6.1145–50)

Paralysis of the tongue is more than just a nasty symptom. For Lucretius, theorist of the origins and workings of language, the loss of the *animi interpres* reduces the victim to a speechlessness that is not only that of infants but also that of our early human ancestors, whose passage into language has been described in the preceding book:

> At varios linguae sonitus natura subegit
> mittere, et utilitas expressit nomina rerum,
> non alia longe ratione atque ipsa videtur
> protrahere ad gestum pueros infantia linguae,
> cum facit ut digito quae sint praesentia monstrent.

> But nature forced humans to produce the tongue's varying sounds, and effectiveness shaped names for things, by a mechanism not very unlike that by which the tongue's initial speechlessness can be seen to push infants toward gesture, causing them to use a finger to point out the things around them. (*De rerum natura* 5.1028–32)

This account of the origins of language has begun with the first halting human communication *vocibus et gestu* (*De rerum natura* 5.1022) and now turns, for comparison, to the animal kingdom, where cattle, dogs, horses, and birds can all be heard making different sounds in different affective situations, from which Lucretius concludes,

> Ergo si varii sensus animalia cogunt,
> muta tamen cum sint, varias emittere voces,
> quanto mortalis magis aequumst tum potuisse
> dissimilis alia atque alia res voce notare.

> And so, if varied feelings force animals, though they are without language, to produce varied sounds, how much more appropriate is it that humans can indicate different things with this or that sound. (*De rerum natura* 5.1087–90)

This is all crucial background, I would argue, to what will follow in the account of the plague, for victims quickly are reduced to expressing their agony through sounds that are not quite words:

> Intolerabilibusque malis erat anxius angor
> assidue comes et gemitu commixta querella,
> singultusque frequens noctem per saepe diemque
> corripere assidue nervos et membra coactans
> dissoluebat eos, defessos ante, fatigans.

> The constant companion of their unbearable suffering was anxious choking and complaint mixed with groaning. And retching, often continuing night and day, drove their muscles and limbs to constant spasms and wore them down, already tired, by exhausting them. (*De rerum natura* 6.1158–62)

A *querella* could be expressed in words, but in the poets, it is just as likely to designate the inarticulate "complaint" of birds and other animals.[46] *Gemitus* likewise designates wordless groaning and moaning, by humans, animals, or even lifeless but resonant things.[47] *Singultus* is the sound of a person sobbing, or gasping for air, or hiccuping; Columella and Pliny will use it of the "clucking" of chickens and other birds.[48] We may perhaps also add to this soundtrack the redundant phrase *anxius angor*, the point of which probably depends on taking the second word to mean not mental "anxiety" but physical "choking," as it does in two passages in Livy and Pliny (where, interestingly enough, it is applied to animals).[49] As, therefore, the plague will strip the body quite literally down to its bones, so it strips human utterance down to its bare essentials, even beyond the "innate, untaught, human semiotic disposition" that Catherine Atherton finds at the heart of Lucretius's theory of language.[50] For these sounds are less products of a will to communicate than they are involuntary symptoms: spasmodic emotive eruptions of sound like those that "dumb" animals are "forced" to "emit" as a consequence of their *varii sensus* (*De rerum natura* 5.1087–88).[51]

Conspicuously involuntary, in fact, are the uncontrollable convulsions suggested by *singultus*, which translates Thucydides' *lunx kenē*, "unsuccessful attempts to vomit" (*Peloponnesian War* 2.49.4). The Latin word, however, would seem to place a greater emphasis on sound, suggesting that Lucretius is up to something not entirely authorized by the Greek, confirmed by the fact that *gemitus* and *querella* correspond to nothing at all in the original. The latter will return, strikingly, at the end of the symptomatology, in a brief vignette that contrasts the *vox blanda* of a caregiver with the *vox querellae* of the now dying patient, i.e., soothing sounds (which, if they were words, offered only empty reassurances) with the final sounds made by this suffering body (Lucretius, *De rerum natura* 6.1245). Let us finally note that, just as in English, *querella* can also denote a medical "complaint," i.e., illness or symptom. In other words, Lucretius essentially lets us hear, from start to finish, the noise of the disease itself, emitted by bodies spoiled of language, infantilized, dehumanized.

But even as the plague take its victims back to a moment of sound (child-like and even animal-like) before language, subtler elements of its description move in another direction entirely. Again, it is the earlier account of the origins of language that offers a key. This ends with a hasty nod to the invention of writing:

> Iam validis saepti degebant turribus aevum
> et divisa colebatur discretaque tellus.
> Tum mare velivolis florebat propter odores
> auxilia ac socios iam pacto foedere habebant,
> carminibus cum res gestas coepere poetae
> tradere, nec multo priu' sunt elementa reperta.
> Propterea quid sit prius actum respicere aetas
> nostra nequit, nisi qua ratio vestigia monstrat.

> Now people lived their lives palisaded by sturdy towers, and the land was farmed in separate marked plots. Then the sea blossomed with sailing ships in search of spices, and people ratified treaties to have reinforcements and allies, when poets first began to record human events for posterity in song—nor was the invention of the

> alphabet much earlier. As a result, our age cannot look back on
> what was done in the past, unless a kind of reason shows us its
> traces. (*De rerum natura* 5.1443–7)

A book later, at the very end of his poem, Lucretius himself, by describing the
famous plague of the Athenians, arguably enters something like the historical
mode first made possible by writing, though his own position is a conspicuously belated one, describing *res gestae* he himself did not witness, through the
intermediary of a writer not of *carmina* but of prose. *Monstrat* here cannot help
reminding us of the *pueri* who, at the beginning of this account, by the same
verb in the same position in the line, point out things around them (*digito quae
sint praesentia monstrent*): from the infant's *praesentia* to the historian's *vestigia*
of the past, humans cannot resist the urge to "show."

Show and Tell

An especially refined ability to "show" with words was prized by ancient rhet-
oricians, who gave the device of vivid description a long list of names, chiefly
enargeia in Greek and *evidentia* in Latin; among the others is one fairly rare
in antiquity but prominent in modern scholarship (on which more below):
ekphrasis.[52] Quintilian offers the following introduction to the longest of his
several discussions of *enargeia*:

> To be able to convey our subject matter clearly and in a way that makes it seem
> visible (*ut cerni videantur*) is a powerful skill. For oratory is less than com-
> pletely effective and does not exercise its full power if it works only on the ears
> and the person judging believes that what he is evaluating has been narrated to
> him, not expressed and made visible to his mind's eye (*non exprimi et oculis
> mentis ostendi*).[53]

"In this category, just as in everything else, the person who especially stands out
is Cicero," Quintilian soon notes, enthusiastically demonstrating his preference
with a quick example:

> Or is anyone so far from able to conjure mental images that upon reading, from
> the *Verrines*, "The praetor of the Roman people stood in his slippers, wearing a
> purple coat and an ankle-length tunic, hanging on some female, on the sea-
> shore," he does not only seem to see, directly, the very person and setting and
> pose, but also construes for himself other unspecified details? For my own part,
> certainly, I seem to see the face and the eyes and the disgraceful petting — and
> the quiet revulsion and frightened shame of those present.[54]

Enargeia was also prized, however, in historians, among whom the acknowledged master was Thucydides, about whom Plutarch comments, "Thucydides, surely, always strives for *enargeia* in his language, since he so strongly wants to make his audience into spectators and to conjure for his readers the astonished and distressed emotions experienced by eyewitnesses."[55] Finally, *enargeia* was also a poetic virtue; its rich and complex evolution especially in Hellenistic literature and criticism (often hand-in-hand with the visual arts) is the subject of a series of penetrating studies by Graham Zanker.[56] Outside Cicero, in fact, Quintilian draws most of his remaining examples of *enargeia* from the poets.

Enargeia often is marked by more or less explicit appeal to the vision of listeners or readers. Not long after the snippet about Verres cited by Quintilian, Cicero exclaims, *Ecce*, and switches to the present tense, as if he and his audience were watching the sordid scene unfold together.[57] In his narrative of the Athenian defeat in the harbor of Syracuse—one of the scenes that inspired Plutarch's praise above—Thucydides cleverly twins his reader's artificial gaze with that of eyewitness spectators onshore, a device prefigured by spectacle of the fleet's original departure, enjoyed by the residents of the Piraeus.[58] Explicit appeals to the reader often take the conditional form of "had you been there, you could have seen . . ." The Lucretian plague includes several such formulations: "you would have been able to see" (*posses . . . videre*), "you would have seen," (*videres*), and even, "you would not have been able to observe" (*nec . . . posses tueri*), all of which go beyond anything in the Greek original.[59] Comparing these to the final scene of the *Catiline* of Lucretius's contemporary, Sallust, which begins, "But once the battle was finally over, then at last you would have seen . . ." (*cerneres*), Peta Fowler notes that both poet and historian are "inviting the reader to contemplate the vividness or *enargeia* of the description," largely consisting, she adds, of "heaps of corpses."[60]

In sum, Cicero's encounter with the Lucretian finale placed a master of Latin rhetorical *enargeia* in front of the translation of a masterpiece of Greek historical *enargeia* into Latin verses that signal *enargeia* with added appeals to the reader's vision. Further enriching, and complicating, this confluence is the fact that the *De rerum natura* elsewhere famously explores both the mechanisms of actual sight as well as the broader phenomenology of vision, true and false—all preoccupations borrowed from Epicurus. To these may be added the importance, to the poem's philosophical arguments, of several key scenes of spectatorship, including, most memorably, those of the proem of book 2, which opens with the wise man actually taking pleasure in the sight of a distant shipwreck, since he knows that this misfortune does not touch him.[61] Complicating matters even further is the fact that antiquity's other technical sense for *enargeia* comes the philosophers, primarily from Epicurus, who used the term to designate evidence from the senses that was clear and distinct—and thus trustworthy.[62] Epicurean *enargeia*, in other words, is at least potentially opposed to rhetorical or literary *enargeia*, which offers anything but the direct, up-close evidence of our own senses and which, therefore, may well seek to deceive.

An influential view of the Lucretian finale sees it as a kind of final exam for the reader who has mastered the poem's series of philosophical lessons and who, therefore, is ready to look impassively on what, for the unenlightened, is instead a heart-wrenching scene of human suffering.[63] Diskin Clay, in elaborating this interpretation, does not discuss *enargeia*, but the term helps to put an even finer point on his argument. The most common purpose of *enargeia* (especially in oratory) is to arouse emotion or even indignation in one's listeners.[64] The wise readers who remain unmoved here, therefore, resist not only the finale's content, but also its persuasive form. At the same time, the Epicurean concept of *enargeia* helps them to cheat a little, arguably with the connivance of their examiner: not only is this dreadful spectacle unverified by the vivid evidence of their own senses, but not even the poet can claim to have seen it himself, since he sees only through the distant eyes of Thucydides. "What has this to do with me?" the wise student asks—and is promoted.

Clay's thesis is as elegant as it is maddening: for the reader to succeed, the poem must, in effect, fail. The honey of poetry, to borrow Lucretius's own famous figure, fully gives way to the wormwood of truth, which, however, for the enlightened, is no longer bitter. In the end, in other words, to take Lucretius seriously as a philosopher, we must finally dismiss any independent ambitions on his part as a poet. Not only does our own appreciation of his artistry rail against this dismissal, but it seems difficult to reconcile with the ancient imitators of his finale—Vergil, Ovid, Lucan, and Silius Italicus—whose own plagues we would have to read as fundamentally different, since these poets cannot be said to share in any way the Epicurean didacticism of their predecessor. A similar gulf likewise opens between Lucretius and his own model, Thucydides. Nevertheless, in the following, I shall not argue that Clay is wrong. Rather, I shall suggest that the emotional detachment that is the product of the poem as philosophy is, in the plague, twinned with an aesthetic detachment required to appreciate the poem *qua* poem. In the latter, by "detachment" I mean that separation of form from content often implicit in aesthetic appreciations, though as we shall see, that very separation is precisely what the plague risks throwing into desperate confusion. First, however, we must shed some new light on a famous consequence of *enargeia*.

The Stillness of the Page

Heinrich Lausberg's *Handbook of Literary Rhetoric* offers an indispensible treatment of *enargeia/evidentia,* which, though largely concerned with digesting sometimes recondite ancient discussions, opens with the following useful introduction, based in part on Quintilian:

> *Evidentia* . . . is the vividly detailed depiction of a broadly conceived whole object . . . through the enumeration of (real or invented) observable details. In *evidentia* the object as a whole is of an essentially static nature, even if it is an event . . . : here we have to do with the description of an image which, though vibrant in its details, is nonetheless held together by the framework of a (more or less relaxable) simultaneity. The simultaneity of the details which determines the static character of the object is the eyewitness's experience of simultaneousness.[65]

This may sound familiar to literary critics, whether or not they are classicists or know *evidentia/enargeia* as a rhetorical category, for its emphasis on "simultaneousness" is very like modern treatments of that more fashionable term, *ekphrasis,* especially that of Murray Krieger's influential 1967 essay, "*Ekphrasis* and the Still Movement of Poetry; or *Laokoön* Revisited," largely responsible for giving the word the critical currency it has enjoyed ever since:

> [A] classic genre was formulated that, in effect, institutionalized this tactic: the *ekphrasis,* or the imitation in literature of a work of plastic art. The object of imitation, as spatial work, becomes the metaphor for the temporal work which seeks to capture it in that temporality. The spatial work freezes the temporal work even as the latter seeks to free it from space. *Ekphrasis* concerns me here, then, to the extent that I see it introduced in order to use a plastic object as a symbol of the frozen, stilled world of plastic relationships which must be superimposed upon literature's turning world to "still" it.[66]

Like several others before and after him, Krieger wrongly thought that the target of literary *ekphrasis* was limited to works of art, an error he later acknowledged; he also would later drift toward *enargeia* as an alternate term.[67] But Krieger is less interested (as, for present purposes, are we) in pinning down an ancient definition of either device than he is in regarding both as emblematic of a characteristic basic to literature generally: its attempt to wriggle out of ordinary time and into space and, thus, into timelessness. Hence he

plays on the two meanings of "still": hardly moving, still here. That the spatial
dimension of this "still movement" is only an illusion, conjured by visual language and deployed against the necessarily temporal nature of language itself,
is something Krieger, here and in his later work, again and again takes to be obvious: linguistic space is an "unattainable dream," "an ultimately vain attempt,"
a "borrowing" that is "inapplicable or can be applied only figuratively," "alien,"
for words "have, literally, no space."[68] But the present book, I hope, already has
made such givens less than obvious, at least for *written* words, which most
emphatically do occupy spaces, both two-dimensional (the page) and three-
dimensional (the book). In other words, if visual/spatial language is an illusion,
then the ostensibly linear language it resists is no less one, belied by any and all
fixity, whether that of writing or, simply, that that of memory itself. Rather
than just reaching for what is "alien" to language, the "stillness" of *ekphrasis/
enargeia* thus points us also toward what, in another sense, was there all along.

Some time ago, in the introduction, we noted that page and book are what
guarantee that a text's words are "all here together, at the same time" (which is
why, of course, I can refer to those comments here, now). But in that same place,
we also observed that the simultaneity of the material text has an analogue in,
e.g., syntax, essential to language as we know it, written or not, and in this chapter, we have compared the synchronic claims of the rhetorical period, spoken
or written. This should caution us against seeming to replace Krieger's visual
essentialism, by which space and stillness legitimately belong only to the visual
arts, with a material one, by which literature must instead borrow these same
qualities from the page. Rather, appeals to either page or painting ultimately
reflect (even if only distantly) the more-than-one-dimensional shape of language itself.

All of this, I would suggest, rather raises the stakes for such appeals. At
least since G. E. Lessing's 1766 *Laocoon, or, On the Limits of Painting and Poetry*,
most scholars of *ekphrasis* and the like, even when differing with Lessing on
other points, have taken as axiomatic his basic contention, namely, that visual
language is trying to do what, in the end, words cannot really do, in a sidelong
or even envious glance at literature's sister arts.[69] This, however, is the one
thing that he and they most surely get exactly wrong, at least regarding the
question of language's "shape." And we might even go so far as to wonder
whether figure and formalism generally—for *figura* and *forma* both mean
"shape"—can best be understood not as wistful glances over the walls of language, but as meditations on the bricks and mortar of the poet's own world.[70]
By way of conclusion, we return to the plague, where we have found urgent
versions of both of the appeals we have just described: to the materiality of
writing, as we saw in chapter 2, and to vision, as we have seen in this one. But

for this final reading, we shall turn again to that formalism which, from mosaic to poetry, most persistently shaped ancient art.

Composition and Decomposition

The Lucretian plague-scene inspired a remarkable tradition of imitators, beginning with Vergil, who closes his third *Georgic* (3.478–566) with an animal plague that intrudes violently into his setting, quite literally stopping agriculture (itself a frequent figure for poetry and the "plowing" of verses[71]) in its tracks. "The entire coloring (*color*) and almost all the lines (*liniamenta*) of this particular plague, in the third book of the *Georgics*, are taken from the description of the plague in the sixth book of Lucretius," notes Macrobius, who then provides a representative list of parallel passages (of which he could have provided more, he assures us), after which he asks, with a wry joke on the double meaning of *membra* as both "phrases" and "limbs" (along the lines of Horace's *disiecti membra poetae*), "Do the parts (*membra*) of this description not seem to you to have sprung from a single source?"[72] Both Lucretius and Vergil in turn influenced Ovid in his plague in the *Metamorphoses* (7.517–613); later joining the tradition were both Lucan (*De bello civili* 6.80–117) and Silius Italicus (*Punica* 14.580–617).[73] This series of poetic plagues opens J. C. Scaliger's discussion, in his *Poetics* of 1561, of Latin poets imitating other Latin poets, and another sixteenth-century commentator, regarding the plague, observes, "The greatest poets . . . can be seen to have ventured here as if onto a common proving ground of artistic skill (*in hunc quasi communem artis ostentandae campum*)."[74]

What made such unpleasant subject matter so irresistible to so many poets (including, surely, others we have lost)? An answer comes from Plato. Socrates observes to Phaedrus that "any discourse must be composed like a living organism, with a body all its own, so that it is neither headless nor footless but has instead a midsection and extremities written so as to fit with one another and with the whole."[75] In fact, the notion that the paradigmatic composed thing is the human body itself underpins most ancient theories of *compositio*. Lucretius's finale, therefore, in which the human body slowly atomizes but the poetry continues to cohere, offers a spectacular paradox: the (anthropomorphic) composition of a scene of (bodily) decomposition. In essence, Lucretius wrests form from the very jaws of formlessness.

This is a rarefied version of the broad problem of poetic representations of ugly subject matter, which Plutarch, in his essay on "How a Young Man Should Appreciate Poetry," analogizes to realistic paintings of "a lizard or an ape or the face of Thersites," in which one may take pleasure in the painter's mimetic accomplishment, "for imitating something beautifully is not the same as imitating something beautiful."[76] In the face of violent or degrading subject matter, the young man "must be taught to praise the talent and skill of the representation, but to denounce and criticize the subject matter it represents."[77] Plutarch's morally and aesthetically fortified student helps us to complete the picture of his Lucretian counterpart (as imagined by Clay), whose Epicurean impassivity before the plague's emotive power, I would argue, not only allows but even is encouraged by his wonder at Lucretius's poetic accomplishment. One might even say that Lucretius has been teaching compositional formalism all along, as a way to understand the world, which, from its atoms up, offers almost endless stories of large bodies made from small ones.[78]

As we already have noted, it was the formalism, not the philosophy, that would matter to Lucretius' imitators, drawn to the plague, as the Renaissance realized, as a chance to prove their artistic mettle (*artis ostentandae*). And at least one early reader, editor or not, saw even the Lucretian original largely in the same light, as a poem "of considerable artistry" (*multae . . . artis*). There can be no doubt that Cicero was fully prepared to understand—and perhaps even envy—what Lucretius *poeta* was doing here. Indeed, in the *Tusculan Disputations*, in two long translations from Greek tragedy—Aeschylus's description of the devouring of Prometheus's liver and Sophocles' account of the dissolution of Hercules' flesh by the centaur's poison—it seems likely that he was experimenting with the same poetic dilemma.[79] In the latter, the tormented hero cries, "Come, son, stand by me, and gaze upon the pitiful, eviscerated body of your mangled father!" We too are supposed to look, with pity but, above all, with admiration: what follows, from its first *serpit*, is consummately Ciceronian stitch work.

In his last surviving treatise, the *De officiis*, Cicero indirectly offers an often quoted definition of composition:

> Ut enim pulchritudo corporis apta compositione membrorum movet oculos et delectat hoc ipso, quod inter se omnes partes cum quodam lepore consentiunt, sic hoc decorum quod elucet in vita movet approbationem eorum quibuscum vivitur ordine et constantia et moderatione dictorum omnium atque factorum.

> As the beauty of the body by the appropriate composition (*apta compositione*) of its members attracts the eyes and provokes delight by the very fact that all its parts agree among themselves with a certain elegance, so this decorum which is evident in life attracts the approval of those in whose company that life is lived with orderliness and consistency and moderation in all things said and done.[80]

Here, however, anthropomorphic *compositio* is applied not to rhetoric or poetics but to the making of a well-ordered life, or at least of a well-ordered public persona. We are reminded that the text in which this advice appears was itself composed precisely in order to stand in for Cicero himself, who forewent a planned visit to his son Marcus in Athens, to whom this treatise is addressed, in order to turn back to Rome and to Antony. Given the treatise's notorious internal inconsistencies, along with the accusations of inconstancy (even from Atticus) that greeted Cicero's abrupt change of plans, we might well observe that, in art as in life, Cicero did not always achieve the calmly coherent *decorum* he describes. Perhaps, however, we should also pause to remember that Cicero soon got his slippery self together long enough to compose the greatest speeches of his career (and arguably of all of Latin literature). He was no poet and not really much of a philosopher, but nothing that survives from antiquity has more often been taken as paradigmatic of *compositio* proper than his oratory, to which even painters of the Renaissance acknowledge a debt.[81] A certain lack of personal composure, let us say, is no obstacle to compositional brilliance. On the contrary, we often are tempted to connect the latter to the former in a number of authors (hardly just Cicero), which is the reason why the rest of Jerome's brief sketch of a tormented Lucretius, true or not, has been greeted by so many as inherently plausible.

Let us close this thought, and this chapter, with a note of Lucretian *apparatus*. Six lines from the poem's end, editors must mark a brief lacuna, because the verse in question is metrically incomplete:

> et unus
> quisque suum pro re < . . . > maestus humabat.[82]

The great Lucretian editor Karl Lachmann observes that "here the parchment appears to have been punctured" (the skin of victims is echoed by the skin that tells their story!) "in the middle of the verse." He then rejects two conjectures made by earlier editors, *utrumque inepte*, and proposes his own supplement: "What Lucretius put here we cannot say, but *compostum* makes sense."[83] The meaning would then be this:

> Each grieving person laid to rest his own loved one, once he was arranged for burial (*compostum*) according to their means.

Given that Lachmann made his fame reconstituting the mutilated Lucretian textual tradition, it is tempting to find in his supplement an epigraph on his own finished work. After all, the textual critic is, like the poet (and like the stargazer), a composer, someone who puts things together. But Lachmann appeals in his note to no new science of stemmatics; this is instead a gesture of pure conjectural *emendatio*, born of the critic's intuition of what the *res*, the poet's style and sense, demands. Since few after Lucretius himself have peered as closely at the tissue of his poetry as did Lachmann, we should perhaps respect his instinct. *Compostum*, indeed, offers a sublimely perverse epitaph for these bodies that, decomposing already in life, are now surrendered to the work of worms. The lost last word, let us say, of a man whose insanity eventually, as Tennyson puts it, "check'd / His power to shape."[84] Perhaps it was the desperate need to shape, the same need that drove Cicero to brilliant oratory and to nervous political heroics, that finally (we are told) drove the better poet mad.

4

THE ERASABLE CICERO

The summer of 59 BC found Cicero in his forty-eighth year and Rome in a state of high anxiety. This was the first summer of the so-called First Triumvirate, and Roman wits had begun to date their documents "in the year in which Julius and Caesar were consuls."[1] Cicero's letters for that year to his dear friend Atticus cover several weeks in the spring, when Cicero was mostly at Anzio and Formia, on the coast between Rome and Naples, and Atticus was in the capital, and then resume in the summer, when Cicero has returned to Rome and Atticus leaves for his usual home in Greece. (For obvious reasons, correspondence between the two exists only for those periods in which they were apart.) Cicero's last letter to Atticus that year was written in October, and apart from a letter to his brother Quintus later in the fall, we next hear from him in a hurried note to Atticus in March of the following year, when he is in desperate flight from Rome into exile.

Let us now look closely at parts of two consecutive letters from July of 59, not for the light they shed on the political intrigues of the day, but for the small place they may be said to hold in the history of erasability as technology and metaphor:

> Sed haec scripsi properans et mehercule timide. Posthac ad te aut, si perfidelem habeo cui dem, scribam plane omnia aut, si obscure scribam, tu tamen intelleges. In iis epistulis me Laelium, te Furium faciam; cetera erunt ἐν αἰνιγμοῖς.

> I wrote this in a hurry—and pretty cautiously. From now on, if I have someone I really trust as courier, I will write everything plainly; otherwise, if I write

obscurely, you will understand all the same. In letters of this latter sort, I'll pretend that I'm "Laelius" and you are "Furius"; everything else will be expressed in enigmas.[2]

De re publica breviter ad te scribam; iam enim charta ipsa ne nos prodat pertimesco. Itaque posthac, si erunt mihi plura ad te scribenda, ἀλληγορίαις obscurabo. Nunc quidem novo quodam morbo civitas moritur . . . Quod scripsero me Furio scripturum, nihil necesse est tuum nomen mutare: me faciam Laelium et te Atticum. Neque utar meo chirographo neque signo, si modo erunt eius modi litterae quas in alienum incidere nolim.

I'll be brief about the republic, since I'm already quite afraid that the very papyrus might betray us. And so, from now on, if I need to write more to you, I'll obscure everything with allegories. Now, indeed, the state is dying of some new kind of disease . . . As for what I wrote about me planning to write to "Furius," there is no real need to change your name: I'll be "Laelius" and you'll be Atticus. And I won't use my handwriting or my seal whenever a letter is the kind I wouldn't want to fall into a stranger's hands.[3]

These two passages will help us to understand some broader themes, but let us first take them on their own terms, by glossing several of their most interesting words and phrases.

charta

Notionally, Roman letters were tablets (*tabulae*, or more commonly, the diminutive *tabellae*; also *codicilli*), and most Roman tablets were of the waxed variety—indeed, the reusable waxed tablet arguably was the most abundant writing surface in the Roman world, though relatively few examples have survived. I say that letters were *notionally* tablets for reasons explained by Festus, who in the second century AD compiled a Latin lexicon: "The ancients (*antiqui*) used tablets (*tabellae*) instead of papyri (*chartae*), and by exchanging these they kept each other informed when absent, whether the reasons for doing so were private or public. For this reason letter-carriers still are called *tabellarii*."[4] Festus based his dictionary on the much earlier work of Verrius Flaccus (who was born in Cicero's lifetime), and the relative chronology implicit in *antiqui* could belong to either scholar, making it difficult to know when the transition from tablet to papyrus (which can never have been absolute) is supposed to have taken place. It is clear in any case that both surfaces were in common use for letters in Cicero's day—indeed, by Cicero himself. Nevertheless, it does appear that Cicero and Atticus restricted themselves to papyrus when corresponding with each other—at least, this is the presumed meaning of a later letter Cicero sends along with two hundred sheets of papyrus, since Atticus has run out and Cicero is worried, therefore, that he will stop writing.[5] An all-papyrus correspondence explains the *volumina* (rolls) in which Cicero and Atticus archived each other's letters not as a transcription but as a continuous montage of segments, pasted on as they arrived.[6]

And so we have opened up quite a spectrum of writing materials. On the one hand is the waxed tablet, normative in the past but still common in Cicero's present for letters, the waxed tablet that had been and would remain the preferred medium for Roman documents like wills and contracts. On the other hand is the papyrus *volumen*, the regular support, throughout most of antiquity, for the literary book. At the center is the *charta* Cicero sent to Atticus, like a waxed tablet because its contents could have been written on one and because it is, in any case, delivered by a "tablet-carrier" (*tabellarius*), but really a papyrus and therefore not destined to return to its sender, erased and rewritten. Much has been said about the *generic* indeterminacy of Cicero's letters (and of letters in general), their "sub-literariness," but what concerns us now is instead their emphatically ambiguous *material* status. Tablet or roll? A letter from Cicero to Atticus was a bit of both.

ne nos prodat
in alienum incidere

Cicero arguably had legitimate cause to worry about others reading his mail. Letters certainly could be lost through the negligence of their couriers: April 59 had seen the loss, in two separate incidents, of a letter from Atticus to Cicero and another from Cicero to Atticus.[7] But deliberate interception was also a possibility. Julius Caesar used secret code for especially delicate correspondence; a passage from Suetonius suggests that this included some still extant letters to Cicero.[8] Cicero himself had excellent reason to know the perils of interception: his final, fatal unmasking of the Catilinarian conspiracy had been achieved by seizing several letters (written, by the way, on waxed tablets) on their way out of Rome under cover of night, one of which, though unsigned[9] and written in very guarded language, nevertheless laid bare the whole plot when unsealed and read to the senate the next day. Authors of several of the letters were forced to acknowledge their seals and their handwriting before the senate; the risk of similar exposure prompts Cicero to propose using neither here (*neque utar meo chirographo neque signo*, "I shall use neither my own handwriting nor my seal").

Nevertheless, there is no evidence that Cicero ever adopted the planned strategy, though it is difficult to believe that every subsequent letter-carrier struck him as *perfidelis*. Certainly the next letter begins scarcely enigmatically: *De re publica quid ego tibi subtiliter?—tota periit*, "Why mince words about the Republic? It's over." No "Laelius" letters follow, though it is of course hard to be sure that this means that none were written: copies of such letters might not have been kept (though it is hard to see why, since other sensitive letters were kept), or, alternatively, the later publisher of the correspondence might have chosen to omit them. We can at least be sure that Cicero did not resort to a scribe prior to the writing of a letter sent a few weeks later, and then his purpose was not disguise: "I don't think you ever before have read a letter from me that was not in my own handwriting—evidence for you of just how busy I am."[10] Under the circumstances, we must take Cicero's proposal to hide his identity as something of an end unto itself—i.e., Cicero in part is playing a game here, and the game is less about any eventual enactment of the masquerade than it is about creating the costume itself. But for more about the rules of this game, let us turn to Cicero's Greek.

ἐν αἰνιγμοῖς ἀλληγορίαις

The simplest explanation of allegory and enigma comes from Quintilian, who places the terms in a tripartite hierarchy, at the bottom of which is metaphor.[11] All three terms refer to metaphorical language, but *metaphora* proper is what Cicero calls *translatio verbi*[12]—a metaphor at the level of a single word. Allegory, in turn, is a metaphor as large as a sentence. Finally, enigma is an especially difficult allegory (*allegoria quae est obscurior*).

We should not overly press Cicero's two letters for technical distinctions; clearly *en ainigmois* and *allēgoriais* mean more or less the same thing here. It is interesting to note that Cicero immediately follows his invocation of allegory with a kind of allegorical beginning, "Now the state is dying from a certain new disease." Perhaps this is a clue to the allegorical language Cicero imagines he might write. But in any case, the only thing that we (and indeed Atticus) can be sure of about Cicero's plan involves neither allegory nor enigma, but rather a simple *translatio verbi*—here, the substitution of one proper name for another. To understand fully the significance of this kind of substitution, we must take a quick plunge into the wider world of Roman waxed tablets. We shall return to allegory in a moment.

Waxed tablets remained the usual material support for Roman documents well after papyrus came to be preferred for letters. In the case of documents that needed to remain works in progress for long periods—accounts are the best example—an erasable surface offered obvious advantages. The use of waxed tablets for permanent documents, like contracts and wills, may seem harder to explain. In part, the conservatism of documentary practices may have resisted changes to which other texts, like letters, were more susceptible. But undoubtedly the most important virtue of tablets was their perceived durability, since clearly they were more resistant to damp, insects, and crumpling. Of course, this produces something of a paradox: waxed tablets are ephemeral because erasable and permanent because durable. Ensuring that the former characteristic did not compromise the latter in the case of documents required elaborate rituals of duplication and, most importantly, sealing, object of a great deal of legal anxiety.[13]

Indeed, while Cicero was writing the letters we are considering, he was also preparing his defense of L. Valerius Flaccus, who would be tried for provincial extortion in August. (In fact, it was during a recess in the trial that Cicero hurriedly dictated his first letter to Atticus not in his own handwriting.) Cicero made alleged suppression or corruption of documents central to his defense and at one point asked the jury to inspect the seals on a tablet presented in evidence by the prosecution. In his surviving speech, Cicero claims that the seals are not in the kind of wax used in Asia, whence the tablets were supposed to come, suggesting either that they have been opened, altered, and resealed, or that they are outright forgeries.[14]

But despite seals and other precautions, documents on waxed tablets could be and often were altered. Just how often? Cicero built early his reputation as an orator out of his successful conduct of legal cases that required him to unravel complex bodies of documentary evidence. Apart from the concealment or outright destruction of documents, erasure was the number-one concern of his detective work. And what is perhaps most striking about these erasures is the fact that the overwhelming majority of them involve the erasure of a person's proper name. Let us consider just one example. The case that made Cicero a star, his successful prosecution of Gaius Verres for corruption as governor of Sicily, was built on literally hundreds of documents.[15] The law had given Cicero as prosecutor broad authority to confiscate documents to be used in evidence, but it excepted the records of the Roman tax-collectors, which Cicero could inspect *in situ* in Sicily but not export. In the records of a certain Sicilian tax-collector, Cicero found numerous records of payment to an otherwise unknown "C. Verrucius."[16] Cicero also noticed that the first four letters of Verrucius's name were always written normally, whereas -*ucius* was always over an erasure (*in litura*). Cicero brings a legal action to compel the tax-collector to confess the obvious truth: "Verrucius" has been substituted for Verres. Cicero's next step is truly remarkable: he has an exact facsimile of the tablets made on papyrus, one which reproduces every letter and every erasure (*litterae lituraeque omnes assimulatae et expressae de tabulis in libros transferuntur*). Cicero would later unroll this copy before the jury in Rome:

> Videtis VERRVCIVM? Videtis primas litteras integras? Videtis extremam partem nominis codam illam verrinam tamquam in luto demersam esse in litura? Sic habent se tabulae, iudices, ut videtis.

> Do you see "Verrucius"? Do you see that the first letters are intact? Do you see that the final part of the name, that porcine tail, is in an erasure, as if it were mired in mud? Gentlemen of the jury, the state of the tablets is exactly as you see here.[17]

One might simply observe that this episode and the many others like it reveal that erasure of a name was a convenient technique—here, in fact, the alteration of just a few letters would have been enough to perpetrate the fraud, had the tablets not fallen under the unforgiving eyes of Cicero. But the sheer number of erased names referred to in Ciceronian oratory suggests that we must connect the phenomenon to a general characteristic of Roman life, one so basic and obvious that it is almost never remarked upon. Plainly put, the Romans were infatuated with their names. We can even see this in account books, for the Romans called the items they contained *nomina*—i.e., the name of the concerned party (such as Verres/Verrucius) is synecdochic for the whole transaction. But of course this is only a small example. The Romans marked time with names, indicating years by the names of the presiding consuls. And anyone who has been to Rome or leafed through a volume of the *Corpus Inscriptionum Latinarum* knows that behind the Romans' so-called "epigraphic habit" was above all a need to leave not just anything but specifically *names* written everywhere.

This obsession could take psychotic turns. It was of course Rome that invented proscription (though compare Greek ostracism), the device by which one could write a name, and so erase a man. (Indeed, one of the cases that first brought Cicero to the Romans' attention was one argued during the First Proscription, in which Cicero accused Sulla's secretary of promising to erase a name from the lists but then reneging.[18]) A different symptom of the same disease is found in the Roman practice of *damnatio memoriae*, the obliteration of the inscribed name (and sculpted representations) of someone who has fallen into political disgrace (usually after death), in which erasure is inflicted on the least erasable of Roman writing materials: stone and bronze.

In a phrase, no Roman citizen was so insignificant that he did not sometimes need his name to be written, and none was so powerful that his name could not one day be erased. Naturally, with the epitaph a central focus of the

Roman epigraphic obsession, the inscription of the name was implicated in hopes and anxieties about death, a fact which ultimately gives rise to elaborate literary and philosophical conceits. Thus Ovid ends his *Metamorphoses* with the hope that his own name will now become "unerasable" (*nomenque erit indelebile nostrum*), leading to the final word of the monumental poem, *vivam*, "I shall live."

All this brings us back to Cicero in 59 BC and, as promised, the question of allegory. It is sometimes forgotten that the Greek word *allēgoria* is ultimately derived from the prefix *all-*, "other," and *agora*, a place to gather either for commerce or politics (what the Romans call a *forum*): in a roundabout way, to speak allegorically (*allēgoreō*, *all-* + *agoreuō*, "to speak in public") is to speak in a way you would not encounter in the *agora*, or at least not in your own. *Allēgoria*, as language notionally brought in from somewhere else (even if only from a different context or register), is thus an extension of—or, if you wish, a further metaphor for—metaphor itself, since *metaphora* refers to "carrying (something) across" (hence *translatio* in Latin) and is itself, therefore, a metaphor for a transference effected through language. Simply put, metaphor and allegory are both imagined as movement, displacement.

This makes the invocation of allegory in an epistolary context especially interesting, since a letter is, if you will, a literal allegory, in that it is carried to another *agora*, i.e., the letter is the text that by definition changes place. But allegory is even more interesting in this particular context, since Cicero's letter is addressed to Titus Pomponius, the man who by trading one *agora* for another—or more precisely, by trading *forum* for *agora*—earned the nickname Atticus, "the Athenian." Atticus is not only the addressee of these letters: he is also their address.

I do not mean to suggest that Cicero was thinking of any of this as he wrote his letters. But the way in which allegory, the letter, and the nickname of Atticus have a common stake in displacement will help us to clarify things as we turn in earnest to the question of changeable names.

Furius
Laelius

Nicknames and other circumlocutions abound in Cicero's correspondence with Atticus, from the earliest surviving letters to the end.[19] The practice represented not a deliberate strategy of secrecy but instead combined a general instinct for discretion with a conspicuous element of play. Two memorable Ciceronian nicknames appear in the correspondence of 59. The first is for the man who soon would orchestrate Cicero's exile, Publius Clodius Pulcher, from whose cognomen, which literally means "beautiful," Cicero fashioned a diminutive, Pulchellus, "Pretty-Boy." The second is for Clodius's notorious sister Clodia, whom Cicero regularly refers to as *Boōpis*, "Cow-Eyed," the Homeric epithet for Hera, probably used by Cicero not only in reference to Clodia's famously sparkling eyes but also to her alleged incestuous affair with her brother (like that of Hera with her brother/husband Zeus). Of course, this very same Clodia (if the traditional identification is right) had another nickname, given to her not by Cicero but by Catullus, who was in love with her, and who in his poetry calls her "Lesbia," after the island of Sappho. Catullus's poems abound in nicknames and epithets, and a need for discretion was certainly present (Clodia, for example, was a married woman), but since the poems are written in a way that assumes that at least some readers will decipher the code and get the poet's full meaning, we must suppose that Catullus too is playing something of a name game. Since this is the poet who describes writing verse as playing on (waxed) tablets (*multum lusimus in meis tabellis*),[20] we can perhaps read his deceptions as symptoms of a world in which names, like love and even poetry itself, are not necessarily written in stone.

But back to Cicero. It is scarcely insignificant that Cicero turns to Homer for Clodia's nickname. Homer's poems were not just classics; they were the principal texts of study for Roman schoolboys. Cicero and Atticus, who were in school together, would have spent much of that time copying out passages (in their waxed tablets) and committing them to memory. When Cicero quotes Homer in the correspondence—and he does so often, and even more often than usual in 59—he is not merely being literary; he is also calling to mind the first years of a friendship now decades old. Indeed, it is not difficult to imagine schoolboys giggling at Juno's bovine epithet and applying it to new targets. In other words, there is every reason to suppose that Cicero and Atticus have been inventing nicknames since their school days.

In fact, Homer is not the only way in which Cicero invokes a pedagogical context in the correspondence of 59. Two consecutive letters from April end with a sentence of Greek:

καὶ Κικέρων ὁ μικρὸς ἀσπάζεται Τίτον τὸν Ἀθηναῖον.

Little Cicero also says hello to Titus the Athenian [i.e., "Atticus"].

καὶ Κικέρων ὁ φιλόσοφος τὸν πολιτικὸν Τίτον ἀσπάζεται.

Cicero the philosopher also says hello to Titus the Athenian, statesman.[21]

"Little Cicero" is Cicero's son, also named Marcus Tullius Cicero, then six years old. Either he wrote down these salutations himself or, perhaps more likely, Atticus is meant to understand that the boy has spoken them, coached, in either case, by his father. Here too is a name game: Cicero's voice is twice displaced, both because he ventriloquizes his son and because the words he speaks are Greek, but in the end, it is still "Cicero" who delivers the letter's parting salutation. These translations, however, leave their mark elsewhere in the second sentence, for Atticus, the man of leisure, is called instead a *politikos*, while "Cicero" has become a philosopher. This role-reversal is in part a reflection of the somewhat uncustomary topography of the spring's correspondence, when it is Atticus who is in Rome and Cicero who is outside (in Formia). But this is no simple invocation of the familiar Ciceronian topos of philosophical *otium* available only outside Rome. Rather, behind the reversal of epithets is a more basic longing, a nostalgia for that long-passed moment when Cicero could have charted for his life a very different course.[22] In 59, before Cicero really had begun his second career as a writer of philosophical dialogues, to write "Cicero philosopher" was to toy with altering the account-books of history.

We are at last prepared to consider the code-names that Cicero chooses for himself and for Atticus in our two letters. "Furius," the name suggested and then discarded for Atticus, unquestionably is borrowed from a particular person of that name: Lucius Furius Philus, friend of Publius Cornelius Scipio Aemilianus and member of his famous coterie of political, philosophical, and literary luminaries of the second century BC. Likewise a member of the so-called Scipionic circle (largely a fiction of Ciceronian origin), and an even closer friend of Scipio, was "Laelius," i.e., Gaius Laelius, to whom was given the nickname Sapiens, "the Wise." Fifteen years later, in 44, Cicero would make this same Laelius the central speaker of his dialogue *De amicitia*, but already in 59, the choice of Laelius "the Wise" and Furius Philus (the cognomen is Greek for "friend") represents a finely wrought conceit for the bond of learning and friendship that has joined Cicero and Atticus since their youth.

Both Furius and Laelius would appear as interlocutors in Cicero's first philosophical dialogue, the *De re publica*, begun in 54 and finished in 51. Cicero would later describe the writing of philosophy not exactly as leisurely retirement but, rather, as the result of forced displacement from public affairs: "In books we gave our opinion, we addressed the people: we considered that philosophy had been given to us as a substitute for service to the Republic."[23] The idealized Scipionic circle, in which Cicero would again and again set his dialogues, provided another country, a "literal allegory," in two senses: another *agora*, in that Cicero's philosophical content and dialogic style were Greek, and another forum, still Roman, but displaced in time to what Cicero regarded as Rome's intellectual golden age. But such dialogues were also allegorical in a more ordinary sense, in that their interlocutors' response to events of the second century thinly mask Cicero's own review of the increasingly bleak political situation of his own day. Indeed, the finale of the *De re publica*, the "Dream of Scipio," is the one Ciceronian text that we, like the relentlessly allegorical readers of the Middle Ages, most readily have ascribed to allegory proper.

There cannot, however, be much question of political caution here: Cicero's fictional dialogues were not anonymous, and a literary man like Caesar could scarcely have failed to perceive their point. Rather, the theme of erasability we have now traced from the bottom to the top of the top of the Roman textual hierarchy—from the documentary to the literary—ultimately produces an inversion of concerns. In the first case (Verres becomes Verrucius), the intent is to impede reading; in the last (Cicero becomes Scipio), the goal seems instead to be to free the author to write. But freedom from what? Cicero does appear in several of his dialogues in his own name, as do a number of his friends, especially Brutus. Here, of course, is another mildly fraudulent name game, in that the contemporary dialogues Cicero reports are largely invented, with Cicero ventriloquizing everyone (including himself, given the fiction). In this regard, the treatises that Cicero and Brutus dedicated to one another in the 40s (Brutus inscribed to Cicero his *De virtute*) should be seen above all as the collaborative prelude to the latter's assassination of Caesar, immediately after which he would shout to the crowd a single name: Cicero.[24] Likewise, Cicero would abandon both literary persona and dialogic form in his last surviving philosophical treatise, the *De officiis*, written in the very weeks in which Cicero prepared himself for his final frontal assault on Mark Antony. Here too, however, we find evidence of a work in progress, for the textual variants in the tradition of the *De officiis* famously suggest that Cicero left the work with cancellations and marginal substitutions not yet integrated into a clean copy. For men like Cicero and Brutus whose deeds, including public speech, would be indelible, the erasable page offered temporary respite from such finalities—until moments like the morning of March 15, when Brutus and the rest traded their styluses for daggers, smuggled into the senate chamber hidden in their writing cases, along with the waxed tablets which, this day, they would not use.[25]

In the event, the assassination of Caesar would turn out not to have been as final as at first it had seemed. Listen to Cicero's continuous revision of his view of the fateful day in letters to Atticus in the months following:

April 10: "Even if everything else is a mess, the Ides of March offer solace." April 12: "So far nothing gives me pleasure besides the Ides of March." April 26: "Let solace come especially from study—but also, to no small degree, from the Ides of March." April 28 or 29: "As you suggest, let us be content with the Ides of March." May 14: "The Ides of March do not offer me as much solace as before." May 22: "Finding solace in the Ides of March is foolish." Later in the same letter: "If things proceed along the lines they seem to be following—prepare yourself for what I am about to say—then I take no pleasure in the Ides of March." Worse follows: "Since killing the master has not made us free, there was no reason to flee this particular master. Trust me, I'm blushing, but there, I've already written the words, and I don't feel like erasing them (*rubeo, mihi crede, sed iam scripseram; delere nolui*)."[26]

Naturally, it is this last line that most captures our attention, for it places erasability at the center of the coy game of confession and concealment that Cicero and Atticus so often played in their letters. In the broadest terms, Cicero could take risks in his letters to Atticus for two reasons. First, these were private letters to a friend and confidant; Cicero could (and, to the scandal of Petrarch, often did) say and do something quite different in public.[27] Second, when he changed his mind, perhaps as the result of a disapproving reply from Atticus, Cicero could subject a sentiment expressed in an earlier letter to revision—even repeated revision, as in the examples just quoted about the "Ides of March," which read like the cancellations and substitutions of a rough draft, though in fact they occur over the course of several letters. But even with such safeguards, there remained a serious danger: Cicero might go too far but so like what he wrote that he was unable to turn back. This is in essence what would happen over the summer and fall of 44, as Cicero, not only in letters but also in unpublished speech and treatise, wrote and revised himself into the man who would be unable to turn away from a public confrontation with Antony.

Cicero's "I don't want to erase" thus has two levels of meaning. First and foremost, Cicero actually likes what he sees, despite his protest that he is blushing (itself a kind of epistolary joke: does one really blush when alone?).[28] But Cicero implicitly blames his unwillingness to undo his lapsus on a material constraint: "I don't want to erase," since erasing papyrus, though certainly possible with a sponge (ancient inks were usually water-soluble) was undoubtedly a messy business and, to judge by surviving papyri, rarer than cancellation (which of course might not conceal enough to avoid a blush).[29] Behind all this is what must be the principal virtue of papyrus for letters between intimates, since using papyrus marks the trust that correspondents must have if they are to move to a relatively unerasable medium on which they write in their own hand without a prior draft. "I worry that the papyrus itself might betray us," Cicero writes back in 59, and though his direct reference is to extraneous readers, he knows, at least unconsciously, that the papyrus always betrays and that this is precisely what he likes about it. To write to Atticus is to surrender to the risk of revealing more than is opportune and then to find oneself unable and, more to the point, unwilling (*delere nolui*) to erase it.

The stakes for the written word were high in 44, and it is not surprising to find Cicero torn between inscription and erasure in the months before he would leave his final, indelible marks on history. (Indeed, in his letters to Atticus from later that year, Cicero would reprise the game of *delere nolui*, though this time in relation not to erasure *per se* but rather to the choice between suppression or publication of the undelivered second *Philippic*.) But disaster loomed on the horizon also in 59, and by way of conclusion, let us consider a final passage from that year's correspondence.

Cicero spent most of April 59 in the tiny seaside town of Anzio, where he had what seems to have been a smallish house, whence he sent Atticus a letter in which, in a brief aside, he expresses a desire to have it all to do over again: "I'm wondering whether I shouldn't stay put and pass this whole period at Anzio, where I would rather have been a *duovir* than at Rome (*ubi quidem ego mallem duumvirum quam Romae fuisse*)."[30] Properly speaking, there is a word missing here. A *duovir* was a member of the local governing board of an Italian municipality; Cicero therefore cannot mean, "Better a *duovir* at Anzio than a *duovir* at Rome." Translators have instead taken Cicero's point to be, "I would rather have been a *duovir* at Anzio than consul at Rome." In such a reading, Cicero might be supposed to have omitted *consulem* out of abhorrence for the superfluousness of saying "consul at Rome"—one could not, after all, be consul anywhere else—whereas reusing *duovir* to mean *consul* works in a literal sense, in that the latter too was one man of a pair; the resulting demotion of Rome's top office makes for a kind of joke: "Better a small-town mayor than mayor of the whole country." Somewhere along the way of the text's manuscript tradition, a scribe sought a more mechanical solution by inserting a *me* before *fuisse*. Translating this as, "Better to have been a *duovir* at Anzio than for me to have been at Rome," doesn't help much; one gets a finer point out of the supplement by instead rendering it as, "Better to have been *duovir* at Anzio than *to have been me* at Rome." Ultimately, however, this is just a variation on the insertion of *consul*, since for the consular Cicero, "having been me" means "having been consul." Indeed, the two words are semantically linked, since Cicero could and does designate the year we call 63 as *me consule*, "when I was consul," a self-indulgent variation on the formula of giving dates by the names of the year's consuls.[31] In this formula may be found the word that is really missing here, for in the end, Cicero's real meaning can only be this: "I would rather have been a *duovir* at Anzio than ever to have been Cicero." At some deep level, it is Cicero's own name that lies *in litura* below *Romae*. But the man who had denied erasure to Verres could scarcely expect, or even want, the same for himself.

5

THE SURFACE OF THE PAGE

I looked dizzily, and beheld a wide expanse of ocean, whose waters wore so inky a hue as to bring at once to my mind the Nubian geographer's account of the *Mare Tenebrarum.*

Edgar Allan Poe,
"A Descent into the Maelström" (1841)

The vast unfathomable abyss, spoken of by the poets, is the great Atlantic ocean; upon the borders of which Homer places the gloomy mansions, where the Titans resided. The ancients had a notion, that the earth was a widely-extended plain; which terminated abruptly, in a vast cliff of immeasurable descent. At the bottom was a chaotic pool, or ocean; which was so far sunk beneath the confines of the world, that, to express the depth and distance, they imagined, an anvil of iron tossed from the top would not reach it under ten days. . . . By the Nubian Geographer the Atlantic is uniformly called according to the present version Mare Tenebrarum. Agressi sunt mare tenebrarum, quid in eo esset, exploraturi. *They ventured into the sea of darkness, in order to explore what it might contain.*

Jacob Bryant,
A New System, or, An Analysis of Ancient Mythology (1775-76)

Is the page flat? Our first impulse is to say yes, else it would not be a page. But to peer closely, even at the finest paper, parchment, or papyrus, is to find the strands and pores and fibers that give every page both the texture and the depth into which the ink must sink without penetrating. And the fact that the page is neither flat nor smooth is clearer still in wax, stone, or clay, where words are not just lines or shapes, but valleys, ridges, and prisms. Far from flat, the page is a terrain, a tissue.

In other words, the page has texture even before it has a text. And by a kind of radical materialism, we might be tempted to say that all the places, from Tartarus to Parnassus, visited by writers, "diggers of wells and builders of houses,"[1] as Michel de Certeau calls them, are re-elaborations and amplifications of that already uneven surface onto and into which texts are made. This chapter will attempt to throw the literary page into relief, restoring to it heights and depths that are neither merely material nor merely metaphorical. We begin with two visions, almost dreams, followed by a nightmare.

Caravaggio's *Narcissus*:[2] a shadowy youth looks down at an even darker pool across a thin horizontal line that divides the painting in two, like a fold. And one need only invert this bifolium to see what he sees, from his point of view: a luscious lake of blackish paint only just tinged by color and barely bothered by form—a magnificent abstraction that spills into the darkness of the "real" world it reflects, embracing, dissecting, dissolving the figure, as if all were spiraling back to that pool of pigments and oil that first appeared at the bottom of the painter's mortar.

Everyone knows the story of Narcissus, for whom long life was prophesied provided he "never come to know himself," and who, having spurned the love of girls and boys, fell in love with his own reflection and pined away, all most memorably described by Ovid. The tale, it has been said, burlesques the Delphic and Socratic injunction to "know thyself," even as it asks serious questions about what self-knowledge is and is not. Narcissus's encounter with his reflection has further been taken as an emblem of that between self and other or, more to the point, of the encounter with the self *as* other, as object. A whole host of questions about gender (especially when one considers Echo's role) and sexuality have been raised by this simultaneously self-constituting and self-destructive erotic gaze. And finally—and this is the most persistent interpretive tradition of all—Narcissus, as both source and spectator of his own reflected image, acts out a parable of the making and viewing of art.[3]

Less often remembered, however, though Ovid tells it too, is the story of Narcissus's pool:

> Fons erat inlimis, nitidis argenteus undis,
> quem neque pastores neque pastae monte capellae

contigerant aliudve pecus, quem nulla volucris
nec fera turbarat nec lapsus ab arbore ramus;
gramen erat circa, quod proximus umor alebat,
silvaque sole locum passura tepescere nullo.

There was a spring, unmuddied, silvery with sparkling waves,
which neither shepherds nor goats who grazed the mountainside
nor any other herd had touched, which no bird or beast or
branch slipping from a tree had disturbed; around it was grass,
nourished by the nearby liquid, as well as a wood which insured
that the space would never be warmed by sunlight.[4]

We have been so ready to see a mirror here that we have overlooked curious
features of its surface and frame. A wood (*silva*) gives way to a grassy margin,
and then to the pool itself. What the pool is filled with is clean (*inlimis*) but not
clear (*argenteus*), its opacity being key to its ability to reflect. In the story that
follows, the things the pool sends back are twice called *signa*, once in the sense
of a marble statue, later, for the sign language of a reflected nod (*Metamorphoses*
3.419, 460). The pool reproduces verbal signs too, but silently; indeed here is
the line that immediately precedes Narcissus's recognition, finally, that this is
his reflection, that it both is and is not he: "You offer back words that do not
reach our ears," *verba refers aures non pervenentia nostras* (*Metamorphoses* 3.462).
If the pool's surface is overly disturbed then the shape it sends back is "obscure"
(*obscuraque moto / reddita forma lacu est*); clarity is restored only when the water
is again "liquefied" (*liquefacta*) (*Metamorphoses* 3.475-76, 486). Liquefied?
Rough water scarcely needs to be liquefied (it already is emphatically so) in
order to become smooth. Such language surely is better suited to the smoothing of the dark wax in a Roman writing tablet, which, like this pool, must be
sheltered from the sun's heating rays, lest it become unable to hold any shape at
all. It seems quite possible, in other words, that what Narcissus saw was not so
much a picture as a poem, one written only just now, its surface still glistening
with waxen whitecaps (*nitidis argenteus undis*) where the stylus has just
plumbed the page's depths.

At the heart of Seneca's bloodiest play, the *Thyestes*, lies a scene of unspeakable
butchery. "Unspeakable," though, is scarcely the right word; the scene is,
rather, unplayable and so, like many such scenes in tragedy, takes place offstage,
described by an eyewitness—in this case, a messenger, rigid with fear, who has,
he tells us, a picture of the deed stuck in his vision (*haeret in vultu trucis imago
facti*), which he soon seeks to translate into words.[5] The removal from the stage

of this scene of horror—what the messenger has witnessed is the murder and dismemberment of Thyestes' sons by his brother Atreus, who cooks and serves their flesh to their unknowing father—does not, in the logic of Senecan drama, undercut its centrality. On the contrary, it is tempting instead to see here a staging of Freudian "repression" (*Verdrängung*): the messenger's narrative potentially remembers not just a *factum* hidden behind the stage but also, metaphorically, some analogous *imago* buried deep in his audience's unconscious.[6]

Before turning once again to questions about the map of the mind, let us devote our attention to a matter somewhat more narrowly topographical. The messenger opens his account with a precise description of a very strange place: the palace of Atreus, scene of the king's gruesome crime. We listen as he begins:

> In arce summa Pelopiae pars est domus
> conversa ad Austros, cuius extremum latus
> aequale monti crescit atque urbem premit
> et contumacem regibus populum suis
> habet sub ictu; fulget hic turbae capax
> immane tectum, cuius auratas trabes
> variis columnae nobiles maculis ferunt.
> Post ista vulgo nota, quae populi colunt,
> in multa dives spatia discedit domus.
> Arcana in imo regio secessu iacet,
> alta vetustum valle compescens nemus,
> penetrale regni, nulla qua laetos solet
> praebere ramos arbor aut ferro coli,
> sed taxus et cupressus et nigra ilice
> obscura nutat silva, quam supra eminens
> despectat alte quercus et vincit nemus.

> Atop the acropolis lies a part of the house of Pelops, facing south, the farthest edge of which rises as high as a mountain and lords over the city, keeping the population, defiant of its kings, in striking range. Here glistens a gigantic hall of massive capacity; majestic columns, variously marked, support its gilded beams. Beyond those parts known to the public, where whole nations come to do homage, the rich house recedes into numerous spaces; in its deepest retreat lies a secret zone, confining an ancient grove in a deep valley, the kingdom's innermost recess. Here no tree tends to spread verdant boughs or be pruned; rather, the yew and the cypress and woods of black ilex nod darkly. Towering over this, an oak looks down on the grove—and dominates. (*Thyestes* 641–56)

The messenger goes on to describe the votive offerings hung on this last tree by successive kings, the Stygian spring that oozes beneath it, and the specters that issue from its waters to haunt the hellish grove.

This house with a forest in place of a Roman peristyle garden[7] might seem an especially grotesque bit of Senecan hyperbole were it not for the fact that a house with a forest inside—along with pastures, vineyards, and a lake—is precisely what Seneca's emperor Nero built in the center of Rome. Indeed, the resemblances, both in look and in feel, between the messenger's phantasmagorical *descriptio loci* and ancient *descriptiones* of Nero's Domus Aurea are striking, to the point that, especially for scholars anxious to connect the play's villain to Rome's famous emperor-gone-bad, the imagined palace starts to look like a grim parody of the one that was all too real.[8] But how exceptional are these apparently twin palace-scapes? In the first place, brick or marble, Rome was a city with a remarkable number of "green spaces," a fact that should be clear enough from the number of attested *horti*, *luci*, and *nemora* that appear in dictionaries of Roman topography. This is the city beautifully reconstructed by Pierre Grimal in *Les jardins romains*, a complex urban landscape that has been given striking visual confirmation by the Neronian-era fresco discovered on the Colle Oppio a few years ago, whatever city it actually represents.[9] It is clear, in other words, that the Domus Aurea's mix of architectural and landscape elements was generically consistent with, rather than exceptional to, the city that surrounded it. Both palaces—Nero's and Seneca's—are thus products of the same general taste, carried to monstrous excess.

The woods add an extra element to consider. In chapter 1, we found in the Vergilian woods an ancient and enduring metaphor for the "poet's workshop"; by Seneca's day (and through to the Renaissance), *silva* was also used in a semi-technical way to designate a particular kind of literary composition. The earliest definition comes from a disapproving Quintilian, who complains about the *vitium* of those writers "who first want to race through the material (*materia*) with the fastest pen possible and who, following the heat of the moment, write extemporaneously; they call this a *silva*."[10] Quintilian's use of the word *materia* points to a meaning of *silva* more common in its Greek counterpart, *hulē*, likewise "woods" but often used to refer to "raw material" (such as, but not limited to, the timber produced by the woods), including the notional raw material of literary composition. Thus *hulē* and *silva* could refer to notes or to something approaching what we call a "rough draft"[11]—this is presumably behind the real or affected spontaneity of the writers Quintilian chides. More or less in this guise, *silva* appears among the commonly used titles rehearsed by Aulus Gellius for works whose authors "had carefully researched varied, miscellaneous, and basically random learning,"[12] the result of wide-ranging note taking like that used by Gellius himself to prepare the work he eventually decides to call *Attic Nights*, after his lucubratory readings while in the Athenian countryside. Gellius helps us to understand that the point of *silva* is its reference to a kind of writing that presupposes reading: the "woods" are thus those of preexisting literature, through which the writer has wandered along paths largely still visible to the reader of the ostensibly less-than-finished work. The highly polished perfection of this form produces the long tradition, from Statius to Poliziano, of using *silva* to title poems born of self-conscious surrender to literary imitation.

However mannered these later developments may seem, they hint at a more general truth: *imitatio* is "one of the inescapable features of Latin literature."[13] And *imitatio* takes us back to the same Seneca, who in one of his letters to Lucilius sets forth a theory of imitation in what would become antiquity's most enduringly influential passage on the subject. There Seneca compares the reader/writer to the bee who flies from flower to flower (from book to book) in order to prepare its honey. Having first stored our collected reading separately, we should then "blend those various tastes into a single flavor so that, even if its sources will be apparent, nevertheless it will reveal itself to be something other than its origin" (*in unum saporem varia illa libamenta confundere ut, etiam si apparuerit unde sumptum sit, aliud tamen esse quam unde sumptum est appareat*).[14]

With this, we again find ourselves in the grove of the palace of Atreus, which happens to be an exercise in precisely the theory of imitation just described—one of countless in Seneca's tragedies, which are characterized by what one recent scholar has called an "overwhelming and oppressive intertextual memory," and another, a "palimpsestic code."[15] The passage's principal source, *unde sumptum sit*, would have been readily apparent to educated members of Seneca's audience, for it is found in Rome's national epic, the *Aeneid*. Vergil describes the palace of Latinus as "a majestic edifice, immense and lofty on a hundred columns, on the city's highest point," adding that it was *horrendum silvis et religione parentum*.[16] Given the second part of the phrase and the general context (this palace is grand but not monstrous), Vergil clearly means *horrendum* in its mildest possible sense: the palace is "awe-inspiring for its woods and the piety of its forefathers." Seneca's point of departure is a deliberate double misreading. First, he will create a palace that genuinely is "hair-raising for its woods." Second, he will pick up on the likely Vergilian wordplay here to imagine a palace that is also *horrens silvis*, "bristling" with trees, perhaps even forging a connection between this passage and Vergil's earlier description of the "shaggy shadow" (*horrens umbra*) cast by the dark woods that overhang the Libyan shore where Aeneas and his men first make landfall.[17] The result is a remarkable conservation of the letter of the source even as its sense is directed into an entirely original *sapor*.

One *locus*, in both the topographical and the textual sense, is thus an *amplificatio*, again in both senses, of the other. This place produced *by* imitation, however, is simultaneously a place *of* imitation: Atreus, with "author-like plotting,"[18] replays the crime of his grandfather Tantalus, invoked at the play's outset, who butchered his son Pelops and served his flesh to the gods. And to this is added yet another layer of meaning, for both crimes, that of Tantalus and that of Atreus, burlesque the Senecan theory of imitation just described: Tantalus hoped by his cookery to dupe the gods (only a distracted Demeter took a bite); Atreus stews the boys' *membra disiecta* into a *sapor* that only briefly fools their father, until recognition of their heads, hands, feet makes it all too horrifically clear *unde sumptum sit*. And the latter story has still another edge, for if the boys are the source of the soup, then *a fortiori* so too is their father and eater Thyestes, inasmuch as he is the source of the boys, now in his belly, become at once womb and tomb. There is much that one could say about these reversals, but perhaps their most striking effect is to transform the recognition scene into a scene of *self*-recognition: among Atreus's macabre witticisms over dinner, hinting at the truth without revealing it, he spares us, "You are what you eat."

Indeed, commentators consistently overlook Seneca's model for this part of the scene, that Ovidian figure for whom disaster had been prophesied should he ever "come to know himself": Narcissus.[19] Thyestes before his soup-bowl is Narcissus before the pool; his reluctant recognition of his sons' separate body parts grimly parodies Narcissus admiring, one by one, the reflected eyes, hair, cheeks, neck, mouth that he does not yet fully recognize as his own.[20] Atreus, in turn, replays the role of Echo, repeatedly throwing Thyestes' words back at him, with pointed modifications. *Redde iam gnatos mihi* ("Now give me my sons back"), demands Thyestes; Atreus replies by turning *Redde iam* into *Reddam* ("I *shall* give them back").[21] Seneca's appeal to the Narcissus story is more than just decorative; indeed, the whole play can be read as a study in mirrors, their reflections set in motion before the action begins: the brothers were supposed to have ruled in alternating years, but Thyestes had slept with the wife of Atreus and had been driven from the kingdom; both in bed and on the throne, the brothers are interchangeable.[22] The recognition scene is as much between brother and brother as it is between father and sons. "Don't you recognize your boys?" taunts Atreus. This time, it is Thyestes who echoes: *Agnosco fratrem* ("I recognize my brother").[23]

What though should *we* see in this page? Should we say, "I recognize Ovid," i.e., *unde sumptum sit*? Or, "I recognize Seneca," i.e., his signature *sapor*? In other words, this highly imitative page, like many others, is self-consciously staged as a scene of reading that is barely distinguishable from writing. Atreus is the author of the atrocity that Thyestes is compelled to read, but in the end, what Thyestes finds in his soup is himself, just as Seneca had looked into Ovid's pool and found there his own play. The same is true of the messenger's speech from which we learn all this: Can we really be sure that the messenger has just been, offstage, in the palace of Atreus? Perhaps he was only in the palace of Latinus, in Vergil; perhaps he has been reading Ovid too; perhaps the lines he learned were not those of this play but, rather, those of other poems, and thus he himself is the author of these amplifications—ostensibly a messenger, he really is playing Seneca himself.

To call such self-indulgent writing narcissistic would be to level a familiar charge at Seneca. But let us remember that Ovid's Narcissus was not a narcissist, or, at least, not a naïve one, for, at least by the end, he knew full well what he was doing. So too, surely, does Seneca. Above all, to suppose that he aims only to stage his own erudition and mimetic virtuosity would be to fail to account for the genuine horror his plays often produce. His secret is not really amplification and hyperbole, achieved by building up his models, making them loom ever bigger, ever closer. Rather, imitation insinuates an architecture *below* his page. "We have seen this somewhere before," we say, and as we peer closer, the page (or stage) gives way, and for a brief moment we worry, with a sinking feeling, that what lies beneath is not a literary memory, but one of our own.[24]

Perhaps we can find a similar authorial strategy at work in the decision of Seneca's pupil and emperor to turn his back on the Palatine palimpsest, the most recent layers of which conserved the traces of his imperial predecessors, stacked on the site of Rome's legendary foundation. To build a palace that told stories other than those of Roman history, Romulus to Claudius, Nero sought not only a *tabula rasa* but a page of a very different shape: concave, not a hill but a valley, with a lake at its bottom and center as focal point. "Now, at last, I begin to live like a human being,"[25] he is reported to have quipped; indignation at this arrogance has obscured his strangely egalitarian point, for a fully convinced tyrant must instead cry, "Now, at last, I begin to live as befits an emperor." One way or another, Nero saw himself—indeed, his "humanity"—represented here, and in part this may be because he shared with his teacher the most basic of poetic principles: the surfaces that best reflect us are the ones that draw us to their (our) depths.

But let us turn from the mirror of a megalomaniac (and of the gilded colossus of himself he erected nearby) and back instead to the pool that reflects Narcissus, who, while we have wandered elsewhere, has been transformed: "His body was nowhere: in place of a body, they find a yellowish flower, with white petals (*folia*) belting its center."[26] Would it be too much to see here the eventual metamorphosis of Narcissus's waxen reverie into a papyrus roll, that yellowish-white assemblage of leaves? What Narcissus wrote on his shimmering tablet, that tablet has now reflected into a book, and that book now bears his name, having replaced him altogether. This is very like what we saw in chapter 2, to say nothing of what happens at the end of the *Metamorphoses*, for all who read Ovid (by which we mean the books and not the man) are compelled by what they hold in their hands to agree with his final prediction that he shall "live on," and that his name shall be "indelible."

If this goes too far, then let us at least see that flower, bicolor and multi-leaved, as a reflection of the complexity of the pool it bends to read. A pool, like a page, is never just a mirror, never fully reducible to its surface. Even when entirely flat (or seemingly so) and fully reflective, it guarantees what no ordinary mirror can, namely, that *there really is something down here*. This is, in part, the reason for Gaston Bachelard's magnificent study of water, *L'eau et les rêves: Essai sur l'imagination de la matière*, which begins with Narcissus: "One cannot dream profoundly with *objects*. To dream profoundly, one must dream with *substances (matières)*. A poet who begins with a mirror must end with the *water of a fountain*."[27] But Bachelard, for whom "matter is the unconscious of form,"[28] says surprisingly little about writing materials. Indeed, he finds significance in the avoidance of the word "blood" by Seneca's rival in horror, Edgar Allan Poe, but it is precisely in a passing mention of Poe's use of the word "inky" that we find the vocabulary Bachelard himself avoids, snatched from a context (given as my epigraph) in which Poe's narrator scales a mountain to look down upon the thus-colored surface of the sea into which will then open the vast, terrible whirlpool of "A Descent into the Maelström."[29] Poe's word choice is not, in fact, an accident, for the whole image maps just how high and deep a story-teller (really the writer) must go, as is clearer still from Poe's other whirlpool, that of the "MS. Found in a Bottle," flung into the sea by its putative author at the very last minute, when he has spun his way almost to the bottom of the world.[30]

Seneca too gives us a whirlpool, invoked as a simile by the chorus of the *Thyestes*, after Atreus offers his brother the kingship:

> So, when waves swell from the deep
> while Corus lashes the Bruttian Sea,
> Scylla echoes from her beaten hollows,
> and sailors at port tremble at the sea
> which greedy Charybdis gulps — then vomits . . .
>
> (*Thyestes* 577–81)

Such a storm has passed, they think:

> But if the force of the winds has slackened,
> the sea spreads out gentler than a pond;

the deep, which ships had feared to furrow,
lies wide open to pleasure-boats, pretty
with sails spread here, spread there:
a chance to count fish below the surface,
where just now, beneath the massive storm,
the Cyclades, shaken, feared the sea.

(*Thyestes* 588–95)

The Chorus is wrong: this placid sea that offers no reflective illusion is, in fact, as meaningless as a blank page; the brothers' truce is a lie; Charybdis was and is the truth; the story is already winding its way toward that awful meal in which all must be recognized.

One could object that it does not always take a whirlpool to get to the bottom of things; many, indeed, have preferred the subtlety of Ovid, who warns, as we have seen, that the overwrought page becomes "obscure." But one way or another, the page must find its depth. Here, of course, we seem to move far beyond anything that belongs to material proper and into the realm of metaphor, the spaces of the mind, the structures of sense. But the page is here too; else we would not tend to speak of "layers"; i.e., not of real depth, but of the iteration of surfaces: layers of the city, layers of the psyche, layers of meaning, woven, stacked. Where pages accumulate, one after another, we have something like a book, that other deep thing which, like a pool, seems to want to reassure us, as it did Narcissus, that there really is something down here, that we are more than just a single, simple reflection.

The author admits this every time she or he grabs a freshly prepared tablet, or smoothes the black wax of one already used, and starts again. Nothing, of course, ensures that these reflections will be flattering, that they will not finally reveal depths we might prefer not to recognize. Such, indeed, is the *Thyestes*, to which we return, by way of conclusion, for one final pool—the one Seneca places at the center of the wood at the center of the palace at the center of his play: "A gloomy spring lies in the dark shade and oozes to a stop in a black pond (*nigra piger / haeret palude*), like the formless liquid (*deformis unda*) of the awful Styx" (*Thyestes* 665–67). The comparison is probably another nod to Ovid's Narcissus, who, after death, continued to seek his reflection in the waters of the river that rings the Underworld (*Thyestes* 504–5).[31] *Deformis*, in this regard, reminds us of *liquefacta*—a superfluous detail, unless this is not water. And indeed, if Narcissus's pool was a tablet, then Seneca's is even more obviously so.

R. J. Tarrant observes that, in the coming lines, "the meaning of *deformis* increases in strength from merely 'unsightly' here to 'disfiguring' and finally to 'lacking [or 'destroying'] all shape.'"[32] But the latter meanings are already present here, if, as seems probable, Seneca is hinting at the well-known property of the water of the Styx (in this case, usually said to be a river locatable somewhere above the earth, though the precise spot varies): namely, that it dissolves everything, even metals and gems; only the hooves or horns of certain animals are immune.[33] Stygian water was the poison reportedly given to Alexander the Great,[34] and Seneca, in his *Natural Questions*, explains exactly how it works: "This . . . water causes extremely rapid damage, with no opportunity for remedy, since, not at all unlike plaster upon contact with water, it stiffens immediately after being swallowed and curdles the body's insides."[35] Seneca's explanation presents something of a paradox, for the water that dissolves everything poisons by doing the opposite: clotting, coagulating, petrifying. It is probably by transferring these effects to their cause that Seneca gives us, in the *Thyestes*, a Stygian spring that oozes to a stop, like the blood that curdles in the veins of its victims—or in the hearer of the tale the messenger is about to tell.[36]

Indeed, the next time we meet the word used to describe the spring's coagulation, *haerere*, is in the messenger's most blood-curdling moment, as the boys' bodies are butchered and cooked: "The cuts of meat, on the one hand, cling (*haerent*) to spits and, placed over gentle fires, drip (*stillant*), while liquid (*latex*) placed on the flames in a glowing cauldron boils up the rest" (*Thyestes* 765-67). By this point, it is clear that the oozing black spring has prefigured this dripping gore and bloody broth. But the sticky pool has echoed in turn an earlier *haerere*, one we already have considered. I shall relate what I have seen, the messenger tells the chorus, "if my heart will stop racing, if my body, stiff with fear, will allow my limbs to move: an image of the savage deed remains stuck in my vision (*haeret in vultu trucis imago facti*)" (*Thyestes* 634-36). We are now prepared to recognize here Seneca's most audacious Ovidian borrowing, for the messenger has begun by echoing Narcissus's very first moments before the pool: "And while he drinks, he is grabbed by the image of his own visible form (*visae correptus imagine formae*). . . He stares, shocked, at himself and freezes, motionless, with the same expression (*vultuque immotus eodem / haeret*), like a statue shaped from Parian marble."[37] Moments like this are, of course, what led Lacan to Narcissus, where he found a model of human psychological development—and a primary myth of twentieth-century thought—in a mirror that gives even as it takes away: Narcissus wins a sense of self, but at the price of his own otherness, his own objectification, as this picture makes him like a statue.[38] Ovid's next lines turn, instead, to the image's other, opposite ability to segment and fragment, as Narcissus picks out for admiration, one by one, the separate parts of his body, a scene gruesomely replayed, as we already have observed, by Thyestes, who must recognize, in the soup below him, the bits and pieces of his own flesh and blood. And in a slightly different vein, we might add that the messenger's exordium, by its resemblance to Narcissus at his pool, reveals that horror is hardly *sui generis* but is simply an amplification of objectification into petrifaction, in part by rendering explicit what is only elegiac in Ovid, namely, the kinship of the image with that perfect objectification that is death.

We could go on, of course: let us summarize by saying that reflective pools, in their dual ability to dissolve and solidify, like Stygian water itself, embrace a whole spectrum of things we have learned to say about representation. But let us pause a moment more over *haerere*, the persistence of which, instead, reveals what theories of representation that assimilate the image to a mirror usually fail to account for: not so much depth (which can be approximated in two dimensions) as fixity. For fixity must always be sought in material that does more than reflect. No sooner has the poet given us a mirror than its waters must be troubled, whipped into froth, waves, whirlpools; it must become mire, muck, black and viscous; it must clot like blood, thicken like gravy, coagulate and stiffen like plaster. For poetry, like the poet's name, is never really "writ in water."

6

✤

THE FOLDED PAGE

In a famous medieval illuminated manuscript known as the Codex Aureus of St. Emmeram, the beginning of the Gospel of John is illustrated, on the facing page, with the somewhat uncanny image of the hand of God.[1] Again and again one can close the book and then reopen it, lifting the hand from the elaborately embellished first words of the Gospel: *In principio erat verbum.* It is as if the illustrator has insinuated between the pages a vision . . .

. . . of the hand of God rising from the page on which it has written its own creation: In the beginning was the word. Suddenly the hand is caught in its own spell; in an instantaneous vacuum it collapses into flatness—and the hand was never really a hand at all, but was itself a word, a pictograph around which a page of parchment has already grown, a page which serves as a reliquary for the dismembered hand of God, who was always already dead through the passion of being written. And beneath this lifeless hand, the words sprout a thicket of tender vines, as the death of the authorial hand of God gives life to the words it wrote not even an instant ago, so that by a curious homeopathy, Death by Representation is resurrected as the Immortality of the Word.

The drama of the page, as this brief reverie reminds us, has seldom been as spectacular as it was for medieval Christians.[2] But for all that this magic seems strange and wonderful, there is a way in which it represents the logical culmination of things we already have seen in this book, as if one of the ancient authors we have tried to imagine had fallen asleep over his draft—and dreamed of God. We turn, therefore, to a rare author who manages to push this vision even farther, until she finally comes back around to where it all began. If we opened with Orpheus, we end, in a sense, with Eurydice.

> I have the untiring love of a mother . . . I throw death out, it comes back, we begin again, I am pregnant with beginnings.
>
> Hélène Cixous,
> "Coming to Writing," 48

In March 841, thirty years before the completion of the Codex Aureus, a Carolingian noblewoman named Dhuoda gave birth to a son in the town of Uzès, not far from Avignon. The boy was born into the chaos that followed the death of Louis the Pious, whose three surviving sons struggled for possession of the disintegrating empire built two generations earlier by Charlemagne. On his father's orders, the infant was taken from his mother even before he was baptized; eight months later, Dhuoda still had not been told his name.[3] This was her second son; the first, William, had been born fourteen years earlier, in November 826.[4]

Then in June one civil war came to an end as Lothar, whose royal claims Dhuoda's husband Bernard, Duke of Septimania, had supported, was defeated at Fontenoy by Louis the German and Charles the Bald. Bernard had abstained from the battle, and in an effort to stabilize his perilous position afterward, he sent his eldest son, William, to Charles as a hostage. On November 30, 841, the day after William's fifteenth birthday, Dhuoda began writing him what she called a *Liber manualis*, "Handbook," framed as a lengthy letter (*Handbook*, XI 2.2–4). It would be their first contact since William had become a virtual prisoner: *Audivi enim quod genitor tuus Bernardus in manus domni te commendavit Karoli regis*, "I have heard that your father Bernard has handed you over to Charles, Lord and King" (*Handbook*, Praefatio 34–35). Dhuoda here is using technical language to describe William's passage into vassalage by the ritual pantomime of the *immixtio manuum*, in which the new lord clasped his hands around the clasped hands of his new vassal.[5] As we will see, these are not the first hands that appear in Dhuoda's *Handbook*, but for us they loom bloodstained over the text, not least because we know that within five years of its writing, both Bernard and William were executed by Charles.[6]

Praesens iste libellus: These are the first three words of Dhuoda's book. *Praesens*, "present," with more or less the same range of meanings as the English adjective. *Iste*, the so-called demonstrative of the second person, "this or that *of yours*." *Libellus*, diminutive of *liber*, "book," a humble name for what is in fact a fairly lengthy text. And so, "This present little book of yours," or, "This little book, present to you."[7] But the drama is lost in the English. Many authors begin by calling attention to *hic liber*, "this book (I am writing)," and so too Dhuoda seems to start: *Praesens*—but this presence is fatefully qualified by what follows immediately, *iste*. By the second word she writes, Dhuoda loses the book she has only just begun: present to William, but already absent to its author.[8]

The speed with which Dhuoda seems to lose ownership of her text is soon echoed by her description of her separation from her second son, born eight months before she began writing:

> Etenim parvulum illum, antequam baptismatis accepisset gratiam, dominus et genitor Bernardus utrique vestrum, una cum Elefanto, praedictae civitatis episcopo, et cum ceteris fidelibus suis, in Aquitaniae partibus ad suam fecit adduci praesentiam.

> And he was still very small, before he had received the grace of baptism, when Bernard, the lord and father of each of you, had him brought into his presence in the area of Aquitaine in the company of Elefantus, bishop of Uzès, and the rest of his circle. (*Handbook*, Praefatio 17–22)

The boy was Dhuoda's only until born, at which point (when he was known to be a male child and potential heir) he was absorbed into an emphatically patriarchal economy of proper names, as two fathers (Elefantus and Bernard) gave him the name Dhuoda is never told—and so rewrote him as their own.

Dhuoda's is a writing born of this erasure of her motherhood. When she begins, *Praesens iste libellus*, she is recapitulating an earlier loss: *parvulus ad suam praesentiam*. For *ad suam praesentiam* is just another way to say *praesens iste*: "presence" is always "yours" or "his," never Dhuoda's, whether she is talking about her "little book" (*libellus*) or her "little boy" (*parvulus*). Indeed, it is hard not to wonder whether Dhuoda was aware of the irony that *parvus liber*, which her diminutives enable her to avoid saying, could mean either.

The lack of presence is, in fact, the occasion for the book that follows, as Dhuoda soon tells us: "But since for a long while now, because of the absence of your presence (*ob absentiam praesentiae vestrae*), under the order of my lord, in whose struggle I rejoice, I have resided in this city, I have seen to it that, out of longing for both of you (*ex desiderio utrorumque vestrum*), this little book, on a scale with my awareness of my own smallness, be written out and delivered (*dirigere*) to you" (Praefatio 23–27). Like any letter, the *Handbook* ultimately assigns presence and absence to author and addressee alike: one of us is here, but here is where the other is not. But what most captures our attention in this sentence is the odd, almost oxymoronic phrase, *ob absentiam presentiae vestrae*, "because of the absence of your presence." This ponderous expression is our first sign that, in her book, Dhuoda will make of absence something palpable.

Dhuoda, *in absentia*, i.e., in the form of her book, addresses her absent son. And she makes her motherhood key to the authority with which she does so:

> Fili, habebis doctores qui te plura et ampliora utilitatis doceant documenta, sed non aequali conditione, animo ardentis in pectore, sicut ego genitrix tua, fili primogenite.

> Son, you will have teachers who may teach you lessons of greater number and of greater use, but you will have none of equal status, with the heart of one burning in her chest, as I your mother have, first-born son. (*Handbook,* I 7.20–23)[9]

Dhuoda's designation of William as *primogenitus*, both here and elsewhere, merits comment. The Carolingians, following old Frankish law, did not inherit by primogeniture; indeed, this is the immediate reason for the civil wars that have made William a hostage. To use *primogenitus* as an epithet for William would not have seemed inappropriate, but neither would it have been automatic. Indeed, Dhuoda seems to have a hidden motive, for *fili primogenite* is juxtaposed immediately to *genitrix tua*. William, it seems, has been made to borrow the uniqueness that Dhuoda argues for herself as mother. The result is a one-to-one relationship of perfect correspondence.

The unique desire between mother and son is waged against the dynastic desires that have commanded their separation, desires Dhuoda characterizes in homosocial terms: "Embrace Charles, your Lord (since God, as I believe, and your father Bernard chose for you to serve him in the budding vigor of your early adolescence), for he is born of a great and noble ancestry on both sides; serve him not only so that you may be pleasing to his eyes, but also that you may, with sense and sensitivity, please both his body and his soul" (*Handbook,* III 4.2–8). The story thus can be told like this: the violent struggles of the ninth century seem to have been occasioned by the fact that a father can have more than one son. Yet Dhuoda reveals the dangerous reverse of this patriarchal coin: William is a hostage because a son can have many fathers—in this passage Bernard, Charles, and even God, plus the *doctores* of the first passage.[10] Against this proliferation of fathers, Dhuoda reminds her son that he has only one mother: "You will have none of equal status (*aequali conditione*), with the heart of one burning in her chest (*animo ardentis in pectore*)."

Nevertheless, motherhood is scarcely a stable concept in the *Handbook*. At the end of a long passage condemning the makers of unjust laws, Dhuoda glosses a famous apocalyptic line from Matthew:

Merito de talibus dicit Evangelista: "Vae pregnantibus et nutrientibus." Pregnans est qui aliena licita inlicite concupiscit. Nutrix, qui tollit non sua, et rapta possidet iniuste.

Rightly about such people the Evangelist says: "Woe to the pregnant and those who are nursing." The "pregnant" is he who unlawfully desires things lawfully belonging to another. "Who is nursing" is he who takes what is not his, and unjustly possesses things which were stolen. (*Handbook*, IV 8.173–6)[11]

The reader pauses perplexed over *qui*. It will not do to say that Dhuoda here is simply being "gender-neutral," for once the masculine relative pronoun defeminizes motherhood, the words that follow denaturalize it entirely. The resignification of motherhood to mark a violent and lawless *male* desire is a stunning move, full of anger and irony. "Medicate what opposes you with its opposite," as the proverb goes, quoted by Dhuoda a few pages earlier (*Handbook*, IV 1.4–5).[12] Indeed, it is difficult not to read as well for the assertion's logical inverse, for surely we can say that Dhuoda herself is *she* who rightfully desires things wrongly another's, *she* who tries to takes back what is hers, what has been stolen from her. And since she shall do so by means of the book she already has analogized to her child, this recoding of motherhood can be seen as the counterpoint to an even more exhilarating resignification and regendering of authorship itself.

We now can return to the beginning of the book to explore further Dhuoda's mothering of her text. There is in fact no single beginning to the book, for Dhuoda begins again and again, introducing two incipits, an epigram, a prologue, a preface, and a table of contents before the *Handbook* begins in earnest. We could interpret these beginnings as signs of Dhuoda's anxiety about her slippery hold on the text, reflecting her slippery hold on her children. But the false starts also introduce a subversive element of play into the book's beginning, play we cannot help reading back into Dhuoda the *genitrix*. As author, Dhuoda is a mother who can give birth when she chooses, who can even change her mind and start over again. And she who could not name her child names her book, defiantly, not once but three times:

Praesens iste libellus in tribus virgulis constat esse erectus: lege cuncta et in fine plenius nosse valebis. Volo enim ut simili modo in tribus lineis secundum auctoritatis seriem utilissimum habeat nomen: id est Norma, Forma et Manualis. Quod utrumque hae partes locutionis in nos specietenus continentur cuncta: Norma ex me, Forma in te, Manualis tam ex me quam in te, ex me collectus, in te receptus.

This present little book rises from the ground in three branches: read every-thing and in the end you will be able to know this more completely. I want it to have a very effective name along three lines, in keeping with the course of its authority—that is, Norm, Form, and Manual, because these classifications of speech are held together completely in us as in a mirror: the Norm out of me, the Form in you, the Manual as much out of me as in you, collected out of me, received in you. (*Handbook,* Incipit 5–12)

Dhuoda next provides an etymology of *manualis*, after which she announces that this will be the one name with which she will refer to the book henceforth:

> Quod volo ut cum ex manu mea tibi fuerit directus, in manu tua libenter facias amplecti eum opus, et tenens, volvens legensque stude opere compleri dignissime. Dicatur enim iste formatus libellus Manualis, hoc est sermo ex me, opus in te . . .

> What I want is that, when it has been directed out of my hand to you, you will willingly see to it that this work is embraced in your hand; and holding it, turning its pages, and reading it, strive for your own completion by putting it most fittingly to work. For let this little book, once it has taken shape, be called *Handbook,* i.e., language out of me, work in you . . . (*Handbook,* Incipit 42–46)[13]

The two passages establish a curious set of oppositions and mediations, which can best be represented by means of a diagram:

Dhuoda		William
Norma	Manualis	Forma
Sermo		Opus

Once again, it is the separation between Dhuoda and William that provides the enabling image of difference; the book is both that which describes their separation (because it is necessitated by it) and also that which links them. And so the book is a *manualis* because it touches each of them, or rather, is touched by each of them—Dhuoda when she writes it, William when he reads it (*ex manu mea . . . in manu tua*).

Yet by a clever loose end Dhuoda already has begun to unravel her text, for she places the *opus* that *manualis* should name on the right side of our diagram. That is to say, the *manualis* common to both of them (*tam ex me . . . quam in te*) names the *opus* that Dhuoda here locates in William alone (*opus in te*). Certainly this gesture conflates William with the book, something we by now expect, but it does more, for it suggests that *manualis* names not the book differentiated across the space of its transmission but rather a difference internal to Dhuoda's own relationship to her *opus*. *Manualis* chiefly designates not the hand that takes up this useful "handbook" but, rather, Dhuoda's own hand in the moment of writing, when this book was "formed" (*formatus*), i.e., written, the process by which language (*Norma/sermo*) becomes a particular text (*Forma/opus*).

But *manualis* implicates the divine author too, as Dhuoda explains in an extended definition of *manus*:

> 'Manus' enim multis intelligitur modis: aliquando Dei potestas, aliquando Filii, aliquando etiam ipse intelligitur Filius. Potestas Dei, sicut ait Apostolus: 'Humiliamini sub potenti manu Dei'; potestas Filii, ut ait Danihel: 'Potestas eius, potestas aeterna'; aliquando ipse Filius, Psalmista dicente: 'Mitte manum tuam de alto,' id est Filium tuum e sumis coelorum. Haec omnia vel his similia operatio et potestas intellegitur sancta, nam manus opus significat perfectum, Scriptura dicente: 'Et facta est super me manus Domini,' hoc est redemptio, quod credentes ad perfectum usque perduxit; item: 'Erat enim manus Domini confortans me,' et item: 'Nam et manus eius cum ipso est.'

> "Hand" is understood in many ways: sometimes the power of God; sometimes that of the Son; sometimes even the Son himself is understood. The power of God, as the Apostle says, "Humble yourself beneath the powerful hand of God"; the power of the Son, as Daniel says, "His power, the eternal power"; sometimes the Son himself, as the Psalmist says, "Send your hand from on high," that is your Son out of the heights of heaven. All these things or things similar to these are understood to be sacred working (*operatio*) and power, for "hand" signifies a work brought to completion (*opus perfectum*), as the Scripture says: "And the hand of the Lord was upon me," that is, redemption, which leads believers all the way to a state of completion. So also: "The hand of the Lord was comforting me." And likewise: "For even his hand is with him." (*Handbook*, Incipit 13–25)

The passage is typical of Dhuoda's daunting complexity. She unfolds a triptych of images apparently unified by the familiar use of *manus* to mean power. But the triptych is a false one: the third image (*ipse Filius*) is an unexpected repetition of the second (*potestas Filii*) and ultimately a doubling of the first (*potestas Patris*), for the Son, we are told, is the incarnated hand of the Father ('*Mitte manum tuum de alto,' id est Filium tuum e sumis coelorum*). For these images, which overlap in a manner far more complicated than that of a triptych, Dhuoda must announce a new hinge: "All these things or things similar to these are understood to be sacred working and power, for 'hand' signifies a work brought to completion" (*Haec omnia vel his similia operatio et potestas intellegitur sancta, nam manus opus significat perfectum*). *Opus* can mean any handiwork, but here and elsewhere it is for Dhuoda connected most immediately with the written *opus*, as we have seen. We might therefore understand the conjunction of *potestas* and *operatio* as the linguistic power of "authority." But this is an authority that Dhuoda entirely inverts in four words: *manus opus significat perfectum*, i.e., the hand (that writes) signifies the work (that it wrote). It is, of course, writing (not the writer) that is supposed to signify. We can circumscribe all writing with the logic of the transcendental signified and say that (all) writing signifies the (ultimate) writer (who is God). But Dhuoda says the opposite (the writer signifies the writing)—and so describes the exact inversion by which the illustrator of the St. Emmeram Gospels announces the death of God. And if the latter illustrates God's death by the sign of his hand, then Dhuoda connects that sign (by making Christ the incarnated hand of God) with God's better known death on (the sign of) the cross.

And so, settling on *Handbook* as her book's single title, Dhuoda turns to contemplate the cross as she ends her incipit:

> For let this little book, once it has taken shape, be called *Handbook*, i.e., language out of me, work in you, even as a certain man has said: "I have planted, Apollo has watered, but God has given increase." What more can I say here, son, unless that, in this undertaking, on the basis of your existing virtues, eager for good work, "I have competed, I have kept the faith, I have finished (*consumavi*) the race successfully." And in whom can these things have force, unless in that one who said, "It is finished (*Consumatum est*)"? For whatever I have begun to draw out in the pages of this *Handbook*, both according to Hebrew speech and according to the Greek alphabet and the Latin language, up to the end I have finished (*consumavi*) my work in him who is called God (*qui dicitur Deus*). (*Handbook*, Incipit 46–56)[14]

Later, Dhuoda will dissect the name of God, finding in its letters and syllables a sacred mystery. Here she anticipates that theme, referring to God as she will again and again, as "he who is called God" (*qui dicitur Deus*). This time, however, the phrase has been prompted by Dhuoda's rather forced claim to have written in Hebrew, Greek, and Latin—actually a pointed allusion to the trilingual inscription of Christ's name that hung over the cross. Immediately before this, Dhuoda has quoted the last words of the crucified Christ: "It is finished," *Consumatum est* (John 19:30). Dhuoda echoes this, moments later, by telling us that she has finished (*consumavi*) her work with God's help. And in a daring *tour de force*, Dhuoda will end her book, many pages hence, with *Consumatum*

est, making God's exact last words her own. More, perhaps, than any other
Christian writer since John (the only evangelist to report these last words),
Dhuoda seems fully to understand the blunt literalism of this final, apparently
impersonal verb, to understand why God is "that one who said, *Consumatum
est*," i.e., he who announces his own death as the otherness of a text he has both
written and become.

Dhuoda follows her incipit with an invocation titled "In the name of the
Holy Trinity," where we cannot help seeing that "name" as the acrostic out of
which the epigram contained in the invocation is written: "Dhuoda sends
greetings to her beloved son William: Read" (*DHVODA DILECTO FILIO
VVILHELMO SALUTEM LEGE*).[15] In the poem the *D* of Dhuoda begins the
Deus of a line in which God is given the epithet *auctor*. Yet from this authorial
beginning the acrostic describes a direction away from Dhuoda/*Deus* the author
toward its final address to the reader: Read.

> Lector qui cupis formulam nosse,
>   Capita perquire abta versorum
> Exin valebis concito gradu
>   Sensu cognosci quae sim conscripta.
> Genitrix duorum masculini sexus,
>   Rogo, ut ores conditori almo :
> Erigat ad summum genitorem prolis
>   Meque cum illis iungat in regnum.

> You, reader, who want to know our formula,
>   Examine the deliberate beginnings of the couplets.
> From there you will be able by quick step
>   To work out who I am, written.
> I, mother of two of masculine sex
>   Ask that you pray to the nourishing founder:
> Lift my offspring to the heavenly Father,
>   And join me with them in the Kingdom.
>
>   (*Handbook*, Epigram 80–87)[16]

Translators since Riché have taken *sim conscripta* to be deponent and have read
the fourth line to mean "You will be able to work out what I have written." But
Dhuoda, who, as we shall see, is fond of *conscribere*, uses it thus nowhere else,
making it clear that that this passive form, addressed to that reader not so
much by the author as by the acrostic poem itself ("You, reader, who want to
know our formula"), means, instead, what it says: "You will be able to work out
who has been written here." And Dhuoda has carefully prepared us to ally this

inscription with the passion of Christ. "Dhuoda to William," in other words, is the device by which Dhuoda has described her slippage, like that of the divine author, into the passivity of being read.

And so she prefaces the following instructions to her epigram:

> . . . hoc opusculum ex nomine meo scriptum in tuam specietenus formam legendi dirigo, gaudens quod, si absens sum corpore, iste praesens libellus tibi ad mentem reducat quid erga me, cum legeris, debeas agere.

> . . . I direct this little work written out of my name into your form of reading, mirror-like, rejoicing that, if I am absent in body, this little book of yours, present to you, may bring to mind what you ought to do regarding me, when you have read. (*Handbook,* Epigram 7–10)

We expect to read "what you should do regarding me when you have read it (the book)," but the word order implies instead "what you should do regarding me when you have *read me.*" This is of course another joke on the fact that the text literally "is written out of my name" (*ex nomine meo scriptum*): D-H-U-O-D-A.

But should we not see ourselves here instead? For in this passage and elsewhere Dhuoda says that her text acts like a mirror (*specietenus*).[17] Modern commentators have been quick to point out that in this image Dhuoda draws upon the genre of "mirrors of princes," handbooks written, usually by clerics, for the moral betterment of young nobles.[18] Indeed, Dhuoda herself suggests such a goal for the book:

> Invenies in eo [opusculo] quidquid in brevi cognoscere malis; invenies etiam et speculum in quo salutem animae tuae indubitanter possis conspicere, ut non solum saeculo, sed ei per omnia possis placere qui te "formavit ex limo."

> You will find in this little work whatever you want to know in brief; you will also find it to be even a mirror in which you can look without hesitation upon the salvation of your soul, so that you can be pleasing not only to this world, but also, in all respects, to him who "formed" you "out of mud." (*Handbook,* Prologue 20–24)

And yet, pages later, the angle of that mirror has changed:

> Ortatrix tua Dhuoda semper adest fili, et si defuerim deficiens, quod futurum est, habes hic memoriale libellum moralis, et quasi in picturam speculi, me mente et corpore legendo et Deum deprecando intueri possis, et quid erga me obsequi debeas pleniter inveniri potes.

Your encourager Dhuoda is always present, son, and if I should fail to be present, which will happen, you have here a little memorial book of morals, and as if into the image of a mirror, you may be able to look upon me by reading mind and body and by praying to God, and you thus are able to discover fully what regarding me you ought to follow. (*Handbook*, I 7.15–20)

Here William is offered the gaze of Perseus—through a mirror held obliquely. But is it really William's vision that is at stake here? A passage we have just considered, written in similar vocabulary, seems to have planted the germ of this image:

> . . . me Dhuodanam, o fili Wilhelme, a te elongatam conspiciens procul, ob id quasi anxia et utilitatis desiderio plena, hoc opusculum ex nomine meo scriptum in tuam specietenus formam legendi dirigo, gaudens quod, si absens sum corpore, iste praesens libellus tibi ad mentem reducat quid erga me, cum legeris, debeas agere.

> . . . looking at myself, Dhuoda, o son William, distanced far from you, and being, because of this, fairly anxious and full of desire to be useful, I direct this little work written out of my name into your form of reading, mirror-like, rejoicing that, if I am absent in body, this little book of yours, present to you, may bring to mind what you ought to do regarding me, when you have read. (*Handbook*, Epigram 5–10)[19]

The vision in this earlier passage seems more complicated than the later one, for here Dhuoda sees herself, and from William's point of view (*a te elongatam procul*). But when Dhuoda later allows her vision to give way to the more ordinary gaze of her reader, other changes she makes to the text complicate matters significantly. In the later version, the simple "what you should do" of *debeas agere* has been replaced with *debeas obsequi*—"what (funeral rites?) you ought to perform." So too the absence in body that characterizes Dhuoda's relationship to William in life (*si absens sum corpore*) has yielded to the absence that is death (*si defuerim deficiens*). This common euphemism makes absence metonymic of death; from here to the end of her book, Dhuoda will instead make death metonymic of absence.

Though in this regard it seems that, for Dhuoda, death will be neither better nor worse than life, she significantly replaces the merely mental reading enjoined to William in the first passage (*ad mentem reducat*) with one he is to undertake mind and body: "by reading mind and body you should be able to look upon me," or—for this is what the text really says—"by reading *me* mind and body you should be able to look upon me." If by this reading Dhuoda at last becomes present to William, it is in the third person that she will do so (*semper adest*), i.e., in the form of the book through which and as which she will be his "encourager." More is at stake in this piece of authorial vanity than meets the eye. Dhuoda later says that William's daily reading of the book will make her a "second mother in mind and body" (*genitrix secunda mente et corpore*) (*Handbook*, VII 1.7–8), not just mapping authorship onto motherhood but suggesting that the one has absorbed the other. And so she who has written both ways — mind and body — expects that she can be read both ways too. But whence a body amidst all these reflections of absences? Indeed, William will see his mother not once but (at least) thrice reflected, "as if in the image of a mirror" (*quasi in picturam speculi*), for surely *quasi* and *pictura* are themselves mirrors. It is as if Dhuoda has placed two or more mirrors facing each other, and their mutual reflection has opened a void between them filled with the very endlessness of their image-making.

This strange prism has a real-world analogue, one ready at hand. For it is the codex book that faces page to page, that finds in a sheet of parchment a surface that is neither flat nor single, but rather, a bifolium. These it stacks, four at a time, sews, and folds, then stacks again, quire after quire, and binds. Dhuoda's view of the page as complex and multiple is already clear in her preference for the verb *conscribere* to mean "to write," where the prefix *con-* suggests that to write is not just to mark but to gather, to accumulate, to assemble.[20] She is hinting, in part, at her research, which she occasionally makes more explicit, as when she tells us that her *Handbook* has been "woven together out of various volumes of books" (*ex diversis librorum voluminibus . . . contextus*) (*Handbook*, IX 1.2–3). But when she uses a compound of the verb that means both "to read" and "to gather," *legere*, she is actually referring to writing: *collegi festinans*, "I composed in haste" (*Handbook*, X 1.11). In other words, these gatherings are not what comes before the book: they are the book itself, the book that stitches together the reflective surfaces of representation and desire (*in hunc codicem libelli ex meo desiderio . . . conscriptum*, "written and gathered into this bound booklet, product of my wish" [*Handbook*, Prologue 30–32]), giving them stuff and substance.[21]

Just *reading* a book is not enough; understanding lies at the end of a journey heavy with materiality: "You have and will have volumes," she tells William, in which he may find what he needs "by reading, leafing through, turning in your mind, examining closely, understanding" (*legendo, volvendo, ruminando, perscrutando, intelligendo*) (*Handbook*, IV 1.40–41). Trite metaphors of textual progress become literal and three-dimensional, mixing book and reader in the same geometry: "For your mind and body I have dictated the little verses found above, below, *and beneath* (*supra, infra et subtus*), along with the rest; I shall not stop instructing you to read them with your mouth and hold them in your heart" (*Handbook*, X 1.24–25). But Dhuoda's most striking evocation of the materiality of the book comes in the penultimate stanza of the book's penultimate poem, the one place where she uses the word *pagina*:

> Mens namque certe mea volvitur antris,
> hoc tamen ortor: ut paginas istius
> iam supra exaratas assidue legas
>   fixas ad mentem.

> My mind, no doubt, is enfolded in shadows, yet I urge you
> to read, continually, this book's pages, already written out,
> above, fastened to your mind. (*Handbook*, X 2.66–69)

This is a place where words accumulate: line after line (*exaratas*, invoking an ancient analogy of writing to the plowing of a field, furrow after furrow[22]), page after page, reading after reading (*assidue*). These must be fasted to the mind (*fixas ad mentem*), but this echoes the earlier binding of a mind that is wound and enfolded (*volvitur*) in shadows, where the verb is that for what one does with a "volume," and the expression, despite its apparent humility, parallels a slightly earlier description of God as the *Handbook*'s ultimate analogy: "Almighty God, in whom all the things already delineated above are most aptly bound together (*volvuntur*)" (*Handbook*, IX 4.21). Even more striking, though, is the stanza's actual binding: the same word, *mens*, is first and last, though the top cover is Dhuoda's mind, and the bottom one, William's. That we wind up with William is no surprise, for the *M* with which the stanza begins is the last letter of his name in the acrostic the entire poem has just formed: *VERSI AD VVILHELMUM*, "verses for William." But since Dhuoda, just before the poem, suggests that her book must be read from its first line "down to its very last syllable" (*usque ad ultimam eiusdem sillabam*), we can hardly fail to notice that the stanza begins with *me* and ends with *me* inverted, reflected (*ment-em*). But "me," of course, is already a reflection of "I," suggesting, finally, that the bookish (and shadowy) space bracketed by these mirrors is not so much that between Dhuoda and William as it is that between Dhuoda and her self.

The book is a space and medium into which, through which, and with which Dhuoda will move. But where to? "Dhuoda to William": again and again she says that the book is "directed" (*directus*) to her son,[23] for the book has an apparent direction, not simply the direction of the reflection that confirms their difference, but the direction of Dhuoda's bodily movement along with that reflection, as she first becomes the text she writes to be her surrogate but eventually assumes the point of view that was supposed to belong to her addressee, William. Nevertheless, Dhuoda has in mind here more than just re-unification with her son in the role of "reader." Already by becoming her text, she has shared the death of God on the pages of the St. Emmeram Gospels. Her book's "direction" is, in fact, a "dirge," a word that comes to us from the opening of the antiphon of the first nocturn of Matins in the Office of the Dead, which, in its double emphasis on direction and vision, Dhuoda may well have in mind: *Dirige, Domine Deus meus, in conspectu tuo viam meam,* "Direct, Lord my God, my way in your sight."[24] But by then confusing herself with William as ideal reader, Dhuoda greatly complicates her own place in this funeral train, looking not only forward to but also back at her own death. Indeed, in the end, William seems little more than the device of Dhuoda's carefully planned othering of herself, for as we shall now see, it is only as William that she can commit her final authorial act.[25]

Dhuoda seems originally to have planned to end the *Handbook* with the acrostic poem we have just considered, followed by the names of William's dead relatives. But her book will have almost as many endings as it did beginnings. Dhuoda's second of several appendices is a section entitled "Returning to Myself, I Grieve" (*Ad me recurrens, lugeo,* where the participle is from the same verb with which she will later instruct William to "return always to this book of yours," *Ad istum . . . semper recurre libellum*). It begins thus:

> Ex nimii amoris dulcedine et desiderio pulcritudinis tuae memetipsam quasi oblitam postponens, 'ianuis clausis,' iterum intus ingredi desidero.

> The sweetness of exceeding love and desire for your beauty cause me to put off the question of my own self, as if forgotten, and "though the doors have been closed," I want to go back in again. (*Handbook*, X 4.2–3)

With *ianuis clausis*, Dhuoda offers yet another daringly Christological description of herself, for the phrase is used at John 20:26, where the resurrected Christ appears to his disciples, though they are meeting behind locked doors. Nor is the choice an accident for this writer preoccupied with hands, for in the passage in John, Christ confronts his doubting Thomas, whom he shows his wounds and instructs, "Stick your finger here and look at my hands and lay your own hand on my side" (*infer digitum tuum huc et vide manus meas et adfer manum tuam et mitte in latus meum*). Reopening the "doors" of her *Handbook*, Dhuoda exposes her own wounds as never before, providing a poignant though brief and sometimes tantalizingly cryptic sketch of herself. "It is no secret to you, in the face of my relentless illnesses and of certain other circumstances . . . that I have endured all these things and others like them . . . in my frail body" (*Handbook*, X 4.8-12). She also offers, for the first time, a pointed reference to debts she has been forced to incur to finance her husband's career; these William is asked one day to repay (*Handbook*, X 4.39-52).

Drawing to a conclusion, Dhuoda reminds William to take care of his younger brother, adds some requests for masses and prayers, and then, "This *Handbook* ends here. Amen. Thanks be to God" (*Finit hic liber Manualis. Amen. Deo gratias.*) (*Handbook*, X 4.64). But this is not, in fact, the end. First comes the brief necrology of William's paternal relations, which Dhuoda has earlier promised that "you will find listed at the end" (*Handbook*, VIII 14.4-5; the list is X 5). Also appended is a guide to reading the Psalms, lifted from Alcuin (*Handbook*, XI 1).[26] After this Dhuoda provides the dates on which she began and ended work on the *Handbook* (November 30, 841, to February 2, 843) (*Handbook*, XI 2.2-8). Only then does the *Handbook* finally end for good: "Here ends, thanks be to God, William's *Handbook*, on the words of the Gospel: 'It is finished' (*Consumatum est.*)."

But in the midst of these additions, just before the treatise on the Psalms, Dhuoda outdoes everything we have seen so far by offering her own epitaph, to which she prefaces precise instructions:

Cum autem et ego ipsa dies finierim meos, nomen meum cum illorum nomini-bus iube transcribi defunctum. Quod volo, et quasi ad praesens totis flagito ni-sibus, ut in loco in quo fuerim sepulta, super ipso tecto sepulchri quod meum operuerit corpus, hos versiculos iube transcribi firmatim, ut cernentes ipsum epythafium sepulchri, pro me indigna dignas ad Deum iubeant fundere preces.

   Sed et istum Manualem quem legis, qui legerit umquam, verba quae sub-tus secuntur meditetur ipse, et me, iam quasi intus reclusam, Deo commendet solvendam.

But when I myself too have finished my days, order my name to be inscribed with the names of those dead. What I want, and as if the moment were present entreat with all my energy, is that in the place in which I am buried, above the very slab of the tomb which covers my body, you order that these verses be transcribed permanently, that they may command those who see the epitaph of the tomb to pour out to God worthy prayers for unworthy me.

   But also may anyone who ever reads this *Handbook* which you are reading ponder the words which follow below, and recommend to God that I, already as if enclosed within them, be released. (*Handbook*, X 6.2-12)

The poem itself, with another acrostic on a form of her name, follows:

Hic, lege, lector, versiculos epitaphii:

+ D + M +

De terra formatum, hoc in tumulo
Dhodane corpus iacet humatum:
    Rex immense, suscipe illam.
Haec namque fragile tellus undique
Suum suscepit coenum ad ymma:
    Rex benignus, illi veniam da.
Ulceris rigata solum
Illi superrestat densa sepulchri:
    Tu, Rex, eius solve delicta.
Omnis aetas et sexus, vadensque
Et revertens hic, rogo, dicite ita:
    Agios magne, eius dilue vincla.
Diri vulneris antro defixa,
Septa fellis, vitam finivit coenosam:
    Tu, Rex, suis parce peccatis.
Anguis ne ille suam obscurus
Animam captet, orantes dicite ita:
    Deus clemens, illi succurre.
Ne hinc pertranseat quis, usque dum legat.
Coniuro omnes ut orent, ita dicentes:
    Requiem illi tribue, Alme,
Et lucem perpetuam ei cum sanctis
Iube, benignus, in finem largiri.
    Amen recipiat post funeris ipsa.[27]

α + ω

Here, reader, read the verses of the epitaph:

+ *Dearly* + *Departed* +

Formed from earth, in this mound
Lies buried the body of Dhuoda:
    Great King, take her up.
For truly this broken soil from all sides
Takes her earth to the depths:
    Kindly King, give her pardon.
She is left with the darknesss of the grave,
Watered only by her sores:
    You, o King, release her bonds.
Every age and sex, coming
And going here, I ask, say this:
    Great Lamb, dissolve her chains.

Fastened to the hollow of an awful wound,
Fenced in by bile, she has finished the earthly life:
    You, o King, forgive her sins.
Lest that dark serpent
Take her soul, praying say this:
    Forgiving God, come to her aid.
May no one pass from this place without stopping to read,
I implore all to pray, saying this:
    Give her rest, o Nourisher.
And command, Kindly One, that light perpetual
Be bestowed on her in the end, together with the saints.
    After she is buried, may she welcome the Amen.
        alpha + omega.

                (*Handbook*, X 6.14–39)

In the introduction to the epitaph, Dhuoda sees herself not in the words that follow (though they will form yet another acrostic poem made out of her name) but behind them (*iam quasi intus inclusam*). Into this vision we too are commanded, for significantly William is no longer her sole audience: "May anyone who ever reads this *Handbook* . . . Here, reader, read . . . Every age and sex . . . May no one pass from this place without reading."[28] She asks us all to pray for her release—from these words, words she instructs William to inscribe firmly (*firmatim*), perhaps to make her tomb a better monument to the inscriptions she has endured, perhaps to make her escape so much more triumphant. In the epitaph itself, she twice asks God to release her from the ropes and chains that bind her (*eius solve delicta . . . eius dilue vincla*), for she is "fenced in by bile" (*septa fellis*), perhaps a bilingual pun on the use of gall as a fixative in medieval ink.[29]

This page is now a mirror in which Dhuoda sees herself, and we as readers are made to remember a much earlier passage we likely passed over as unremarkable, one in which Dhuoda seemed to provide the most predictable explanation of the mirror image:

> in speculis mulierum demonstratio apparere soleat vultu, ut sordida extergant, exhibentesque nitida

> a showing of the face customarily appears in the mirrors of women, so that they may rub out blemishes, and reveal parts clear and beautiful (*Handbook*, Prologue 10–2)

But let us take a closer look at what seems conventional, for women at their mirrors are not usually said to "rub out blemishes" but, rather, to conceal them. Thus Isidore, in the midst of a long section on "ornament" that Dhuoda may have in mind here, describes women's work before their mirrors as one of addition and supplementation:

> Specula sunt in quibus feminae vultus suos intuuntur. Dictum autem speculum vel quod ex splendore reddatur, vel quod ibi feminae intuentes considerent speciem sui vultus et, quidquid ornamenti deese viderent, adiciant.

> Mirrors are where women go to see their own faces. It is called a mirror (*speculum*) either because it reflects as a consequence of its shininess (*splendor*), or because the women who look there examine the appearance (*species*) of their faces and add whatever embellishment they see is missing.[30]

Dhuoda's emphasis instead on erasure makes it clear that, already in her Prologue, the mirror works like a page: the "blemishes" (*sordida*—"stains") she sees here are none other than the words that are written there, and that the page is the pristine surface (*nitida*) revealed by their erasure. Many pages later, Dhuoda will water the darkness of the tomb with her sores, the sores that lie beneath each letter carved onto the page of her epitaph, drawing on a long Christian tradition of seeing bloody bodies—especially martyred bodies—as texts.[31] And though Isidore elsewhere describes ink as the sacramental blood of Christ, he makes the pen the agent of that blood's dissemination.[32] Dhuoda observes instead that it is the page that bleeds that ink, the page that for medieval readers and writers was almost always made of skin.

Something more about Dhuoda's ending is illuminated by what we learned in chapter 1 (and which we have encountered many times since). There we saw that the page has two main tenses: reading and writing. The writer exists only where the page is blank; everywhere that there are words, the writer has become a reader. Writers know (or at least seem to hope) that they are only the first readers of their words; others will follow. But Dhuoda makes these future readers into a future-perfect writer: a different Orpheus, her son William, must complete these lines by transcribing them onto her tomb. But because Dhuoda already imagines things from this point of view, she is like a Eurydice who sees herself from even farther off than Orpheus did, peering at her inscription through its eventual transcription. And the blank page is not only the vanishing point of this gaze: it is also its source. For the Dhuoda who looks back at these words is, in this vision, one who has been released from her chains—a resurrected body looking back at a prelapsarian one, a blank page facing a blank page, with not only her own book, her own life, but all writing and all human history between.

The blank page is not only a Christian fetish; since Isak Dinesen's story of
that name, it has been something like a feminist icon for the possibility of a text
that means without inscription.[33] But this ideal did not keep Dinesen from
writing, nor did it stop Dhuoda. In part this is because Dhuoda simultaneously
has in mind a model of *écriture féminine* more along the lines of that of Cixous
("I, too, overflow . . ."[34]): what twentieth-century feminist writers would
imagine as a page neither blank nor hymeneal, but menstrual, i.e., one that
bleeds without the aid of any pen(is). This is not Dhuoda's metaphor, at least
not explicitly, but she shares with her later counterparts a strategy of resistance
by substitution: her own writing slowly crowds out all the other inscriptions
her body/page has endured.

But there is a more general authorial anxiety at work here, one Dhuoda
shares not only with Dinesen but also with Orpheus. The author loses not only
the words she or he writes: already with the very first stroke of the first of these,
a writer loses the blank page, that space of pure potential whose eloquence the
pen can never quite match. All one can do is turn the page and start again—
and again, and again, as does Dhuoda, with her half-dozen beginnings, with
her oscillation between the eminently practical and the utterly mystical, now
in prose, now in verse, in search of a language, a subject, a form, a figure that
will trace the contours of the page without obscuring what lies below. Foolish
authors, by contrast, try to fill the page, as if unaware of what, after its boundedness, is the page's most certain materiality: write and rewrite, cancel and
underline, gloss and comment, and still, in the end, there will be more page
than ink.

"Write things that look like me," we heard the page say in our introduction.
Dhuoda finds a number of these, not all of which entirely resemble one another: womb, tomb, an outstretched hand, a poem, the face of God, Dhuoda's
own, the tower at Uzès in which she lived and wrote, the limits that surround
every life, even that of a king. Perhaps, of course, it is instead the page that is a
picture of one of these. But which? Probably we shall never finally settle on an
order for these metaphors. Let us simply say that, once we start writing, the
page is always before us, staring us in the face, inescapable. Except, perhaps,
for that apparent escape that comes when, yielding to the blankness that was
there when we began, we end.

NOTES

Introduction

1. Roland Barthes, "The Death of the Author," *Aspen* 5+6 (1967), no pagination.

2. From the extensive bibliography we may single out, from before Barthes, William K. Wimsatt and Monroe C. Beardsley, "The Intentional Fallacy," *Sewanee Review* 54 (1946): 468-88, revised in William K. Wimsatt, *The Verbal Icon: Studies in the Meaning of Poetry* (Lexington, 1954), 2-18, and from after him, Michel Foucault, "What Is an Author?" in *Language, Counter-Memory, Practice*, ed. and trans. Donald F. Bouchard and Sherry Simon (Ithaca, N.Y., 1977), 113-38, and Stanley Fish, *Is There a Text in This Class? The Authority of Interpretive Communities* (Cambridge, Mass., 1980), especially the title essay, 303-21.

3. Persius, *Satires* 3.10-16. Here as often in Persius, the question of who is speaking to whom, when, is fraught. My punctuation follows the Oxford Classical Text (OCT) of W. V. Clausen, ed., *A. Persi Flacci et D. Iuni Iuvenalis Saturae* (Oxford, 1959) and the much-discussed intuition of A. E. Housman, "Notes on Persius," *Classical Quarterly* 7 (1913): 18, that "Persius is both the subject and the speaker" of most of the poem, in which he "holds parley with himself." Whether this makes the poem strictly autobiographical (as Housman argues) is another question: note that the narrator is about to study (*an tali studeam calamo?*) rather than to poetize, though for Persius, student of philosophy and philosophical poet, the two activities were never distant. But for a subtler reading, see D. M. Hooley, *The Knotted Thong: Structures of Mimesis in Persius* (Ann Arbor, 1997), 202-29.

4. Gertrude Stein, *Look at Me Now and Here I Am: Writings and Lectures, 1909-45*, ed. Patricia Meyerowitz (London, 1971), 213-15.

5. Barthes, "Death of the Author," n.p.

6. Shane Butler, *The Hand of Cicero* (London and New York, 2002).

7. The most significant possible exceptions are the Homeric epics, which the influential work of Milman Parry in the 1920s and '30s sought to prove were composed

orally, though the precise time at which (and way in which) writing began to shape an originally oral tradition of tales about the Trojan War remains—and probably always will remain—a matter of speculation and debate. For a brief introduction to the question, see R. B. Rutherford, *Homer, Greece and Rome: New Surveys in the Classics* 26 (Oxford, 1996), 9–15. Most of Parry's publications on the subject may be found in Milman Parry, ed., *The Making of Homeric Verse: The Collected Papers of Milman Parry* (Oxford, 1971), with a survey of Parry's career and views by Adam Parry, ix–lxii. Parry's formidable influence, combined with Homer's archetypal status in literary history, has contributed to an exaggerated sense of ancient poetry's "orality" in general; Homer's early tradition is instead exceptional, and the Homer known by Greeks and Romans of the historical period was, in any case, one that circulated in books, from which even professional rhapsodists now learned their lines (Xenophon, *Memorabilia* 4.2.10). The reading, sometimes by professionals, of poetry to an audience was, by contrast, an important influence on poets throughout antiquity, but the proper key is not orality but performance. On Roman *recitationes*, see Adriano Pennacini, "L'arte della parola," in Guglielmo Cavallo, Paolo Fedeli, and Andrea Giardina, eds., *Lo spazio letterario di Roma antica*, vol. 2, *La circolazione del testo* (Roma, 1989), 254–67.

8. "Whatever they may do, authors do *not* write books. Books are not written at all. They are manufactured by scribes and other artisans, by mechanics and other engineers, and by printing presses and other machines," Roger Stoddard, "Morphology and the Book from an American Perspective," *Printing History* 9.1 = 17 (1987), 4. Guglielmo Cavallo and Roger Chartier, eds., *A History of Reading in the West*, trans. Lydia G. Cochrane (Amherst, 1999), 5.

9. Catullus, *Poems* 1 and 50. This is our first encounter with the waxed tablet (sometimes called the stylus tablet), usually made by slightly hollowing out a rectangular surface on a small panel of wood (or other material) and coating it with wax; this would be inscribed with a sharp stylus, and the writing then could be erased by smoothing the wax, usually with the blunt end of the same stylus. Multiple sheets could be hinged or otherwise bound to produce diptychs or larger polyptychs. Such tablets were in use throughout antiquity and the Middle Ages; for the Romans, at least, they probably were the most commonly used writing surface of all. On waxed (and other) tablets generally, see Elisabeth Lalou, ed., *Les tablettes à écrire de l'Antiquité à l'Epoque Moderne, Bibliologia* 12 (Brepols, 1992); for the Romans, see especially the contributions by Robert Marichal, "Les tablettes à écrire dans le monde romain" (165–85) and by Mario Carpasso, "Le tavolette della Villa dei Papiri ad Ercolano" (221–30), both with illustrations. Mostly about medieval tablets is the very helpful article of Richard H. Rouse and Mary Rouse, "The Vocabulary of Wax Tablets," in Olga Weijers, ed., *Vocabulaire du livre et de l'écriture au moyen âge: Actes de la table ronde, Paris 24–26 septembre 1987* (Brepols, 1989), 220–30. For extensive photographs of the sizeable archive of documentary waxed tablets from the mid-first century AD found in Murecine, Italy, see Giuseppe Camodeca, ed., *Tabulae Pompeianae Sulpiciorum (TPSulp.): Edizione critica dell'archivio puteolano dei Sulpicii* (Rome, 1999), vol. 2. Clay and waxed tablets as literary supports are discussed by Michael Haslam, "The Physical Media: Tablet, Scroll, Codex," in John Miles Foley, ed., *A Companion to Ancient Epic* (Oxford, 2005), 145–50, who notes that the Romans reserved the waxed variety for drafts but that the Near East also employed these for "library texts" (148).

10. L. Roman, "A History of Lost Tablets," *Classical Antiquity* 25.2 (2006): 351–88, offers an elegant reading of the presence of writing materials in Catullus and other

Roman poets, though the conclusion that tablets and the like must be overcome in order to achieve a complete and thus immaterial/immortal poem somewhat misses the mark.

11. Amy Richlin briefly treats writing as metaphor for corporal punishment and sexual violence in Catullus in *The Garden of Priapus*, rev. ed. (New York, 1992), 150, 154–56, and in "Cicero's Head," in James I. Porter, ed., *Constructions of the Classical Body* (Ann Arbor, 1999), 197–98. Ovid's use of tablets (and slaves) as instruments of and surrogates for the elegiac "I" is briefly explored by Kathleen McCarthy, "*Servitium Amoris: Amor Servitii*," in Sandra R. Joshel and Sheila Murnaghan, eds., *Women and Slaves in Greco-Roman Culture: Differential Equations* (London and New York, 1998), 182–84.

12. For more on the shape of digital "pagespace," with useful (for reasons that will be clear below) corrections to an earlier view of such as being unique in its invitation to readings that are not "linear," see Jerome McGann, *Radiant Textuality: Literature after the World Wide Web* (New York, 2001), 147–50, who observes "the need for a thoroughgoing retheorization of our ideas about books and traditional textuality in general." Note, furthermore, that the apparent unboundedness of the digital page is, for the user, at any given moment, only an unseen potential, regulated by that other heir (the legitimate one?) to the printed page, the screen; indeed, professional Web designers are taught to avoid making pages that "scroll" (itself a suggestive echo of the book, though it represents not so much a survival as a rediscovery).

13. "In a really well-made roll it [the join] may be very difficult to detect," Eric G. Turner, *The Terms Recto and Verso: The Anatomy of the Papyrus Roll, Papyrologica Bruxellensia* 16.1 (Brussels, 1978), 15. Turner provides a schematic drawing of how this worked in practice on page 14. The terms *sc[h]ida* and *pagina* are used together with their distinct meanings by Pliny the Elder, *Natural History* 13.24.80; discussion in Theodor Birt, *Das antike Buchwesen in seinem Verältniss zur Litteratur* (Berlin, 1882), 225. See also William A. Johnson, *Bookrolls and Scribes in Oxyrhynchus* (Toronto, 2004): "In laying out the columns the scribe did not pay attention to the glue joins (*kollēseis*) between the manufactured sheets (*kollēmata*). The point is not controversial, but I do not know that it has ever been documented. Examination of the point of *kollēsis* reveals no statistical tendency for the column of writing to avoid the join" (88); Johnson too provides a schematic drawing that illustrates this as fig. 1 (x). Johnson offers by far the most thorough and careful description of ancient book-rolls to date, though his precision leads him to understate the very continuity with which I am concerned here: "The aesthetic of the codex depends upon the page. . . . The codex page has no true counterpart in the roll. The physical presence of the page, with it block of text surrounded by upper, lower, and side margins, cannot be paralleled in the roll, where upper and lower margins are continuous and where the intercolumn belongs to no single column but (excepting start and end) to two. . . . [W]e must leave behind the image of a notional 'page' consisting of a written column plus the surrounding margins, for that makes no sense in the context of the roll" (86). As is readily apparent, Johnson's details actually suggest both continuities and discontinuities; his conclusion depends on seeing the latter as amounting to an "aesthetic" rupture regarding the page's "physical presence," subjective categories that he does not really explain. More to the point, Johnson's salutary advice not to retroject the codex onto the roll sidesteps the crucial fact that Latin speakers, moving in the opposite direction, saw enough of a continuity from column to page to use the same word for both; where Johnson sees margins, variously shared, they saw, first and foremost in each case, blocks of text.

14. That this is the result of imitation of papyrus-roll exemplars is argued by E. A. Lowe, "Some Facts about Our Oldest Latin Manuscripts," *Palaeographical Papers, 1907–1965* (Oxford, 1972), 201.

15. Pauly and Wissowa et al., *Realencyclopädie der classischen Altertumswissenschaft* 18.2, col. 2312. The use of multiple columns did not vanish, however; indeed, two columns remained common for biblical texts, in part to make more efficient use of their *per cola et commata* layout; see the photographs and descriptions in E. A. Lowe, *Codices Latini Antiquiores* (Oxford, 1934–72).

16. The following discussion is based largely on the article for *pagina* in the *Thesaurus Linguae Latinae* 10.1, fasc. 1, coll. 84–91; the article for *pagina* in Pauly and Wissowa et al. 18.2, coll. 2310–12; and the entries for *pagina, pagus,* and *pango* in the *Oxford Latin Dictionary*. Regarding *pagina,* of particular interest is the definition of the second-century grammarian Sextus Pompeius Festus (as preserved by Paulus Diaconus, *Epitoma Festi,* ed. Lindsay, 247): *paginae dictae, quod in libris suam quaeque optineat regionem, ut pagi; vel a pangendo, quod in illis versus panguntur, id est figuntur,* "*paginae* are called thus because, in books, each one possesses its own territory, like districts (*pagi*), or else from planting/fixing (*pangere*), since on them verses are fixed, i.e., carved." Joseph de Ghellinck, "'Pagina' et 'sacra pagina': Histoire d'un mot et transformation de l'objet primitivement désigné," *Mélanges Auguste Pelzer, Université de Louvain: Recueil de travaux d'histoire et de philologie,* 3rd series, vol. 26 (Louvain, 1947), 23–59, offers an excellent survey of extended and metaphorical uses of *pagina* in antiquity and the Middle Ages. For an interesting exploration of the influence of *pango/pagina* on Romance, see Leo Spitzer, "*Pageant* = Lat. *Pagina,*" *American Journal of Philology* 64.3 (1943): 327–30, though his conclusion that the English *pageant* depends on *pagina* but means not "page" but "something well-constructed and prepared for a purpose" seems an unnecessarily complicated solution.

17. On the extraordinary persistence of such imagery, see Ernst Robert Curtius, *European Literature and the Latin Middle Ages* (Princeton, N.J., 1990 [1953]), 313–14; also Rouse and Rouse, "Vocabulary of Wax Tablets," 228.

18. A. Ernout and A. Meillet, *Dictionnaire étymologique de la langue latine: Histoire des mots,* 4th ed. (Paris, 1994), s.v. *pagina,* do not express a clear preference for one of the two ancient etymologies, noting, "*Pagina* a commencé par être un terme d'agriculture; il désignait une treille," for which they cite Pliny, *Natural History* 17.169, where *pagina* designates a small section of a vineyard (thus, a small *pagus,* with, again, either etymology equally applicable); they then note the meaning of "une colonne d'écriture, une page" and give the comparandum of *exarare.* (Pliny provides also the only other ancient example of *pagina* to mean something other than "page" *vel sim.,* using it, at *Natural History* 16.225, to designate one of the wooden "panels" of a folding or double door.) The two are not, of course, mutually exclusive, and the contamination between marking and demarking must, in fact, have been early in the case of *pagus,* since farmers could (and still do) use the plow for both. Compare the Etruscan rite of marking the border of a city with the plow, employed by Romulus for the first outline of the Palatine city of Rome. P. Oxy. 2088 apparently refers to the Palatine as a *pagus,* site of Roma Quadrata and the "first" of the several *pagi* of which the city was eventually comprised: Arthur S. Hunt, ed., *The Oxyrhynchus Papyri,* vol. 17 (London, 1927), 113–15. Egidio Forcellini, *Lexicon Totius Latinitatis,* 4th ed. (Padova, 1864–1926), vol. 3, 543–44, after first offering the unlikely suggestion that the "fastening" implied by *pango/pagina* could be that of

strips of the papyrus plant to one another in order to produce a papyrus sheet, provocatively suggests that the page is made of verses fastened to verses, just as these are made of letters fastened to letters, cautioning that the *pagina* is thus the space given over to writing and not the entire surface. John B. Van Sickle informs me that he will take up the meaning of *pagina* along lines similar to those followed here in his forthcoming translation of and commentary on Vergil's *Eclogues*: *Virgil's* Book of Bucolics: *The Ten Eclogues in English Verse* (Baltimore, 2010).

19. "Common to the original sense of the word is the idea of boundedness, demarcation, the drawing of lines to mark off and order. This easily extends to the chart or diagram of the demarcated area, which in turn modulates to the outline of the literary work. From the organized space, plot becomes the organizing line," suggests Peter Brooks, *Reading for the Plot: Design and Intention in Narrative* (New York, 1984), 12, regarding a possible "subterranean logic connecting these heterogeneous meanings." But on this and other questions about the "shape" of narrative, I am delighted to be able to point readers to a major new study by my colleague Alex Purves, *Space and Time in Ancient Greek Narrative* (Cambridge, 2010).

20. William V. Harris, "Why Did the Codex Supplant the Book-Roll?" in John Monfasani and Ronald G. Musto, eds., *Renaissance Society and Culture: Essays in Honor of Eugene F. Rice, Jr.* (New York, 1991), 71–85, reviews earlier discussions of this transition and offers his own synthesis and refinements. See now also the review of the debate by Mario Capasso, *Introduzione alla papirologia* (Bologna, 2005), 113–22.

21. The codex was able to swell greatly in size only after the further innovation (often overlooked) of the use of multiple gatherings (i.e., fascicules or "quires") in its assembly. Nevertheless, T. C. Skeat, "The Origins of the Christian Codex," *Zeitschrift für Papyrologie und Epigraphik* 102 (1994): 263–68, argues even more emphatically than in his earlier publications that a codex capable of holding four gospels not only could have existed in the earliest period, but must have.

22. Eusebius modeled his tables in part on Origen's *Hexapla*, which arranged six versions of the Old Testament in side-by-side columns in large codices, "perhaps the first book—as opposed to official documents—ever to display information in tabular form: in columns intended to be read across rather than down the page," as it is described by Anthony Grafton and Megan Williams, *Christianity and the Transformation of the Book* (Cambridge, Mass., 2006), 17, who offer an engrossing reconstruction of such books and of the uses they suppose. James O'Donnell, *Avatars of the Word from Papyrus to Cyberspace* (Cambridge, Mass., 1998), 55–56, finds in Eusebius a clear example of the codex's invitation to "nonlinear" reading, "the genesis of the revolution in how words could be used," which he traces forward to our own electronic media.

23. On the persistent importance of nonlinear biblical reading and its reliance on the codex, see Peter Stallybrass, "Books and Scrolls: Navigating the Bible," in Jennifer Andersen and Elizabeth Sauer, eds., *Books and Readers in Early Modern England* (Philadelphia, 2002), 42–79 .

24. Thus Skeat, "Origins of the Christian Codex," 265, emphasizes the roll's "panoramic aspect": "In reading a roll the reader's eyes travel continuously over the text without interruption, like the smooth sequence of the frames of a cinematograph film, melting into each other, in contradistinction to the blinkered vision of the codex reader, to whom the text appears in a series of disjointed snapshots." Skeat had offered an earlier version of this notion in "Roll Versus Codex—A New Approach," *Zeitschrift für Papyrologie und*

Epigraphik 84 (1990): 297–98, where he notes "the advantages of a panoramic or narrative presentation," comparing the book-roll to the Parthenon frieze and Trajan's Column. Skeat's view is repeated with approval by Guglielmo Cavallo, "Between *Volumen*
and Codex: Reading in the Roman World," in Cavallo, *History of Reading in the West*, 88.

25. In the age of the book-roll, the page finds a comparandum in the necessity of
stretching long texts across multiple rolls, since practicality and convention kept the
maximum size of a papyrus roll fairly regular. Cavallo, *History of Reading in the West*, 65,
sees the exploitation of this material constraint to mark textual divisions, yielding
"books" in the sense of the major sections of a larger "work," as "an overall discipline of
how to structure a book." Haslam, "Physical Media: Tablet, Scroll, Codex," 144, draws
the connection between page and book: "Something all the media have in common is
materiality, and a text which in consequence is artificially broken up. Until the codex
becomes sufficiently capacious to accommodate epics in their entirety, the text has to be
parceled out over more than a single carrier object . . . And whether or not a text can be
contained within the compass of a single manuscript, it still has to be interrupted at frequent (ideally regular) intervals, turned into a succession of blocks of text, whether sides
or columns or both."

26. Other exceptions, as Peter Stallybrass points out to me, include the numbered
tablets that held the *Epic of Gilgamesh* and the consistent pagination of printed copies of
the Talmud that enabled talented rabbis to perform the "pin test," proving they knew
every word located at a particular position on any given page.

27. A caput in this sense is a paragraph marked by the protrusion of its first few
letters into the left margin (like the "head" of a nail or the like); the device seems first
to have been used for the division of legal texts into clauses but was later used by, e.g.,
Cicero: see my "Cicero's *Capita*," *Litterae Caelestes: Rivista annuale internazionale di
paleografia, codicologia, diplomatica e storia delle testimonianze scritte* 3 (2009): 9–48, which
supersedes my treatment of the same subject in "*Litterae Manent*: Ciceronian Oratory
and the Written Word" (PhD diss., Columbia University, 2000), 177–305.

28. On the period, see chapter 3.

Chapter 1. The Backward Glance

1. Bibliography on the Orpheus story through the ages is too vast to summarize, but
the following are good places to start: Charles Segal, *Orpheus: The Myth of the Poet* (Baltimore, 1989); W. K. C. Guthrie, *Orpheus and Greek Religion: A Study in the Orphic
Movement* (London, 1935); Gustaf Fredén, *Orpheus and the Goddess of Nature*, Acta Universitatis Gothoburgensis 64.6 (1958); John Block Friedman, *Orpheus in the Middle Ages*
(Cambridge, Mass., 1970); Judith E. Bernstock, *Under the Spell of Orpheus: The Persistence of a Myth in Twentieth-Century Art* (Carbondale, Ill., 1991). On the question of
when exactly the "turning tabu" became part of the story, see John Heath, "The Failure
of Orpheus," *Transactions of the American Philological Association* 124 (1994): 163–96. The
idea for the present paper first took form in the classroom, in an ongoing course on
Ovid and his reception, too briefly co-taught with Sean Keilen, for whose thoughts on
the later Orpheus see *Vulgar Eloquence: On the Renaissance Invention of English Literature* (New Haven, Conn., 2006).

2. Vergil, *Georgics* 4.485–503; Ovid, *Metamorphoses* 10.53–63. They are discussed
together by Segal, *Orpheus*, 36–94. C. M. Bowra, "Orpheus and Eurydice," *Classical*

Quarterly 2.3/4 (1952), 125, supposes that the device of the glance as what sends Eurydice to her second doom was the invention of a lost Hellenistic poet who "took up an ancient idea that, when gods or ghosts of the underworld are summoned, men should avert their eyes."

3. Vergil, *Georgics* 4.485–502.

4. Ovid, *Metamorphoses* 10.53–63.

5. Later tellings will emphasize Orpheus's moral failure. Already for the author of the pseudo-Vergilian *Culex*, the backward glance betrays a lack of sexual self-control (*oscula cara petens rupisti iussa deorum*, 293). Boethius briefly reviews the fatal moment and comments, "This tale applies to any of you are trying to lead your mind to the daylight above, for anyone who, overcome, bends his glance toward the pit of Hell, loses whatever of value he is carrying with him, as he looks on those below" (*Consolation of Philosophy* 3.12.52–58). For the remarkable transformations of this lesson in the medieval commentary tradition on Boethius, see Friedman, *Orpheus in the Middle Ages*, 86–145.

6. The count is that of John Sparrow, *Half-Lines and Repetitions in Virgil* (Oxford, 1931), 29.

7. "Like an orator, he ended when he had made his point" (*oratorie finivit ubi vis argumenti constitit*), as the "Daniel Scholiast" puts it, commenting on the half-line at 4.361. See Sparrow, *Half-Lines*, 24–25, who reviews other proponents of this view prior to his own partial endorsement. Sparrow's is the definitive study of the phenomenon; his sometimes maddeningly prevaricating language attempts to strike a compromise on the question of the origins of the *hemistichia*, arguing (conclusions concentrated on 45–46) that some certainly are simply unfinished while others occur in contexts in which we might expect a daring poet to truncate a line and are probably deliberate, though it is impossible, he finally cautions, to know whether these latter would have survived Vergil's final, anxious polish.

8. The principal and most reliable source is the *Vita* included among the fragmentary remains of the Vergilian commentary of Aelius Donatus and generally thought to reproduce, without significant alteration, that by Suetonius, with whose works it is printed in, e.g., the Loeb Classical Library. This and other sources are examined, with an eye to the question of the *hemistichia*, by Sparrow, *Half-Lines*, 7–18.

9. Philip Hardie, *Virgil: Aeneid Book IX* (Cambridge, 1994), 24–25, provides a brief discussion of and additional bibliography for and against the theory that the episode was written separately. More generally, the passage enjoys a small but especially brilliant scholarly bibliography, which may roughly be divided into two camps: (1) readings of the episode as a commentary on ancient or Roman or specifically Augustan ideologies of violence and heroism (and the commemoration of either or both) or (2) readings of the episode as a literary tour-de-force unusually rich in intertextual (and intratextual) play. The present study offers mostly the latter, but for a skillful and provocative integration of both kinds of reading, see Sergio Casali, "Nisus and Euryalus: Exploiting the Contradictions in Virgil's Doloneia," *Harvard Studies in Classical Philology* 102 (2004): 317–54.

10. It is impossible to capture in English the drama of the Latin's word order. "L'ampio stacco fra *ipsa* e *capita*, l'uno al principio, l'altro alla fine della proposizione, dà un orrido spicco alle teste confitte," notes, for example, Antonio La Penna, "Lettura del nono libro dell'*Eneide*," in Marcello Gigante, ed., *Lecturae Vergilianae*, vol. 3: *l'Eneide* (Naples, 1983), 318. For a spear as a pen, in a passage whose backward turn is related to what I shall suggest in this chapter, see *Aeneid* 1.478.

11. For far more on the episode as a miniature of the whole, see Don Fowler, "Epic in the Middle of the Wood: *Mise en Abyme* in the Nisus and Euryalus Episode," in Alison Sharrock and Helen Morales, eds., *Intratextuality: Greek and Roman Textual Relations* (Oxford, 2000), 89–113. On the pair's (and the narrative's) mazelike path, see Penelope Reed Doob, *The Idea of the Labyrinth from Classical Antiquity through the Middle Ages* (Ithaca, N.Y., 1990), 242–43.

12. *noctisque per umbram / castra inimica petunt, multis tamen ante futuri / exitio.* Note the remarkable temporal frame implied by *ante futuri*, where the second word indicates the nearer limit (this is what is going to happen from this point on), and the first describes a farther one, though with ambiguity in which the careful reader hears a foreboding, for though they will in fact leave the camp, they will never proceed on their mission.

13. Many readers will at once recognize Vergil's mode here as an "ecphrastic" one (*ekphrasis* and *enargeia* will receive a fuller treatment in chapter 3); note, however, that while the ecphrasis of a work of art (real or imagined) often animates its object (by allowing the motion natural to narrative to contaminate what is notionally static), its normal effect is to slow or stop movement and time. One wonders, in fact, whether Vergil may deliberately play on the archetypal ecphrasis of the shield of Achilles in Homer, *Iliad* 18.478–608, or, nearer still, on the example of his own shield of Aeneas one book back (8.617–728), inviting us to compare the animated armor there with the static arms here. Regarding the scene's stillness and silence, Michael C. J. Putnam, *The Poetry of the Aeneid: Four Studies in Imaginative Unity and Design* (Cambridge, Mass., 1965), 50, rightly compares the sight that greets the Greeks who emerge from the Trojan Horse at 2.252–3: *. . . fusi per moenia Teucri / conticuere; sopor fessos complectitur artus.* In his discussion of book 9 (49–63), Putnam notes a number of other striking connections between the Nisus/Euryalus episode and both earlier and later passages in the poem.

14. Cf. the sights that greet Aeneas in Elysium, *Aeneid*, 6.651ff.

15. As in 9.243, Vergil pointedly underscores that Nisus is guiding the journey and thus the narrative; in fact, he has been doing so since his opening provocation to Euryalus (9.184–87), which, according to Fowler, "Epic in the Middle of the Wood," 98, "figures him metapoetically as a surrogate author."

16. *via facta per hostis.*

17. Cf. Fowler, "Epic in the Middle of the Wood," 110–11; Hardie, *Virgil: Aeneid Book IX*, 141 (with a long list of other Vergilian woods).

18. Cf. Stephen Hinds, *Allusion and Intertext: Dynamics of Appropriation in Roman Poetry* (Cambridge, 1997),12–14, discussing Vergil's forest at *Aeneid* 6.179–82 and its nod to Ennius.

19. Perhaps we can even find in the variety of trees that comprise the Orphic forest a general nod to the variety of woods used to make ancient tablets (both waxed and unwaxed, i.e., inscribed in ink), on which see Robert Marichal, "Les tablettes à écrire dans le monde romain," in Elisabeth Lalou, ed., *Les tablettes à écrire de l'Antiquité à l'Epoque Moderne, Bibliologia* 12 (Brepols, 1992), 171–72; R. Pintaudi and P. J. Sijpesteija, eds., *Tavolette lignee e cerate da varie collezioni* (Florence, 1989), 203–6 (limited, however, to a group of late-antique/early medieval unwaxed tablets in the Vatican Library); and Russell Meiggs, *Trees and Timber in the Ancient Mediterranean World* (Oxford, 1982), 81, 292, 296, 445. Cypress, the first of Orpheus's trees, is the source of a Hellenistic tablet mentioned in the accounts of the Delian temple commissioners (Meiggs, *Trees and Timber,*

445); it is instead the wood of a bookworm-resistant book-box (as the line is explained by Porphyry) in Horace, *Ars Poetica* 332.

20. We are also, potentially, in or near the Underworld, another figure for poetry, and particularly for literary memory. For Aeneas in book 6, the way to Hell passes first through the woods, *itur in antiquam silvam* (6.179), to which Hell's darkness is later compared (6.271); for both, Aeneas needs help from his "learned" (*docta*) guide, whose warning that Hell's inhabitants are not so much real as *cava sub imagine formae* (6.293) could as easily be said of poetry's fictions. "It is never quite clear—and was probably never meant by Virgil to be clear—where woods end and underworld begins," notes Putnam, *Poetry of the Aeneid*, 55–59, who makes brilliant and beautiful connections (with a somewhat less convincing moral) between the Nisus and Euryalus approaching the woods and Aeneas's *katabasis* in book 6. Cf. Hardie, *Virgil: Aeneid Book IX*, 27; Fowler, "Epic in the Middle of the Wood," 112. The general link between woods and Hell belongs, of course, to a vast tradition; thus Dante, following Vergil, opens the *Inferno* in a *selva oscura*.

21. On *stetit* and *respicit*, see Putnam, *Poetry of the Aeneid*, 53–54.

22. This is a good place to note the pair's earlier appearance in the footrace of *Aeneid* 5.286ff., among the resemblances of which to their later adventure is the troubled linear trajectory by which Nisus, near victory, slips in a puddle of sacrificial blood and deliberately brings down his nearest competitor, Sirio, allowing Euryalus, until then in third place, to win. Sirio is "spun backward" (*revolutus*) in the bloody sand; cf. Ovid's later description of Eurydice's disappearance: *revolutaque eodem est* (*Metamorphoses* 10.63). Curiously, Nisus and Euryalus first appear by name in another half-line (5.294, *Nisus et Euryalus primi* . . .).

23. *Me, me, adsum qui feci, in me convertite ferrum* . . .

24. Catullus, *Poems* 11.21–24.

25. Homer, *Iliad* 8.306ff; 10.254ff. For additional possible echoes (of Lucretius and even Sophocles), see Fowler, "Epic in the Middle of the Wood," 96–97. Vergil, in turn, would be imitated by many here, including Ovid, describing the death of Hyacinthus (*Metamorphoses* 10.190ff.).

26. For a fuller catalogue of the connections between these two passages and with their model in the *Georgics*, see J. Heurgon, "Un exemple peu connu de la Retractatio virgilienne," *Revue des Etudes Latines* 9 (1931): 258–68. Cf. Putnam, *Poetry of the Aeneid*, 53–55. Monica R. Gale, "Poetry and the Backward Glance in Virgil's Georgics and Aeneid," *Transactions of the American Philological Association* 133 (2003): 323–52, argues that their shared backward glance embodies lessons to both poet and prince about the ideological use of the past.

27. Vergil had already reprised these last lines word for word to describe Aeneas's attempt to embrace his father's shade in the Underworld (6.700–2).

28. Vergil, *Georgics* 4.497–502. This passage is patterned, in turn, on the language Homer uses to describe Achilles' vain effort to embrace the shade of Patroclus at *Iliad* 23.99–101; discussion of this and other Homeric intertexts in Joseph Farrell, *Virgil's Georgics and the Traditions of Ancient Epic: The Art of Allusion in Literary History* (New York, 1991), 321–24. *Iamque vale* are the parting words of Anchises to Aeneas (*Aeneid* 5.738) and of Camilla to Acca (ibid., 11.827). Vergil would again echo Orpheus's speechlessness when Dido turns away from the departing Aeneas, who is "getting ready to say many things," *multa parantem / dicere* (4.390–91).

29. Pausanias, *Description of Greece* 10.26.1; Ennius, *Annals* (ed. Skutsch, whose comments on the passage are suggestive) 1.36 (frag. 29).

30. Some, like Percellius Fastus, author of a lost critique of Vergil titled *Furta*, might even say "theft": any loss is scarcely the imitator's.

31. Quintilian, *Institutes of Oratory* 10.5.9, on which see Heinrich Lausberg, *Handbook of Literary Rhetoric: A Foundation for Literary Study* (Leiden, 1998), 484-85 (§ 1104).

32. Suetonius, *Life of Vergil* 22.

33. Ovid, *Metamorphoses* 11.64-66.

34. Ellipses in original; these are the book's last words.

35. The line imagined here is, of course, that of dactylic hexameter; other metrical forms create additional end-points beyond that of the line (to say nothing of the metrical breaks *within* the hexameter line and others). Rhyme, in other traditions, offers further emphasis and possibilities, as does the stanza, the very name of which (literally, "room") echoes the boundedness of the page itself, or the sonnet, with its punctuating couplet. On the shaping and sectioning of ancient pastoral by "refrains and anaphora and other kinds of blocking maneuvers," adding up to a "stanzaic pattern," see Thomas G. Rosenmeyer, *The Green Cabinet: Theocritus and the European Pastoral Lyric* (Berkeley, 1969), 94-95.

36. Rainer Maria Rilke, *Sonnets to Orpheus*, trans. M. D. Herter Norton (New York, 2006), 24-25 (Sonnet 1.5); Herter translates more or less literally, "And he obeys, while yet he oversteps," but others struggle more to capture the enigmatic meanings of and ambiguous relationship between "obeying" and "overstepping" here.

37. Ovid, *Metamorphoses* 10.55.

38. Horace, *Satires* 1.4.62.

39. Vergil, *Georgics* 4.457-59; Ovid, *Metamorphoses* 10.8-10 (who mentions the snake but not Aristaeus).

40. Maurice Blanchot, *The Gaze of Orpheus and Other Literary Essays*, trans. Geoffrey Hartman (Barrytown, N.Y., 1981), 99.

41. Helen Stroud, *Engendering Inspiration: Visionary Strategies in Rilke, Lawrence, and H. D.* (Ann Arbor, Mich., 1995), 180ff.

42. H. D. (Hilda Doolittle), *Collected Poems 1912-1944*, ed. Louis L. Martz (New York, 1983), 50.

43. Ovid, *Metamorphoses* 3.463. My thanks to Micaela Janan for a long discussion about how best to render Narcissus's words in English. In her forthcoming book on Ovid's Theban cycle, she prefers, "That one [of yours] I am!"

44. Ovid, *Metamorphoses* 1.487, where Daphne asks her father for the same gift of chastity Diana obtained from her own father. Throughout Ovid's description, Daphne's looks and habits are Diana's.

45. Pliny, *Natural History* 13.21.69. If he is partially right, then the "bark" in question is presumably the rind of the papyrus plant. Before bark, he tells us in the same passage, the ancients wrote on palm leaves.

46. Ovid, *Metamorphoses* 10.83-85.

47. Already we can see how Ovid weaves the story's reflection of the storyteller into the self-reflectiveness of storytelling itself: the first three stories are all pederastic and so mirror what we have just been told about Orpheus; the third points back to the first, with which it shares Apollo as lover; the first (told by the narrator) takes us in turn back to the whole poem's first erotic episode, likewise about Apollo, who, as the god of poetry

pursuing the girl who will become poetry's emblem (Daphne, the laurel, an evergreen, like the cypress), patently figures the author himself (even more poignantly so if read in the light of *Amores* 1.1). And this recursive web becomes only more elaborate in the stories to follow. Cf. Philip Hardie, *Ovid's Poetics of Illusion* (Cambridge, 2002), 65–70, with useful links to Freud and Lacan on desire and repetition.

48. Ovid, *Metamorphoses* 10.734–35: *nec plena longior hora / facta mora est.*

49. Vergil, *Georgics* 4.500–502.

50. Ovid, *Metamorphoses* 10.57–59.

51. Ibid., 3.426–29: *dumque petit petitur . . . In mediis . . . bracchia mersit aquis nec se deprendit in illis.* Cf. 3.458: *cumque ego porrexi tibi bracchia, porrigis ultro.*

52. Ibid., 10.63.

Chapter 2. Myself Sick

1. For additional close commentary on Thucydides' opening sentence, and especially on his verb, *xunegrapse*, see Darien Shanske, *Thucydides and the Philosophical Origins of History* (Cambridge, 2006), 18ff. Nicole Loraux, "Thucydide a écrit la guerre du Péloponnèse," *Metis* 1 (1986): 139–61, offers a lavish meditation on the same sentence and its apparent "effacement" of the historian in order to produce "la guerre en personne" (161). Against this reading, however, Lowell Edmunds, "Thucydides in the Act of Writing," in Roberto Pretagostini, ed., *Tradizione e innovazione nella cultura greca da Omero all'età ellenistica: Scritti in onore di Bruno Gentili*, vol. 2 (Rome, 1993), 852, surveying the work's other invocations of its own being-written, finds Thucydides omnipresent in "a self-conscious textuality" by which "Thucydides the historian . . . becomes less important than Thucydides the writer." My own reading of the plague will be consistent with elements of both of these apparently contrasting views.

2. On names at the beginnings of Greek philosophical and historical works (and the apparently Eastern origins of the practice), see John Marincola, *Authority and Tradition in Ancient Historiography* (Cambridge, 1997), 271–73. Especially striking is the beginning of Hecataeus, *Genealogies*, "Hecataeus of Miletus speaks (*mutheitai*) thus: I write (*graphō*) the following . . ." (*FGrHist* 1 F 1a), where the historian's description of who he is (third- or first-person?), what he is doing (speaking? writing?), and when (present tense) contrasts usefully with the later adaptation of the same convention by Thucydides, who instead introduces himself as the third-person author of what is emphatically a text and at least notionally a *fait accompli* (though as Edmunds, "Thucydides in the Act of Writing," 837–38, explains, these traits are not stable throughout the work).

3. It is highly unlikely the "Thucydides" of 1.117.2 is the historian: see Simon Hornblower, *A Commentary on Thucydides*, vol. 1 (Oxford, 1991), 191. Thucydides' only other appearance as a direct participant in the events he describes is thus at 4.104–7, where "Thucydides, son of Olorus and the one who wrote these things" (4.104.4) is shown maneuvering against the Spartan commander Brasidas, on which passage see Marincola, *Authority and Tradition*, 182–85, followed by discussion of later historians as direct participants in their histories. Thucydides does briefly mention his exile in his so-called "second preface" at 5.26.5, but "[s]ince his exile has no consequences for the war, its mention is reserved for the place where it does have importance, on Thucydides' activities as an historian" (ibid., 184).

4. Thucydides, *Peloponnesian War* 2.48.3.

5. "To show," of course, is seldom an innocently visual concept in the historians. Compare and contrast the language of "showing" (*apodexis*) in the opening sentence of Herodotus's *Histories*. Nevertheless, Thucydides' *dēlōsō*, followed by a passage rich in virtuosic *enargeia*, means more (i.e., less) than "clarify" or "explain," insisting instead on the word's root meaning: "I shall show," i.e., "I shall make you see." For a brief introduction to the vast subject of the relationship between seeing, hearing, and saying in ancient historiography (and earlier, in Homer), including the privileged place of autopsy, see Marincola, *Authority and Tradition*, 63–86. See also François Hartog, "l'oeil de Thucydide et l'histoire 'véritable,'" *Poétique* 49 (1982): 22–30.

6. As Marincola (184–85, n.52) notes, Thucydides uses of himself the first person "for statements of opinion, reasoning, inference, autopsy, and methodology, that is, anything that affected the history *qua* history"; the third person is used "for formal openings and closings"—like the preface and the frequent markers of the ends of the single years of "the war (of) which Thucydides wrote (*xunegrapse*)"—and also "when he is an historical character." This last, however, arguably leaves out the plague, where Thucydides' direct involvement is marked instead by a participle (*nosēsas*). His verb (*dēlōsō*), as Marincola notes, belongs to the first-person category, since the author speaks "as investigator or as one with superior knowledge"; the same correctly observes that 4.104–7 "is not an autoptic statement." The plague is thus unique in the entire history for the explicit way in which it stitches together Thucydides as author, eyewitness, and participant.

7. When Thucydides actually wrote his introduction is, of course, a different question. "What is certain is that Thucydides did not complete his work," notes Tim Rood, *Thucydides: Narrative and Explanation* (Oxford, 1998), 52.

8. Probably Thucydides was not unaware that this made him an extreme example of *pathei mathos* ("learning from experience" or "suffering"), a proverb known to us from Aeschylus, *Agamemnon* 177.

9. Thucydides, *Peloponnesian War* 2.48.3. Many editors seclude various parts of the (pleonastic?) τὰς αἰτίας . . . σχεῖν of the manuscripts, given in full here but with a simplified translation.

10. A. W. Gomme, *A Historical Commentary on Thucydides*, vol. 2 (Oxford, 1956), 161. Simon Hornblower, *Thucydides* (London, 1987), 2, offers this somewhat less than decisive improvement: "Not only his detailed description of its symptoms, but his fondness for seeing even strictly non-medical matters in medical terms . . . can reasonably be ascribed to a natural amateur interest in a serious illness one has suffered from oneself. The experience was surely (in the vulgar sense) traumatic."

11. Adam Parry, "The Language of Thucydides' Description of the Plague," *Bulletin of the Institute of Classical Studies* 16 (1969): 106–18, largely responding to D. L. Page, "Thucydides' Description of the Great Plague at Athens," *Classical Quarterly* n.s. 3 (1953): 97–119. Subsequent bibliography is summarized by Hornblower, *Commentary* (316–17), to which add Thomas E. Morgan, "Plague or Poetry? Thucydides on the Epidemic at Athens," *Transactions of the American Philological Association* 124 (1994): 197–209, who argues that, regarding medical terminology, "the truth lies somewhere in the middle" between Page and Parry. Hornblower too eventually sides in part with Page, insofar as Thucydides employs "rich medical vocabulary" that is "not at variance with medical usage" and "which leaves on the reader a strong *impression* of clinical precision"; thus Parry, in finding "a positive abhorrence of the technical" by Thucydides "goes too far" (322). Hornblower rightly notes, however, that medical fluency, however measured,

does not necessarily mean a primarily medical purpose; as he puts it, "there was more than one Thucydides" (317).

12. Ibid., 116. That the plague is integral to the history of the war is also suggested by the deployment of disease as metaphor later in the work, on which see Hornblower, *Commentary* (480), commenting on 3.82; Lisa Kallet, "The Diseased Body Politic, Athenian Public Finance, and the Massacre at Mykalessos (Thucydides 7.27-29)," *American Journal of Philology* 120 (1999): 223-44, summarized in her *Money and the Corrosion of Power in Thucydides* (Berkeley, 2001), 134-37. But on the general question of the metaphorical reach of disease in Greek thought and literature, see now G. E. R. Lloyd, *In the Grip of Disease: Studies in the Greek Imagination* (Oxford, 2003), with an anthology of relevant texts, who proposes (8-13) that "metaphor" actually sells short the polysemy of disease in Greek thought (discussion of Thucydides [120-27], with text and translation [134-41]), and Robin Mitchell-Boyask, *Plague and the Athenian Imagination: Drama, History and the Cult of Asclepius* (Cambridge, 2008), who largely agrees with Lloyd (18-19; discussion of Thucydides [41-43]). Nevertheless, reading (or writing) the plague as metaphor is hardly less alienating, in the particular case of Thucydides, *autos nosēsas*, than is his transformation into a clinician: this is the timeless lesson of Susan Sontag's *Illness as Metaphor* (New York, 1978), supplemented by *AIDS and Its Metaphors* (New York, 1989).

13. Dionysius of Halicarnassus, *Thucydides* 24.

14. Dionysius of Halicarnassus, *Demosthenes* 39.

15. Demetrius, *On Style* 2.48. The arrangement Demetrius admires is hard to capture in English. The Greek actually ends with *on*, participle of the verb "to be." A lesser writer, suggests Demetrius, would have moved this monosyllable back one word, allowing the sentence to end more euphoniously with *on etunchanen* (instead of *etunchanen on*).

16. This motion actually already begins in the preceding section's description of the disease "descending" (*katebē*) through Egypt and "falling upon" (*enepese*) Athens (48.1.1). Simon Swain, "Man and Medicine in Thucydides," *Arethusa* 27.3 (1994): 303-27, notes that Thucydides' use of *empiptein* and the like, here and elsewhere, "recalls medical talk" (306) but often points to the social and political consequences of "a wholly unexpected visitation, one outside human control, which affects not only men's bodies but crucially their minds also" (307), such as but not limited to disease. Doubtless we can detect an echo of the frequent "descent" of the passions and of divine vengeance on mortals in tragedy, on which see Ruth Padel, *In and Out of the Mind: Greek Images of the Tragic Self* (Princeton, N.J., 1992), 53, 129-32.

17. For a brief but incisive exploration of how the plague account is consistent with Thucydides' attempt to record the "symptoms" of human conflict, see Luciano Canfora, *Tucidide: L'oligarca imperfetto* (Pordenone, 1991), 30-34.

18. René Girard, "The Plague in Literature and Myth," *"To Double Business Bound": Essays on Literature, Mimesis, and Anthropology* (Baltimore, 1978), 512. Girard, however, finds a somewhat different crisis for language in the plague, "less than theme, structure, or symbol, since it symbolizes desymbolization itself" (530). Girard's more or less anthropological point is to connect the plague in literature and myth to "a certain pervasive violence in our relationships" (526); he sidesteps the question of what (else) the plague meant for those who, like Thucydides, knew the real thing.

19. Jeffrey S. Rusten, ed., Thucydides, *The Peloponnesian War, Book 2* (Cambridge, 1989), 186. Morrison Marshall, "Pericles and the Plague," in E. M. Craik, *"Owls to*

Athens": Essays on Classical Subjects Presented to Sir Kenneth Dover (Oxford, 1990), 167–
69, reviews additional attempts to translate the sentence but proposes instead taking
kreisson logou to refer to the limits of human reason; it would thus represent a quiet
attempt to excuse Pericles "for not taking advance account of *this* possibility," i.e., of a
disaster that was "beyond calculation" or "beyond all expectation." Marshall is followed
by Hornblower, *Commentary*, 323. Swain, "Man and Medicine in Thucydides," 313–14,
usefully compares Thucydides 3.82.2, where *eidos* is used to indicate difference in detail,
but ignores this in order to suggest "beyond reason / understanding" for *kreisson logou*.
Ugo Fantasia, ed. and trans., Thucydides, *La guerra del Peloponneso, Libro 2* (Pisa,
2003), 133 and 440, though he rightly cites the important comparandum of Xenophon,
Memorabilia 3.11.1, where *kreisson logou* is used of a woman's "indescribable" beauty,
settles on "caratteristiche . . . tali da superare ogni previsione." But the plainest meaning
is best; cf. Rex Warner, trans., Thucydides, *History of the Peloponnesian War* (New York,
1972), 153: "Words indeed fail when one tries to give a general picture of this disease."
    20. Cf. Gregory Crane, *The Blinded Eye: Thucydides and the New Written Word*
(Lanham, Md., 1996), 29, on the dilemma of the whole history: "No account could ever
fully describe an event so complex as the Peloponnesian War. More generally, texts are
inherently reductive, in that they must convert lived experience into a linear stream of
words. A text can make plain many things that are not clear to the observer on the spot
(note Thucydides' comments at 1.22.3 on how confusing many informants found the
events in which they participated), but no one could seriously argue that Thucydides'
account could encapsulate the experiences of thousands of participants in a conflict that
spread across the Greek world and lasted for an entire generation."
    21. Or to put this another way, a disease's "essence" (to give the extended meaning
of *eidos* some of its philosophical freight) is first and foremost "what it looks like" (*eidos*
narrowly meant), but the latter combines both the general (here is the disease so that you
can recognize it should it return) and the specific (I cannot really capture the disease),
with the latter emphasized here. The word is frequent with a variety of meanings in the
Hippocratic corpus: see C. M. Gillespie, "The Use of Εἶδος and Ἰδέα in Hippocrates,"
Classical Quarterly 6.3 (1912): 179–203.
    22. Cf. François Hartog, "Herodotus and the Historiographical Operation," trans.
Wayne R. Hayes, *Diacritics* 22.2 (1992): 83–93, on Thucydides' opening words, which
suggest that "the work can be read both as a funeral inscription and as the memorial of
an initial absence—namely, that of Thucydides of Athens" (92).

Chapter 3. Latin Decomposition

    1. Jerome, *Chronicon* (ed. Helm) 94 BC.
    2. Karl Lachmann, *In T. Lucretii Cari De rerum natura libros Commentarius* (Berlin,
1850), 63: *neque a philosphia alienum sed nulli certae disciplinae addictum.*
    3. Lucretius, *De rerum natura libri sex*, ed. H. A. J. Munro, 4th ed. (Cambridge,
1893), vol. 2, 3.
    4. Lucretius, *De rerum natura libri sex*, ed. Cyril Bailey (Oxford, 1947), vol. 1, 21.
    5. Giuseppe Solaro, ed., *Lucrezio: Biografie umanistiche* (Bari, 2000), 33.
    6. John Masson, *Lucretius: Epicurean and Poet* (London, 1907), 38.
    7. Ibid., 39.
    8. First argued by J. Woltjer, "Studia Lucretiana," *Mnemosyne* 23 (1895), 222–27.

9. "Insomma tutta la notizia biografica nota a Girolamo appare costruita, a partire dalla martellante denuncia della 'follia' dell'autore, su quel che sembrava ricavarsi dall'opera stessa di Lucrezio," concludes Luciano Canfora, *Vita di Lucrezio* (Palermo, 1993), 30, who returns often in the course of this engaging book to the question (always answered negatively) of the reliability of Jerome's biography, with notes to earlier skeptics. More on the same in the also lively Leofranc Holford-Strevens, "*Horror Vacui* in Lucretian Biography," *Leeds International Classical Studies* 1.1 (2002): 1-23.

10. Cicero, *Ad Quintum fratrem* 14 = 2.10(9).3. David Sedley, *Lucretius and the Transformation of Greek Wisdom* (Cambridge, 1998), opens his monograph (1-2) with this letter in order to explore not the connection between Cicero and Lucretius but, rather, that between the latter and Empedocles (a Latin version of which Cicero mentions in the following sentence); he returns once or twice to Cicero as philosopher but never as poet.

11. This interpretation is the conclusion, after an exhaustive examination of other possibilities (the *crux* is *tamen*, sometimes emended by editors), of Henry Wheatland Litchfield, "Cicero's Judgment on Lucretius," *Harvard Studies in Classical Philology* 24 (1913): 147-59. As my translation suggests, I myself tend to see the *tamen* as marking a shift from Quintus's quoted opinion to Cicero's own additional view of the poem's *ars*; in any case, our problem is produced precisely by the fact that Cicero could count on Quintus, as author of the letter to which he replies, to understand at once the elliptical formulation that perplexes us.

12. Lucilius 84-85 (Marx and Warmington), 74-75 (Krenkel). *Lexis* transliterates the Greek λέξεις.

13. Donald A. Russell, in his Loeb of Quintilian, *The Orator's Education* (Cambridge, Mass., 2001), vol. 4, 224, n.128, makes the interesting suggestion (which he attributes to W. Trimpi) that *vermiculatus* follows play inherent in the Greek καμπαί, "twists," and κάμπαι, "caterpillars."

14. E. H. Warmington, ed. and trans., *Remnants of Old Latin*, vol. 3 (Cambridge, Mass., 1938), 29, tries to reproduce the effect with French: "How charmingly are *ses dits* put together—artfully like all the little stone dice of mosaic in a paved floor or in an inlay of wriggly pattern!"

15. Cicero, *De oratore* 3.171. Strictly speaking, Crassus is talking about the "placement" of words *in sequence*, but *componere* and *struere* push the image into (at least) two dimensions. Strictly linear "placement" is better served by the phrase *consecutio verborum*, used by Cicero at *Partitiones oratoriae* 18 in reference to meter. An analogous tension between sequence and the two- and three-dimensional structures that contain it is found in ancient mnemotechnics, which, in fact, arrange verbal material into *loci*: for an introduction, see Frances A. Yates, *The Art of Memory* (Chicago, 1966), 1-26. The key discussion is that of the *Rhetorica ad Herennium*, which at 3.30 compares the *dispositio* and *collocatio* of remembered "images" to writing and the *loci* themselves to wax or papyrus; almost paradoxically, the sequential organization of the *loci* enables us to remember their contents along any trajectory, "from the top, from the bottom, or from the middle."

16. Cicero, *Orator* 149-50.

17. Cicero, *De oratore* 1.150.

18. Cf. Quintilian, *Institutio oratoria* 4.2.127: *perire artem putamus nisi appareat, cum desinat ars esse si appareat.*

19. On their dates of composition, see Nino Marinone, *Cronologia Ciceroniana* (Rome, 1997), 191-92.

20. Cicero, *Brutus* 274.

21. Quintilian will later restore the negative connotation of the Lucilian passage in application precisely to the question of rhetorical "flow" (*oratio, quae ferri debet et fluere*), urging his reader not to pursue prose-rhythm too *vermiculate*, "vermiculately" (*Institutio oratoria* 9.4.113).

22. Cf. Quintilian, *Institutio oratoria* 1.11.3 (*nam si qua in his ars est dicentium, ea prima est ne ars esse videatur*); 4.2.126 (quoted above); Ovid, *Metamorphoses* 10.252 (*ars adeo latet arte sua*), regarding Pygmalion's statue. More of the same (and their *Nachleben*) in Paolo D'Angelo, *Ars est celare artem: Da Aristotele a Duchamp* (Macerata, 2005).

23. Simon Hornblower and Antony Spawforth, *The Oxford Classical Dictionary*, 3rd rev. ed. (Oxford, 2003).

24. Aratus, *Phaenomena*, ed. and trans. Douglas Kidd (Cambridge, 1997), xi.

25. Ibid., 175.

26. Cicero, *De oratore* 1.69.

27. "The stars and poetry go together for the Romans," observes Emma Gee in her excellent "Cicero's Astronomy," *Classical Quarterly*, 51.2 (2000): 533. Gee emphasizes the philosophical implications of finding *ordo* and *ratio* in the arrangement of both stars and words, and although she is more concerned with Cicero (who later translated Aratus; discussion below) than with his model, she suggests that some of what Cicero develops "is already inherent in his Stoic source" (534).

28. Aratus, *Phaenomena* 45–50.

29. A somewhat more mechanical Aratean interest in the placement of words on the page can be found, as James Zetzel points out to me, in his use of acrostics, the one certain example of which is in 783–87, on which see Kidd, Aratus, *Phaenomena*, 445–46.

30. Cicero, *Aratea* (or *Phaenomena*), frag. 8 (ed. Ewbank), known from *On the Nature of the Gods* 2.42 and Priscian 14.6.52.

31. Black-and-white images of the entire mosaic in P. G. P. Meyboom, *The Nile Mosaic of Palestrina: Early Evidence of Egyptian Religion in Italy* (Leiden, 1995).

32. Plutarch, *Life of Cicero* 2.3. For a detailed account of Cicero's poetry and its reception, see the introductory material of the edition of W. W. Ewbank, ed. *The Poems of Cicero* (London, 1933).

33. Tacitus, *Dialogus de oratoribus* 21.6. Rare efforts to revise this judgment tend to make things only worse; thus John W. Spaeth, Jr., "Cicero the Poet," *Classical Journal* 26.7 (1931): 500–512, concludes, excruciatingly, "But that [Cicero] could find time in such a busy life as was his to write verse and to write it passably well should move us to greater admiration of his achievement. He probably does not deserve a place on the heights of Parnassus; but he is well worthy of a habitation on the slopes" (512).

34. Cicero, *Marius*, frag. 2 (ed. Ewbank); Cicero 17 in Edward Courtney, *The Fragmentary Latin Poets* (Oxford, 1993), 177–78 (which see on present-tense *abiecit*); known from *On Divination* 1.47.106. Antonio Traglia, *La lingua di Cicerone poeta* (Bari, 1950), 41, faults the excessive use of participles (which, however, are part of what gives the scene its crucially static quality, on which more below). A much more enthusiastic reading is provided by Enrica Malcovati, *Cicerone e la poesia* (Pavia, 1943), 270–72, who notes Cicero's model in Homer, *Iliad*, 12.200–7, as does Sander Goldberg, *Epic in Republican Rome* (New York and Oxford, 1995), 141–44, who compares Vergil, *Aeneid* 11.751–56.

35. On *technopaignia*, see Marco Fantuzzi and Richard L. Hunter, *Tradition and Innovation in Hellenistic Poetry* (Cambridge, 2004), 40–41. On the broad phenomenon

through the ages and across cultures, see Dick Higgins, *Pattern Poetry: Guide to an Unknown Literature* (Albany, 1987). "But all poetry, even in its most traditional forms, asks the reader to decipher the text in spatial as well as linear terms," rightly observes Jerome J. McGann, *The Textual Condition* (Princeton, N.J., 1991), 113, regarding the ultimate point of the calligrammic high-jinks of Apollinaire, Blake, Pound, and others.

36. Ancient discussions of the period are collected by Heinrich Lausberg, *Handbook of Literary Rhetoric: A Foundation for Literary Study* (Leiden, 1998), 414–25 (§§ 923–47).

37. Perhaps lurking behind some of these snakes is Plato's description of that perfectly self-contained first creature at *Timaeus* 32d-34a, sometimes taken to depend on the *ouroboros* or tail-biting dragon found in mythologies around the world.

38. Cicero, *Orator* 204.

39. On the importance both of written preparation before speaking and of publication afterward (or even instead of oral delivery), see Shane Butler, *The Hand of Cicero* (London, 2002).

40. Plato, *Phaedrus* 275a.

41. Horace, *Ars Poetica* 1–9.

42. On the meaning and sources of Horace's *simplex . . . et unum*, see C. O. Brink, ed., *Horace on Poetry*, vol. 2 (Cambridge, 1971), 77ff. But in downplaying Ciceronian influence (79–80), primarily by exposing the forced *Quellenforschung* of earlier scholars seeking to establish a clear link, passage to passage, between the *Ars Poetica* and Cicero's rhetorical works, Brink arguably misses (as did they) more general affinities of the sort briefly explored here.

43. Compare the potter's wheel that figures the work of the poet in Horace, *Ars Poetica* ll. 21–22, from which emerges not an elegant amphora but a simple jug.

44. The female torso, though contrasted to the fishy tail, offers only an ambiguous reprieve, since it too, in part through its nod to the body of a siren (and the general ancient view of female bodies behind both), is already semimonstrous.

45. Lucretius, *De rerum natura* 3.720–21 (hereafter cited in text).

46. *OLD querela*, citing, for this latter meaning (2), Cicero, *Aratea* 221.

47. *OLD gemitus*.

48. *OLD singultus*.

49. *OLD angor*. *Pace* Bailey, op. cit., vol. 2, 1161, regarding the one other appearance in Lucretius of *anxius angor* (at 3.993), Cicero's distinction between *anxietas* and *angor* at *Tusculan Disputations* 4.27 does not fully explain the repetitious)even if not tautologous) phrase. The earlier passage regards the torments of Tityos, *quem volucres lacerant atque exest anxius angor* (3.993), where at least a secondary meaning of *angor* as "choking" would offer grimly clever play on the line's second, metaphorical image of eating. Diskin Clay, *Lucretius and Epicurus* (Ithaca, N.Y., 1983), 264, attempting a philosophical reading of the phrase at 6.1158, notes that it has "no warrant in Thucydides' Greek."

50. Catherine Atherton, "Lucretius on What Language Is Not," in Dorothea Frede and Brad Inwood, eds., *Language and Learning: Philosophy of Language in the Hellenistic Age, Proceedings of the Ninth Symposium Hellenisticum* (Cambridge, 2005), 107.

51. For more on all of this, see Brooke Holmes, "*Daedala Lingua*: Crafted Speech in *De rerum natura*," *American Journal of Philology* 126 (2005): 554–60.

52. Other terms include *hupotupōsis, diatupōsis, repraesentatio, illustratio, demonstratio, descriptio*, and *sub oculis subiectio*, a list I borrow from Ann Vasaly, *Representations: Images of the World in Ciceronian Oratory* (Berkeley, 1993), 90. Lausberg, *Handbook of*

Literary Rhetoric, 359–66 (§§ 810–19) compiles (under the rubric *evidentia*) ancient terms and discussions. On *repraesentatio,* see now James Ker, "Roman Repraesentatio," *American Journal of Philology* 128.3 (2007): 341–65. Ruth Webb, "Imagination and the Arousal of the Emotions in Greco-Roman Rhetoric," in Susanna Morton Braund and Christopher Gill, eds., *The Passions in Roman Thought and Literature* (Cambridge, 1997), 112–27, offers a good introduction to the role of *enargeia* in Greco-Roman oratory; see also the brief but rich discussion in Vasaly, *Representations,* 89–104. A fuller survey of *enargeia* in ancient rhetorical theory is given by Alessandra Manieri, *l'immagine poetica nella teoria degli antichi:* Phantasia *ed* enargeia (Pisa, 1998), 123–54.

53. Quintilian, *Institutio oratoria* 8.3.62. Cf. 4.2.63ff.; 6.2.32ff.

54. Ibid., 8.3.64–5. This gushing review is very like that of *enargeia* in the oratory of Lysias by Dionysius of Halicarnassus (*Lysias* 7). Interestingly, he later returns (11.3.90) to the same Ciceronian *exemplum* to discuss the inappropriate use of gesture to render a scene more vivid through, in essence, pantomime. Webb, "Imagination and the Arousal of the Emotions," 122–24, offers some brief comments on the earlier passage.

55. Plutarch, *Moralia* (*De gloria Atheniensium*) 347a. On this passage and on historical *enargeia* generally, see Andrew D. Walker, "*Enargeia* and the Spectator in Greek Historiography," *Transactions of the American Philological Association* 123 (1993): 353–77. Cf. Manieri, *l'immagine poetica,* 155–64.

56. Graham Zanker, "Enargeia in the Ancient Criticism of Poetry," *Rheinisches Museum für Philologie* 124 (1981): 298–311; *Realism in Alexandrian Poetry: A Literature and Its Audience* (London, 1987); "Pictorial Description as a Supplement for Narrative: The Labour of Augeas' Stables in *Heracles Leontophonos*," *American Journal of Philology* 117.3 (1996): 411–23; *Modes of Viewing in Hellenistic Poetry and Art* (Madison, 2004). On poetic *enargeia* see also Manieri, *L'immagine poetica,* 173–92.

57. Cicero, *In Verrem* II 5.87.

58. Thucydides, *Peloponnesian War* 7.71; 6.30–31. See Walker, "*Enargeia* and the Spectator," for extensive analaysis of the Syracusan scene, its ancient critical reception, and later imitations.

59. Lucretius, *De rerum natura* 6.1257; 6.1268; 6.1163 (where the observation, being of "heat," is not strictly visual). On the departures from the Greek, see Clay, *Lucretius and Epicurus,* 262–63.

60. Peta Fowler, "Lucretian Conclusions," in Monica R. Gale, ed., *Lucretius* (Oxford, 2007), 226, originally published in D. H. Roberts, F. M. Dunn, and D. P. Fowler, ed., *Classical Closure: Reading the End in Greek and Latin Literature* (Princeton, N.J., 1997), 112–38. Note, however, that the spectacle Sallust claims to offer is of the *audacia* and *vis animi* of the Catilinarians—i.e., here, as often, *enargeia* ultimately enables us not only to see events but to see into their causes and meanings.

61. Lucretius, *De rerum natura* 2.1–4. Acting the part of a victim of shipwreck is mentioned by Quintilian, as a school-exercise in the generation of pity in an audience, immediately following one of this discussions of *enargeia* (*Institutio oratoria* 6.2.36). On crude paintings of shipwrecks, either as ex-votos or as alms-inducing advertisements of their plight by victims reduced to begging, see H. H. Huxley, "Storm and Shipwreck in Roman Literature," *Greece and Rome* 21.63 (1952): 123–24, discussing Cicero, *De natura deorum* 3.89; Persius, *Satires* 1.88–90; Juvenal, *Satires* 12.28; Phaedrus, *Fabulae* 4.23.24–25. In other words, shipwrecks seem to have been somewhat emblematic of what, even when only represented, can arouse strong emotions; its choice by Lucretius to make his point is, therefore, scarcely accidental. One also wonders whether Thucydides and his

famously pathos-stirring account of the Athenian defeat at Syracuse (see above), is also on Lucretius' mind here.

62. G. Zanker, "Enargeia," 308–9, also noting use of the term earlier by Theophrastus and later by the Stoics. Cf. Manieri, *l'immagine poetica*, 113–22; A. A. Long, *Hellenistic Philosophy: Stoics, Epicureans, Sceptics*, 2nd ed. (Berkeley, 1986), 22–23.

63. Gerhard Müller, "The Conclusions of the Six Books of Lucretius," in Monica R. Gale, ed., *Lucretius* (Oxford, 2007), 234–53, first published in German in 1978, argues that the plague is to be understood, "secondly, as an extreme case of human helplessness in the face of terrible disaster, and therefore as an antithesis to Epicurean peace of mind" (251); Lucretius expects the reader "to remember everything that he has learned about true philosophy through the whole poem, to see the story of the Athenian disaster in the right light" (253). But the definitive version of the "final test" hypothesis is that of Clay, *Lucretius and Epicurus*, 257–66.

64. Webb, "Imagination and the Arousal of the Emotions," 120–21.

65. Lausberg, *Handbook of Literary Rhetoric*, 359 (§ 810). I have omitted parenthetical citations of Quintilian.

66. Murray Krieger, "*Ekphrasis* and the Still Movement of Poetry; or *Laokoön* Revisited," in *Ekphrasis: The Illusion of the Natural Sign* (Baltimore, 1992), 265–66; the essay was first published in 1967. The rapidly expanding bibliography on *ekphrasis* (ancient and not) in the wake of Krieger (and a few important predecessors) is surveyed by D. P. Fowler, "Narrate and Describe: The Problem of Ekphrasis," *Journal of Roman Studies* 81 (1991): 25, oddly omitting, however, Krieger himself; partially updated by James A. Francis, "Metal Maidens, Achilles' Shield, and Pandora: The Beginnings of 'Ekphrasis,'" *American Journal of Philology* 130 (2009): 1–23. Ruth Webb's *Ekphrasis, Imagination and Persuasion in Ancient Rhetorical Theory and Practice* (Farnham, U.K., 2009) reached me as this book was in press.

67. Krieger, "*Ekphrasis* and the Still Movement of Poetry," 6–9, attributing the "narrow meaning" to Leo Spritzer and nodding toward "a fuller history of the term's usage," without, however, abandoning the former, "the heart of the word's meaning for me," though he will "broaden the range of possible ekphrastic objects by re-connecting ekphrasis to all 'word-painting.'" For a brief history of the term in modern scholarship, see Ruth Webb, "*Ekphrasis* Ancient and Modern: The Invention of a Genre," *Word and Image* 15 (1999): 7–18. Graham Zanker has several times laid out the cases for preferring *enargeia* and against the misunderstanding of *ekphrasis*: "Enargeia" provides the full argument; see also *Realism*, 39–43; "Pictorial," 412; new evidence from the Posidippus papyrus in *Modes*, 175, n.2.

68. Krieger, *Ekprhasis: The Illusion*, xvii, 9, 31, 13, 10.

69. G. E. Lessing, *Laokoon, oder, Über die Grenzen der Mahlerey und Poesie* (Berlin, 1766). By contrast, there have been efforts to complicate the flip side of this contention, by observing how poetry's ability to "animate" a described art-object parallels the actual experience *in time* of a work of visual art: regarding antiquity, see especially Eleanor Winsor Leach's dazzling *The Rhetoric of Space: Literary and Artistic Representations of Landscape in Republican and Augustan Rome* (Princeton, N.J., 1988), where the basic problem is spelled out (8–14).

70. For a broader case for the contamination of form with matter in ancient thought (*pace* Plato), see James I. Porter, "The Disgrace of Matter in Ancient Aesthetics," in Ralph Rosen and Ineke Sluiter, eds., *Kakos: Badness and Anti-Values in Classical Antiquity* (Leiden, 2008), 283–314.

71. See pages 7–8.

72. Macrobius, *Saturnalia* 6.2.7 (*Ipsius vero pestilentiae, quae est in tertio Georgicorum, color totus et liniamenta paene omnia tracta sunt de descriptione pestilentiae quae est in sexto Lucretii*); 6.2.14 (*Nonne vobis videntur membra huius descriptionis ex uno fonte manasse?*).

73. The tradition would resume in the Renaissance with, e.g., Angelo Poliziano's *Epicedion in Albieram* and *Sylva in scabiem* and Girolamo Fracastoro's *Syphillis* or *De morbo gallico*. On the presence of the plague in Western literature, including and beyond the Thucydidean-Lucretian tradition, see Jürgen Grimm, *Die literarische Darstellung der Pest in der Antike und in der Romania, Frieburger Schriften zur romanischen Philologie* 6 (Munich, 1965). Specifically on the Vergilian plague and its Lucretian intertext, see also Joseph Farrell, *Vergil's Georgics and the Traditions of Ancient Epic: The Art of Allusion in Literary History*, New York, 1991; David West, "Two Plagues: Virgil, Georgics 3.478–566 and Lucretius 6.1090–1286," in David West and Tony Woodman, ed., *Creative Imitation and Latin Literature* (Cambridge, 1979), 71–88. For details on the echoes of Lucretius and Vergil in Ovid's plague, see Franz Bömer, *P. Ovidius Naso, Metamorphosen: Kommentar*, vol. 3 (Heidelberg, 1976), 331–56.

74. J. C. Scaliger, *Poetices libri septem* (Lyon, 1561; repr. Stuttgart, 1964), 263–65 (book 5, chaps. 10–11). Jacobus Pontanus, *Symbolarum libri xvii Virgilii* (Augsburg, 1599; repr. New York, 1976), vol. 1, col. 522: *Videntur praecipui poetae, ut notavit Delrius, in hunc quasi communem artis ostentandae campum excurrisse*, adding, *valde enim elaboratae sunt*, "for the products show considerable effort."

75. Plato, *Phaedrus* 264c. On the healthy body as rhetorical model, see Larue Van Hook, *The Metaphorical Terminology of Greek Rhetoric and Literary Criticism* (Chicago, 1905), 18–20. On *compositio* generally (and its constitutive parts, like the anthropomorphically named *membrum*), see Lausberg, *Handbook of Literary Rhetoric*, 411–60 (§§ 911–1054). (On the coincidence of "rhetoric" and "poetics" in ancient literary theory, see ibid. 19–21 [§ 35].) The Renaissance was supremely sensitive to these metaphors and to the aesthetic ideal to which they point, and the best account of ancient theories of composition comes, in fact, in the riveting study of their pictorial *Nachleben* by Michael Baxandall, *Giotto and the Orators: Humanist Observers of Painting in Italy and the Discovery of Pictorial Composition, 1350–1450* (Oxford, 1971).

76. Plutarch, *Moralia* 18a–d.

77. Ibid., 18d.

78. In fact, the student of Lucretian atomism and especially of its consequent theories of vision will have found much in this chapter that sounds familiar, starting with the aesthetic principles of Lucilius and Cicero. This raises an obvious question: both in Lucretius and beyond, does atomistic theory underpin compositional theory, or the other way around? Probably this is a chicken-or-egg choice, but it seems worth noting that Lucretius would have been taught to compose words, and doubtless even verses, long before he went looking for atoms. More specifically, one might explore how both atomism and compositional theory conjure a *horror vacui* at the heart of which lies a fatal attraction, as James I. Porter, "Lucretius and the Poetics of Void," in Annick Monet, ed., *Le jardin romain: Epicurisme et poésie à Rome: Mélanges offerts à Mayotte Bollack* (Villeneuve d'Ascq, 2003), 197–226, brilliantly observes for the former. Porter offers his own reading of the plague (200–203) as a picture of death as the voiding of void (bodies packed onto bodies), greeted instead by the fear of the voiding of bodies (fought over, though dead, at the poem's end). Life actually requires both—as, let us add, does art.

79. Cicero, *Tusculan Disputations* 2.23–26; 2.20–22.

80. Cicero, *De officiis* 1.98.

81. Baxandall, *Giotto and the Orators*.

82. Lucretius, *De rerum natura* 6.1280–81.

83. Lachmann, *In T. Lucretii Cari*, 426. He actually writes *conpostum*.

84. Alfred Tennyson, "Lucretius," in *The Holy Grail and Other Poems* (Boston, 1870), 167.

Chapter 4. The Erasable Cicero

1. Suetonius, *Life of Julius Caesar* 20.

2. Cicero, *Letters to Atticus* 39 = 2.19.5.

3. Ibid. 40 = 2.20.3.

4. Festus (ed. Lindsay), 490–92.

5. Cicero, *Letters to Atticus* 97 = 5.4.4.

6. Ibid. 177 = 9.10.4; Cornelius Nepos, *Life of Atticus*, 16.3. Discussions in Nicholas Horsfall, ed., *Cornelius Nepos: A Selection, Including the Lives of Cato and Atticus* (Oxford, 1989), and in D. R. Shackleton Bailey, *Cicero's Letters to Atticus*, vol. 1 (Cambridge, 1965), 60. On archival rolls of this general sort (*tomoi sunkollēsimoi*), see Orsolina Montevecchi, *La papirologia*, rev. ed. (Milan, 1988), 15.

7. Cicero, *Letters to Atticus* 28 = 2.8.1, where Cicero learns that couriers have lost a letter from Atticus on the road from Rome, and 33 = 2.13.1, where Cicero explains that a previous letter of his, enclosed, had accidentally been returned to its sender.

8. Suetonius, *Life of Julius Caesar* 56; cf. Aulus Gellius, *Attic Nights* 17.9; Isidore, *Etymologies* 1.25; Suetonius, *Life of Augustus* 88.

9. I.e., anonymous, with the name of the sender suppressed in opening and closing salutations. The letter did bear the sender's seal. On the whole affair, see Shane Butler, *The Hand of Cicero* (London and New York, 2002), 85–102.

10. Cicero, *Letters to Atticus* 43 = 2.23.1.

11. Quintilian, *Institutio oratoria* 8.6.52.

12. Cicero, *De oratore* 3.155.

13. For more on waxed tablets, see the introduction.

14. Cicero, *Pro Flacco* 37–38.

15. Butler, *Hand of Cicero*, 35–60.

16. Cicero, *Against Verres* 2.2.186ff.

17. Ibid., 2.2.191. Further discussion in Butler, *Hand of Cicero*, 33–34. "Porcine tail" is a joke on the literal meaning of Verres' name.

18. The speech is the *Pro Sexto Roscio Amerino*, on which see Butler, *Hand of Cicero*, 14–23.

19. Cf. D. R. Shackleton Bailey, *Cicero's Letters to Atticus*, vol. 1, 279, 405.

20. Catullus, *Poems* 50.2.

21. Cicero, *Letters to Atticus* 29 = 2.9.4; 30 = 2.12.4; cf. 35 = 2.15.4.

22. Cicero had made the regret explicit in *Letters to Atticus* 25 = 2.5.2: *Sed quid ego haec, quae cupio deponere, et toto animo atque omni cura philosophein? Sic, inquam, in animo est. Vellem ab initio. Nunc vero, quoniam quae putavi esse praeclara expertus sum quam essent inania, cum omnibus Musis rationem habere cogito.* "But why am I worrying about such things, when I want to put all such aside and devote every thought and effort to

the pursuit of knowledge? I tell you, I'm seriously thinking about it. If only I had done so from the start. But now, having learned first-hand the extent to which all I thought glorious is really meaningless, I'm ready to do business with all the Muses."

23. Cicero, *De divinatione* 2.7; cf. Butler, *Hand of Cicero*, 110.

24. Cicero, *Philippics* 2.28–30.

25. Dio Cassius, *Roman History* 44.16.1. Cf. Suetonius, *Life of Julius Caesar* 82. Cicero would later quip, "If, as the saying goes, the pen had been mine, I would have finished the whole play, not just one act" (*Philippics* 2.34). Sean Gurd, "Cicero and Editorial Revision," *Classical Antiquity* 26.1 (2007): 49–80, explores the circulation and (collective) revision of unfinished texts as a powerful republican symbol for Cicero, Brutus, and friends.

26. Quoted from Butler, *Hand of Cicero*, 108. The letters are 358 = 14.4.2; 360 = 14.6.1; 367 = 14.13.3; 368 = 14.14.3; 376 = 14.22.2; 381 = 15.4.2–3.

27. Petrarch, *Letters on Familiar Matters* 24.3 and 4.

28. Carlin Barton, *Roman Honor: The Fire in the Bones* (Berkeley, 2001), 213, n.66, notes this example of "blushing even when one is not in the presence of others," possible for an honorable man, but here prompted by Atticus's virtual presence through the letter.

29. The sponge was probably more useful on those elusive members of the Roman family of writing surfaces, parchment notebooks, praised for an erasability comparable to that of wax by Martial, *Epigrams* 14.7; cf. Horace, *Ars poetica* 388–90. Martial sends a "Punic sponge" along with a papyrus book of poems at *Epigrams* 4.10 in case the recipient does not like them, but doubt about the precise point of his closing assertion that only "one erasure," not "many" will resolve matters (by cleaning the whole roll, as seems also to be the effect of the sponge at Suetonius, *Life of Augustus* 85? or by erasing just Martial's name in order to enable the recipient to plagiarize?) makes it hard to know how to take the passage as evidence of normal practice, as does the fact that the poem indicates (absurdly) that the book has just been copied and that its ink is not yet dry. On sponges, parchment, water-soluble inks, and the erasure of papyrus, see Jocelyn Penny Small, *Wax Tablets of the Mind: Cognitive Studies of Memory and Literacy in Classical Antiquity* (London and New York, 1997), 148–49, 293.

30. Cicero, *Letters to Atticus* 26 = 2.6.1.

31. E.g., at *Pro Sulla* 11, where the phrase is opposed to *Lepido et Volcacio consulibus*, and again at 52, where it ends a long temporal expression, *ea nocte quae consecuta est posterum diem Nonarum Novembrium me consule*.

Chapter 5. The Surface of the Page

The epigraphs to this chapter are drawn from Edgar Allan Poe, *The Complete Works of Edgar Allan Poe*, ed. James A. Harrison (New York, 1965), vol. 2, 226–27; and Jacob Bryant, *A New System, or, An Analysis of Ancient Mythology*, 2nd ed., vol. 3 (London, 1776; repr. New York 1979), 59–61. On Bryant as Poe's source (and on Bryant's "Nubian" one), see Kent Ljungquist, "Poe's Nubian Geographer," *American Literature* 48.1 (1976): 73–75.

1. Michel de Certeau, "Reading as Poaching," in *The Practice of Everyday Life*, trans. Steven F. Rendall (Berkeley, 1984), 174.

2. Now housed in the Galleria Nazionale d'Arte Antica of Palazzo Barberini in Rome. The ups and downs of its attribution to Caravaggio need not concern us here.

3. The vast bibliography can only be sampled here. Ovid, *Metamorphoses* 3.339–512, and the other ancient textual sources, as well as prior scholarship on them, are discussed

by Louise Vinge, *The Narcissus Theme in Western European Literature up to the Early 19th Century* (Lund, 1967), 1-41. A similar survey of the myth in ancient literature and art, with a sophisticated exploration of its themes (and of their post-classical resonance), is offered by Maurizio Bettini and Ezio Pellizer, *Il mito di Narciso: Immagini e racconti dalla Grecia a oggi* (Turin, 2003): 35-215. Narcissus in the ancient visual arts (and in poems which offer *ekphraseis* thereof) is the specific subject of John Elsner, "Naturalism and the Erotics of the Gaze: Intimations of Narcissus," in Natalie Boymel Kampen, *Sexuality in Ancient Art: Near East, Egypt, Greece, and Italy* (Cambridge, 1996): 247-61, where the emphasis is on Narcissus as an emblem for the visually and erotically constituted nexus of self and other and its relationship to art-objects. The fullest treatment of Narcissus as artist is Gianpiero Rosati, *Narciso e Pigmalione: Illusione e spettacolo nelle* Metamorfosi *di Ovidio* (Florence, 1983). In a somewhat similar theoretical vein to Elsner's, though regarding the Ovidian version (placed in a broader context of Roman sexual and philosophical spectatorship), see now Shadi Bartsch's *The Mirror of the Self: Sexuality, Self-Knowledge, and the Gaze in the Early Roman Empire* (Chicago, 2006), 86-94; also Patricia B. Salzman-Mitchell, *A Web of Fantasies: Gaze, Image, and Gender in Ovid's* Metamorphoses (Columbus, Ohio, 2005), 56-59 and 93-95. Also noteworthy is Philip Hardie, "Lucretius and the Delusions of Narcissus," *Materiali e discussioni per l'analisi dei testi classici* 20/21 (1988): 71-89, reprised and expanded in his *Ovid's Poetics of Illusion* (Cambridge, 2002), 143-72, who offers subtle readings of key phrases and passages in Ovid. One of the most provocative accounts of the Ovidian episode remains (despite occasional inexactitude about the Latin) John Brenkman, "Narcissus in the Text," *Georgia Review* 30 (1976): 293-327, who, among other things, recognizes that Narcissus's *imago* is not exactly a picture: "'Iste ego sum'—that articulation also links the voice of the self with its other, the 'image.' What is this *imago* of the voice? Certainly it is not another voice, as was the echo (*imagine vocis*, 385) that Narcissus failed to recognize as the repetition of his own speech. The movement of the lips reflected in the water is the *silent, spatial, visible repetition of the voice*. It is the other of speech. Indeed, grouped around the reflected image is an entire cluster of predicates that have traditionally been assigned to writing" (317).

4. Ovid, *Metamorphoses* 3.407-12 (hereafter cited in text).

5. Seneca, *Thyestes* 635-36. For some, *all* of Seneca is unplayable and was written to be read, not performed; for a recent review of the debate, see A. J. Boyle, *Tragic Seneca: An Essay in the Theatrical Tradition* (London and New York, 1997), 10-11. A modern synthesis (if not a consensus) seems to be emerging by which the tragedies are seen not as texts too readerly to have been played, but as plays which stage (literally or figuratively, thus leaving open the question of performance) acts of reading and response. Thus C. A. J. Littlewood, *Self-Representation and Illusion in Senecan Tragedy* (Oxford, 2004), 172: "Senecan tragedy is written as drama. Whether or not the plays were staged they have the literary form of theatrical events. Representations in the tragedies of theaters and spectators are therefore powerful vehicles of self-consciousness inasmuch as they offer images of the production and reception of specifically dramatic literature. In a similar way as the tragic chorus, traditionally as much spectator as actor, offers a model of audience response so representations of spectacles and spectators are formal devices through which actual readers and spectators are made to reflect upon their response to the dramatic events."

6. On my own mind in much of the following is Freud himself as a crafter of metaphors for the psychic apparatus, from "A Note upon the 'Mystic Writing-Pad,'" in *The Standard Edition of the Complete Psychological Works of Sigmund Freud*, ed. and trans.

James Strachey (London, 1953–74), vol. 19, 227–32, to the fantasy of a Rome whose archeological layers can be seen simultaneously, in "Civilization and Its Discontents," ibid., vol. 21, 70. Each model insists on both surface and depth; especially suggestive is the fact that Freud's "Mystic Writing-Pad" finds its psychological depth in wax, as do the ordinary waxed tablets that we have just seen figured in Ovid (and that we shall again see below, in Seneca).

7. Cf. R. J. Tarrant, ed., *Seneca's* Thyestes (Atlanta, 1985), 184–85.

8. Cf., e.g., Tacitus, *Ann.*, 15.42; Suetonius, *Nero*, 31.1–2. On *descriptiones loci*, see Tarrant, *Seneca's* Thyestes, 183. Any theory of Senecan parody hinges, of course, on the controversial question of the play's date, on which see Tarrant, 10–13 (where a date as late as 60–62 is tentatively preferred).

9. Pierre Grimal, *Les jardins romains*, 3rd ed. (Paris, 1984); see esp. chaps. 5 and 6. See also Nicholas Purcell, "Town in Country and Country in Town," in Elisabeth Blair MacDougall, ed., *Ancient Roman Villa Gardens* (Washington, 1987), 185–203. The Colle Oppio fresco, discovered in 1997 and now generally known as the *Città dipinta* ("Painted City"), still awaits publication; for a brief introduction in English, see Eugenio La Rocca, "The Newly Discovered City Fresco from Trajan's Baths, Rome," *Imago Mundi* 53 (2001): 121–24. Seneca's own gardens are mentioned by Tacitus, *Annals* 14.52 and Juvenal, *Satires* 10.16. On the specific subject of groves, both painted and real, in Roman aristocratic houses, see Bettina Bergmann, "Exploring the Grove: Pastoral Space on Roman Walls," in John Dixon Hunt, ed., *The Pastoral Landscape, Studies in the History of Art* 36 (Washington, 1992), 21–46.

10. Quintilian, *Institutio oratoria* 10.3.17: *Diversum est huic eorum vitium qui primo decurrere per materiam stilo quam velocissimo volunt, et sequentes calorem atque impetum ex tempore scribunt: hanc 'silvam' vocant.* For the real-world distinction between *lucus*, *nemus*, and *silva*, see Servius on Vergil, *Aeneid* 1.310; he calls the last *diffusa et inculta*.

11. Cf., in addition to the Quintilian just cited, Suetonius, *De grammaticis* 24.4.

12. Gellius, *Attic Nights* Pref. 5–6: *Nam quia variam et miscellam et quasi confusaneam doctrinam conquisiverant, eo titulos quoque ad eam sententiam exquisitissimos indiderunt. Namque alii Musarum inscripserunt, alii Silvarum . . .*

13. D. A. Russell, "De imitatione," in David West and Tony Woodman, eds., *Creative Imitation and Latin Literature* (Cambridge, 1979), 1.

14. Seneca, *Moral Epistles* 84.5. The image's post-classical influence was augmented by its reprise by Macrobius, *Saturnalia* 1.Praef.2.

15. Alessandro Schiesaro, *The Passions in Play:* Thyestes *and the Dynamics of Senecan Drama* (Cambridge, 2003), 223; A. J. Boyle, *Tragic Seneca*, 85ff.

16. Vergil, *Aeneid* 7.170–72. Servius, commenting on 170, claims that Vergil is describing the house of Augustus on the Palatine. For more extensive discussion of Seneca's Vergilian intertext, see Tarrant's comments on the passage (*Seneca's* Thyestes, 183ff.). Compare also the grove in the middle of Carthage at *Aeneid* 1.441ff. On other echoes of *Aeneid* 7 in the prologue (and in the "second prologue" in act 2), see Schiesaro, *Passions in Play*, 32–36.

17. Vergil, *Aeneid* 1.165.

18. Schiesaro, *Passions in Play*, 49, who, in the pages that follow, beautifully pursues the relationship between *nefas*, inspiration, and sublimity in the poetic machinations of Atreus. The butcher as poet and playwright is even more grotesquely central to the most famous imitation *of* Seneca's *Thyestes*: Shakespeare's *Titus Andronicus*.

19. Ovid, *Metamorphoses* 3.348, where Narcissus's mother is told that he will live long only *si se non noverit*. Seneca's chorus is probably already invoking the story at *Thyestes* 403, where they remark on the weight of death on one who dies *ignotus sibi*.

20. Ovid, *Metamorphoses* 3.420ff.

21. Seneca, *Thyestes* 997–98.

22. Cf. Schiesaro, *Passions in Play*, 139.

23. Seneca, *Thyestes* 1005–6. Cf. Thyestes' "internal" echo of *adeste* at 1002–3. James Ker has pointed out to me a "pre-echo" of these reflections at line 220: *fas est in illo quidquid in fratre est nefas*.

24. Cf. Schiesaro, *Passions in Play*, 224: "The analysis of intertextuality, especially this particular brand of Senecan self-conscious, metadramatic intertextuality, can fruitfully move towards an evaluation of rhetorical features as they interact with the psychological processes of the reader." Seneca often seems to be aiming for something like the sublime as described by Pseudo-Longinus, *On the Sublime* 7.2–3.

25. *Eiusmodi domum cum absolutam dedicaret, hactenus comprobavit ut se diceret quasi hominem tandem habitare coepisse* (Suetonius, *Life of Nero* 31.2).

26. Ovid, *Metamorphoses* 3.509–10.

27. Gaston Bachelard, *Water and Dreams: An Essay on the Imagination of Matter*, trans. Edith R. Farrell (Dallas, 1983), 22.

28. Ibid., 50.

29. Ibid., 102. Bachelard once before mentions "ink," likewise in connection to Poe (54).

30. Poe, *Complete Works*, vol. 2, 1–15. Jean Ricardou, "'Le Caractère singulier de cette eau,'" *Critique* (1967): 718–33, brilliantly argues that *The Narrative of Arthur Gordon Pym*, with its strange substances and elaborate white/black imagery, offers "un voyage au bout de la page."

31. But if the image alludes to the Ovidian Narcissus, the language is borrowed from Vergil's description of Hell as visited by Orpheus, where he sees the shades *quos circum limus niger et deformis harundo / Cocyti tardaque palus inamabilis unda / alligat et novies Styx interfusa coercet* (*Georgics* 4.478–80; partially reused at *Aeneid* 6.438–39), on which see Michael Putnam, *Virgil's Poem of the Earth: Studies in the Georgics* (Princeton, N.J., 1979), 300. Note here especially the *deformis* which Seneca will transfer from the reeds to the water and, more generally, the sluggishness (*tarda*) and fixity (*alligat, coercet*) by which Vergil is figuring the inescapability of death (and, as Putnam notes, the binding force of law). Ovid twins Narcissus and Orpheus (as we saw in chap. 1); Seneca goes one step farther by linking the Ovidian former to the Vergilian latter.

32. Tarrant, *Seneca's Thyestes*, 187. Brackets in original.

33. See, e.g., Vitruvius, *On Architecture* 8.3.16; Pliny, *Natural History* 30.149; Pausanias, *Description of Greece* 8.18.5–6. These and other ancient sources on the water's properties are collected and discussed by Cristiano Castelletti in the splendidly abundant commentary of his edition of Porphyry, *Sullo Stige* (Milan, 2006), 63–68.

34. Castelletti, Porphyry, *Sullo Stige*, 240–41, reviews the ancient sources.

35. Seneca, *Natural Questions* 3.25.1: *haec . . . aqua summa celeritate corrumpit, nec remedio locus est, quia protinus hausta duratur, nec aliter quam gypsum sub umore constringitur et alligat viscera*.

36. Seneca simultaneously gives form to Hell's stickiness as a trap from which there is no escape: cf. Vergil, *Aeneid* 6.425, where the Styx is an *irremeabilis unda*.

37. Ovid, *Metamorphoses* 3.418-19. *Haerere* is the verb for love's tenacious hold on Echo at 3.395.

38. Jacques Lacan, "The Mirror Stage as Formative of the Function of the I as Revealed in Psychoanalytic Experience," in *Ecrits: A Selection*, trans. Alan Sheridan (New York, 1977), a version of which was first given as a lecture in 1936. On Lacan and Narcissus, see Gayatri Chakravorty Spivak, "Echo," *New Literary History* 24 (1995), 7.

Chapter 6. The Folded Page

1. Munich, Bayerische Staatsbibliothek, Clm 14000, foll. 97v-98r. The pages here described are reproduced in color in Robert G. Calkins, *Illuminated Books of the Middle Ages* (Ithaca, N.Y., 1983), plates 6 and 7. The manuscript was produced in 870 for the Carolingian emperor Charles the Bald.

2. For a more extended vision of the medieval book, see the classic chapters on "The Book as Symbol" in Ernst Robert Curtius, *European Literature and the Latin Middle Ages* (Princeton, N.J., 1990 [1953]), 302-47. "Much more than a sign or a symbol, in certain circumstances the Bible codex embodied the actual presence of the incarnate Christ as the Word of God to dramatic effect," notes Claudia Rapp, "Holy Texts, Holy Men, and Holy Scribes: Aspects of Scriptural Holiness in Late Antiquity," in William E. Klingshirn and Linda Safran, eds., *The Early Christian Book* (Washington, 2007), 199. See also Jesse M. Gellrich, *The Idea of the Book in the Middle Ages: Language Theory, Mythology, and Fiction* (Ithaca, N.Y., 1985).

3. Dhuoda, *Handbook* I 7.25-26. Here and throughout, references are to Dhuoda's text are to *Manuel pour mon fils, Sources Chrétiennes* no. 225 bis, ed. Pierre Riché (Paris, 1991), a revision and expansion of Riché's critical edition and French translation first published in 1975 as no. 225 in the same series. There are two English translations of the *Handbook*: one by Carol Neel, *Handbook for William: A Carolingian Woman's Counsel for Her Son* (Washington, D.C., 1991), and, with a facing Latin text reproduced from Riché, by Marcelle Thiébaux, *Dhuoda, Handbook for Her Warrior Son: Liber Manualis* (Cambridge, 1998). Both offer commentary, and the latter provides a substantial introduction. Dhuoda offers extraordinary difficulties for the translator: her thought is extremely complex, but her grasp of Latin grammar and syntax is often tenuous, in part as the result of a limited—though not negligible—education, in part under heavy influence from whatever vernacular she spoke. On the subject of her Latin, see Bengt Löfstedt, "Zu Dhuodas Liber manualis," *Arctos: Acta Philologica Fennica* 15 (1981): 67-83. In their understandable quest to produce a readable translation, Riché, Neel, and Thiébaux often underrepresent Dhuoda's complexity. For a lively and illuminating introduction to Dhuoda and her *Handbook*, see Peter Dronke, *Women Writers of the Middle Ages* (Cambridge, 1984), 36-54. Additional bibliography on Dhuoda is reviewed by Steven A. Stofferahn, "The Many Faces in Dhuoda's Mirror: The *Liber Manualis* and a Century of Scholarship," *Magistra: A Journal of Women's Spirituality in History* 4:2 (1998): 89-134. Sophisticated work on Dhuoda, however, has lagged behind that on later medieval women writing in the vernacular.

4. Dhuoda, *Handbook*, Praefatio 6-7 (hereafter cited in text).

5. Thiébaux, *Dhuoda, Handbook for Her Warrior Son*, 20.

6. See the introduction to Riché's edition (21), where the relevant bibliography for the fates of Bernard, William, and the younger son is summarized.

7. Neel, *Handbook for William*, translates, "The little book before you . . ."

8. Compare, of course, the poignant use of *iste* by the Ovidian Narcissus, discussed in chap. 1.

9. On the general question of Dhuoda's construction of her own "authority," see M. A. Claussen, "Fathers of Power and Mothers of Authority: Dhuoda and the *Liber manualis*," *French Historical Studies* 19.3 (1996): 785–809.

10. Overlapping vocabulary highlights this slippage: Charles is *dominus* (Praefatio 35), *senior* (III 4.2 and VIII 6.2). Bernard is *dominus* to William (Praefatio 18–9), *senior* (Praefatio 24) to Dhuoda herself, and in relationship to William's uncle Thierry, Bernard is "his *dominus* and our *senior*" (VIII 15.9). *Genitor*, however, is used only of Bernard.

11. The citation is from Matt. 24:19.

12. *Contrariis etenim contraria sunt opponenda medicamina.*

13. For *opere compleri dignissime*, cf. IV 4.52, *opere compleveris digno*; translators have taken *compleri* to be deponent, but a passive meaning, referring to William's own completion by/as (rather than of) the *opus*, gives a finer point. This deliberate ambiguity (to complete the work, i.e., to read it and follow its advice, is to be completed by it, i.e., to become its final product) receives its most complex expression at IV 8.100: *inobliviosus lector factorque operis studearis compleri dignissimo*. In the following sentence, Neel translates *sermo* and *opus* as "lesson" and "task"; Thiébaux, as "words" and "actualization." Both thus undo the pun on the book as *opus*, though they capture Dhuoda's first layer of meaning.

14. Dhuoda's first two biblical quotations (1 Cor. 3:6, 2 Tim. 4:7), as is often the case in the *Handbook*, match no known Latin translation.

15. As the title suggests, a Trinitarian template lurks below the consubstantiability Dhuoda assigns to writer and written. In fact, she will later redefine *manus*, the third and favored member of her book's trinity of names, as "holy work unto the flowing largesse of the Holy Spirit," *manus: hoc opus intellige sanctum in dationem Sancti Spiritus manantem* (IV 4.98–9), with play on *manantem* and *manus*. Dhuoda may be thinking in part of Luke 23:46, where Christ entrusts his spirit "into the hands" of the Father (*Pater in manus tuas commendo spiritum meum*).

16. Riché and others take *genitorem* in the penultimate line to be the object of *erigat*, and *prolis*, therefore, to be genitive: "Qu'il élève jusqu'au ciel le père de ces enfants." But the jarring intrusion of Bernard here seems unlikely; better to understand *prolis* as accusative and to take *genitorem* with *summum*. Peter Godman, *Poetry of the Carolingian Renaissance* (London, 1985), 274–77, represents Dhuoda by this poem, for which he gives an English translation and brief notes; in his introduction he notes the "liturgical model" and "origins in chant" of her verse, calling her a member of a "poetic avant-garde" (53).

17. Dhuoda again uses the word to describe how her book works at X 3.3.

18. Discussion in Riché, *Manuel pour mon fils*, 12–14. See also Claussen, "Fathers of Power and Mothers of Authority," 3, with a list of contemporary *specula* and additional bibliography. On the genre, see Hans Hubert Anton, *Fürstenspiegel und Herrscherethos in der Karolingerzeit*, Bonner Historische Forschungen 32 (Bonn, 1968), with brief notes on Dhuoda's place in the tradition on 86–87. The instructive mirror, however, is also one of many attributes that Dhuoda shares with later female mystics. Margery Kempe, *The Book of Margery Kempe*, ed. Sanford Meech and Hope Allen (London, 1940), 186, describes a vision in which Christ "ordains" her to be a "mirror" for the correction of others. On mirrors in the works of Mechtild of Magdeburg and Marguerite of Oingt

(who titled one of her works *Speculum*), see Caroline Walker Bynum, *The Resurrection of the Body in Western Christianity, 200-1366* (New York, 1995), 334–41. Christian writers who invoke mirrors inevitably have in mind Paul, 1 Cor. 13:12, *videmus nunc per speculum in aenigmate, tunc autem facie ad faciem*, "For now we see through a glass, darkly; but then face to face" (King James Version), and Dhuoda is surely no exception, though she nowhere cites the verse.

19. Dhuoda's "distance" here echoes God's (from humanity) at I 3.2–4, borrowed in turn from the Psalms.

20. *Conscribere* used at, e.g., ibid., Epigram 83; Prologue 30.1–2; I 7.28–29 (where it is paired with Dhuoda's "embrace" of the book itself: *hunc codicellum Manualis a me comprensum, et in tuo nomine conscriptum*); II 1.4, 1.45–6; III 2.16; VI 1.3; X 2.3.

21. Might Dhuoda's *conscribere* thus cast unexpected light of Thucydides' *xungraphein* (chap. 2), suggesting that it too means more than "compile," hinting already at the text's stake in its own material presence?

22. On the medieval persistence of which, see Curtius, *European Literature*, 313–14.

23. *Handbook*, Incipit 43; Epigram 8; Prologue 7–8, 15, 29; Preface 27; I 1.4, 7.24; III 10.2; IV 1.68; X 2.3.

24. At a broader level, Dhuoda, by "directing" her book, shares another verb with the divine director, her authorial counterpart. Cf. Psalm 24 (25):5, *dirige me in veritate tua*, quoted by Dhuoda at II 4.5.

25. An anonymous reader of the present book in manuscript interestingly notes that Dhuoda's absorption by William undoes and reverses birth: she is now part of him.

26. The text is Alcuin (or Pseudo-Alcuin), *De psalmorum usu liber*.

27. Riché, followed by Thiébaux, suggests emending *ipsa* to *ipsam* to make Christ (Amen) welcome Dhouda and not *vice versa*. But the reversal in the text as-is is hardly out of character.

28. Dhuoda actually has foreseen additional readers all along: *illos ad quos hunc libellum ad relegendum ostenderis*, "those to whom you may show this book for rereading" (I 1.10–11).

29. The Latin word *galla* (gall) is not used for bile, properly called *fel* in Latin, and instead refers only to oak or iron gall, used in ink. In Old High German, however, *galla* (etymologically related to Latin *fel*) means "bile." Riché believes that Dhuoda spoke a Germanic language, and at another point in the text her argues for a pun based on a false Latin/German cognate (68, n.4).

30. Isidore, *Etymologiae* 19.31.18.

31. To give one example among countless (and one which Dhuoda might well have known), Prudentius, *Crowns of Martyrdom* 3.135–40, describes the martyr Eulalia, "counting the marks" made on her body by her torturers and crying, "Look, Lord: you are being inscribed on me! What joy to read these letters that record your victories, Christ! The very crimson of my drawn blood speaks your holy name."

32. Isidore, *Etymologiae* 6.14.3: "The nib [of a pen] is divided into a dyad, though unity is conserved its full body; this, I believe, is the product of a mystery which enables Old and New Testament to be signified in its two points, through which is expressed the sacrament of the Word, poured out with the blood of the Passion" (... *acumen in dyade dividitur, in toto corpore unitate servata, credo propter mysterium, ut in duobus apicibus Vetus et Novum Testamentum signaretur, quibus exprimitur Verbi sacramentum sanguine Passionis effusum*). It is difficult not to compare Isidore's mystery of the pen to Derrida's use of

hymen (both membrane and marriage, barrier and union) as a deconstructive emblem, theorized in *La dissémination* (Paris, 1972). Cf. Gayatri Chakravorty Spivak's slight revision of the Derridean hymen (which moves it away from Isidore and closer to our present concerns), "the always folded (therefore never single or simple) space in which the pen writes its dissemination," in her "Translator's Preface" to Jacques Derrida, *Of Grammatology* (Baltimore, Md., 1976), lxvi; see also her review of Derrida's *Glas* (Paris, 1974), "*Glas*-Piece: A *Compte Rendu*," *Diacritics* 7.3 (1977): 6.

33. Isak Dinesen, "The Blank Page," in *Last Tales* (New York, 1957), 99–105. In the story, a convent responsible for weaving linens for a royal house receives, in return, the latter's nuptial bedsheets, stained with the virginal blood of each new princess bride. These the nuns frame and hang in a long corridor, admired by visitors like an gallery of cryptic paintings. But it is one sheet, entirely unmarked, that prompts the deepest reveries.

34. Hélène Cixous, "The Laugh of the Medusa," *Signs* 1.4 (1975): 876.

BIBLIOGRAPHY

All translations from Greek or Latin in this book are the author's own unless otherwise indicated. A specific edition of an ancient or medieval text appears below (usually under the name of its author) only if it has directly been cited in the notes.

Anton, Hans Hubert. *Fürstenspiegel und Herrscherethos in der Karolingerzeit.* Bonner Historische Forschungen 32. Bonn, 1968.

Aratus. *Phaenomena.* Edited and translated by Douglas Kidd. Cambridge, 1997.

Atherton, Catherine. "Lucretius on What Language Is Not." In Dorothea Frede and Brad Inwood, eds., *Language and Learning: Philosophy of Language in the Hellenistic Age, Proceedings of the Ninth Symposium Hellenisticum,* 101-38. Cambridge, 2005.

Bachelard, Gaston. *Water and Dreams: An Essay on the Imagination of Matter.* Translated by Edith R. Farrell. Dallas, Tex., 1983.

Barton, Carlin. *Roman Honor: The Fire in the Bones.* Berkeley, Calif., 2001.

Bartsch, Shadi. *The Mirror of the Self: Sexuality, Self-Knowledge, and the Gaze in the Early Roman Empire.* Chicago, 2006.

Barthes, Roland. "The Death of the Author." *Aspen* 5+6 (1967): n.p.

Baxandall, Michael. *Giotto and the Orators: Humanist Observers of Painting in Italy and the Discovery of Pictorial Composition, 1350-1450.* Oxford, 1971.

Bergmann, Bettina. "Exploring the Grove: Pastoral Space on Roman Walls." In John Dixon Hunt, ed., *The Pastoral Landscape, Studies in the History of Art* 36, 21-46. Washington, D.C., 1992.

Bernstock, Judith E. *Under the Spell of Orpheus: The Persistence of a Myth in Twentieth-Century Art.* Carbondale, Ill., 1991.

Bettini, Maurizio, and Ezio Pellizer. *Il mito di Narciso: Immagini e racconti dalla Grecia a oggi.* Turin, 2003.

Birt, Theodor. *Das antike Buchwesen in seinem Verältniss zur Litteratur.* Berlin, 1882.

Blanchot, Maurice. *The Gaze of Orpheus and Other Literary Essays.* Translated by Geoffrey Hartman. Barrytown, N.Y., 1981.

Bömer, Franz. *P. Ovidius Naso, Metamorphosen: Kommentar*. Vol. 3. Heidelberg, 1976.

Bowra, C. M. "Orpheus and Eurydice." *Classical Quarterly* 2.3/4 (1952): 113–26.

Boyle, A. J. *Tragic Seneca: An Essay in the Theatrical Tradition*. London and New York, 1997.

Brenkman, John. "Narcissus in the Text." *Georgia Review* 30 (1976): 293–327.

Brooks, Peter. *Reading for the Plot: Design and Intention in Narrative*. New York, 1984.

Bryant, Jacob. *A New System, or, An Analysis of Ancient Mythology*. 2nd ed. Vol. 3. London, 1776. Reprint, New York, 1979.

Butler, Shane. "Cicero's *Capita*." *Litterae Caelestes: Rivista annuale internazionale di paleografia, codicologia, diplomatica e storia delle testimonianze scritte* 3 (2009): 9–48.

———. *The Hand of Cicero*. London and New York, 2002.

———. "*Litterae Manent*: Ciceronian Oratory and the Written Word." PhD diss., Columbia University, 2000.

Bynum, Caroline Walker. *The Resurrection of the Body in Western Christianity, 200–1336*. New York, 1995.

Calkins, Robert G. *Illuminated Books of the Middle Ages*. Ithaca, N.Y., 1983.

Camodeca, Giuseppe, ed. *Tabulae Pompeianae Sulpiciorum (TPSulp.): Edizione critica dell'archivio puteolano dei Sulpicii*. Rome, 1999.

Canfora, Luciano. *Tucidide: L'oligarca imperfetto*. Pordenone, 1991.

———. *Vita di Lucrezio*. Palermo, 1993.

Capasso, Mario. *Introduzione alla papirologia*. Bologna, 2005.

Carandini, Andrea, ed. *La leggenda di Roma*. Vol. 1, *Dalla nascita dei gemelli alla fondazione della città*. 2nd ed. Milan, 2006.

Casali, Sergio. "Nisus and Euryalus: Exploiting the Contradictions in Virgil's Doloneia." *Harvard Studies in Classical Philology* 102 (2004): 317–54.

Cavallo, Guglielmo, and Roger Chartier, eds. *A History of Reading in the West*. Translated by Lydia G. Cochrane. Amherst, Mass., 1999.

Cicero. *Cicero's Letters to Atticus*. Edited and translated by D. R. Shackleton Bailey. Vol. 1. Cambridge, 1965.

———. *The Poems of Cicero*. Edited by W. W. Ewbank. London, 1933.

Cixous, Hélène. "Coming to Writing." In *"Coming to Writing" and Other Essays*, translated by Deborah Jensen, 1–58. Cambridge, Mass., 1991.

———. "The Laugh of the Medusa." *Signs* 1.4 (1975): 875–93.

Claussen, M. A. "Fathers of Power and Mothers of Authority: Dhuoda and the *Liber manualis*." *French Historical Studies* 19.3 (1996): 785–809.

Clay, Diskin. *Lucretius and Epicurus*. Ithaca, N.Y., 1983.

Courtney, Edward. *The Fragmentary Latin Poets*. Oxford, 1993.

Crane, Gregory. *The Blinded Eye: Thucydides and the New Written Word*. Lanham, Md., 1996.

Curtius, Ernst Robert. *European Literature and the Latin Middle Ages*. Princeton, N.J., 1990 [1953].

D'Angelo, Paolo. *Ars est celare artem: Da Aristotele a Duchamp*. Macerata, 2005.

de Certeau, Michel. "Reading as Poaching." *The Practice of Everyday Life*. Translated by Steven F. Rendall. Berkeley, Calif., 1984.

de Ghellinck, Joseph. "'Pagina' et 'sacra pagina': Histoire d'un mot et transformation de l'objet primitivement désigné." *Mélanges Auguste Pelzer. Université de Louvain: Recueil de travaux d'histoire et de philologie*. 3rd series. Vol. 26, 23–59. Louvain, 1947.

Dhuoda. *Handbook for Her Warrior Son: Liber Manualis*. Edited and translated by Marcelle Thiébaux. Cambridge, 1998.

———. *Handbook for William: A Carolingian Woman's Counsel for Her Son*. Translated by Carol Neel. Washington, D.C., 1991.

———. *Manuel pour mon fils. Sources Chrétiennes* no. 225 bis. Edited and translated by Pierre Riché. Paris, 1991.

Dinesen, Isak. "The Blank Page." In *Last Tales*, 99–105. New York, 1957.

Doob, Penelope Reed. *The Idea of the Labyrinth from Classical Antiquity through the Middle Ages*. Ithaca, N.Y., 1990.

D(oolittle), H(ilda). *Collected Poems 1912–1944*. Edited by Louis L. Martz. New York, 1983.

Dronke, Peter. *Women Writers of the Middle Ages*. Cambridge, 1984.

Edmunds, Lowell. "Thucydides in the Act of Writing." In Roberto Pretagostini, ed., *Tradizione e innovazione nella cultura greca da Omero all'età ellenistica: Scritti in onore di Bruno Gentili*. Vol. 2, 831–52. Rome, 1993.

Elsner, John. "Naturalism and the Erotics of the Gaze: Intimations of Narcissus." In Natalie Boymel Kampen, *Sexuality in Ancient Art: Near East, Egypt, Greece, and Italy*, 247–61. Cambridge, 1996.

Ernout, A., and A. Meillet. *Dictionnaire etymologique de la langue latine: Histoire des mots*. 4th ed. Paris, 1994.

Fantuzzi, Marco, and Richard L. Hunter. *Tradition and Innovation in Hellenistic Poetry*. Cambridge, 2004.

Farrell, Joseph. *Virgil's Georgics and the Traditions of Ancient Epic: The Art of Allusion in Literary History*. New York, 1991.

Fish, Stanley. *Is There a Text in This Class? The Authority of Interpretive Communities*. Cambridge, Mass., 1980.

Forcellini, Egidio. *Lexicon Totius Latinitatis*. 4th ed. Padova, 1864–1926.

Foucault, Michel. "What Is an Author?" In *Language, Counter-Memory, Practice*, edited and translated by Donald F. Bouchard and Sherry Simon, 113–38. Ithaca, N.Y., 1977. Originally published in the *Bulletin de la Société française de Philosophie* 63.3 (1969): 73–104.

Fowler, Don. "Epic in the Middle of the Wood: *Mise en Abyme* in the Nisus and Euryalus Episode." In Alison Sharrock and Helen Morales, eds., *Intratextuality: Greek and Roman Textual Relations*, 89–113. Oxford, 2000.

———. "Narrate and Describe: The Problem of Ekphrasis." *Journal of Roman Studies* 81 (1991): 25–35.

Fowler, Peta. "Lucretian Conclusions." In Monica R. Gale, ed., *Lucretius*, 199–233. Oxford, 2007. Originally published in D. H. Roberts, F. M. Dunn, and D. P. Fowler, eds., *Classical Closure: Reading the End in Greek and Latin Literature*, 112–38. Princeton, N.J., 1997.

Francis, James A. "Metal Maidens, Achilles' Shield, and Pandora: The Beginnings of 'Ekphrasis.'" *American Journal of Philology* 130 (2009): 1–23.

Fredén, Gustaf. *Orpheus and the Goddess of Nature. Acta Universitatis Gothoburgensis* 64.6. Göteborg, 1958.

Freud, Sigmund. "Civilization and Its Discontents." In *The Standard Edition of the Complete Psychological Works of Sigmund Freud*, edited and translated by James Strachey. Vol. 21, 57–124. London, 1953–74.

———. "A Note upon the 'Mystic Writing-Pad.'" In *The Standard Edition of the Complete Psychological Works of Sigmund Freud*, edited and translated by James Strachey. Vol. 19, 227–32. London, 1953–74.

Friedman, John Block. *Orpheus in the Middle Ages*. Cambridge, Mass., 1970. Reprint, Syracuse, N.Y., 2000.

Gale, Monica R. "Poetry and the Backward Glance in Virgil's *Georgics* and *Aeneid*." *Transactions of the American Philological Association* 133 (2003): 323–52.

Gee, Emma. "Cicero's Astronomy." *Classical Quarterly* 51.2 (2000): 520–36.

Gellrich, Jesse M. *The Idea of the Book in the Middle Ages: Language Theory, Mythology, and Fiction*. Ithaca, N.Y., 1985.

Gillespie, C. M. "The Use of Εἶδος and Ἰδέα in Hippocrates." *Classical Quarterly* 6.3 (1912): 179–203.

Girard, René. "The Plague in Literature and Myth." In *"To Double Business Bound": Essays on Literature, Mimesis, and Anthropology*. Baltimore, Md., 1978.

Godman, Peter. *Poetry of the Carolingian Renaissance*. London, 1985.

Goldberg, Sander. *Epic in Republican Rome*. New York and Oxford, 1995.

Gomme, A. W. *A Historical Commentary on Thucydides*. Vol. 2. Oxford, 1956.

Grafton, Anthony, and Megan Williams. *Christianity and the Transformation of the Book*. Cambridge, Mass., 2006.

Grimal, Pierre. *Les jardins romains*. 3rd ed. Paris, 1984.

Grimm, Jürgen. *Die literarische Darstellung der Pest in der Antike und in der Romania. Frieburger Schriften zur romanischen Philologie* 6. Munich, 1965.

Gurd, Sean. "Cicero and Editorial Revision." *Classical Antiquity* 26.1 (2007): 49–80.

Guthrie, W. K. C. *Orpheus and Greek Religion*. London, 1935.

Hardie, Philip. "Lucretius and the Delusions of Narcissus." *Materiali e discussioni per l'analisi dei testi classici* 20 (1988): 71–89.

———. *Ovid's Poetics of Illusion*. Cambridge, 2002.

Harris, William. "Why Did the Codex Supplant the Book-Roll?" In John Monfasani and Ronald G. Musto, eds., *Renaissance Society and Culture: Essays in Honor of Eugene F. Rice, Jr.* New York, 1991.

Hartog, François. "Herodotus and the Historiographical Operation." Translated by Wayne R. Hayes. *Diacritics* 22.2 (1992): 83–93.

———. "L'oeil de Thucydide et l'histoire 'véritable.'" *Poétique* 49 (1982): 22–30.

Haslam, Michael. "The Physical Media: Tablet, Scroll, Codex." In John Miles Foley, ed., *A Companion to Ancient Epic*, 142–63. Oxford, 2005.

Heath, John. "The Failure of Orpheus." *Transactions of the American Philological Association* 124 (1994): 163–96.

Heurgon, J. "Un exemple peu connu de la Retractatio virgilienne." *Revue des Etudes Latines* 9 (1931): 258–68.

Higgins, Dick. *Pattern Poetry: Guide to an Unknown Literature*. Albany, N.Y., 1987.

Hinds, Stephen. *Allusion and Intertext: Dynamics of Appropriation in Roman Poetry*. Cambridge, 1997.

Holford-Strevens, Leofranc. "*Horror Vacui* in Lucretian Biography." *Leeds International Classical Studies* 1.1 (2002): 1–23.

Holmes, Brooke. "*Daedala Lingua*: Crafted Speech in *De rerum natura*." *American Journal of Philology* 126 (2005): 527–85.

Hooley, D. M. *The Knotted Thong: Structures of Mimesis in Persius.* Ann Arbor, Mich., 1997.

Hornblower, Simon. *A Commentary on Thucydides.* Vol. 1. Oxford, 1991.

———. *Thucydides.* London, 1987.

Hornblower, Simon, and Antony Spawforth. *The Oxford Classical Dictionary.* 3rd rev. ed. Oxford, 2003.

Housman, A. E. "Notes on Persius." *Classical Quarterly* 7 (1913): 12–32.

Hunt, Arthur S., ed. *The Oxyrhynchus Papyri.* Vol. 17. London, 1927.

Huxley, H. H. "Storm and Shipwreck in Roman Literature." *Greece and Rome* 21.63 (1952): 117–24.

Johnson, William A. *Bookrolls and Scribes in Oxyrhynchus.* Toronto, Ont., 2004.

Kallet, Lisa. "The Diseased Body Politic, Athenian Public Finance, and the Massacre at Mykalessos (Thucydides 7.27–29)." *American Journal of Philology* 120 (1999): 223–444.

———. *Money and the Corrosion of Power in Thucydides.* Berkeley, Calif., 2001.

Keilen, Sean. *Vulgar Eloquence: On the Renaissance Invention of English Literature.* New Haven, Conn., 2006.

Kempe, Margery. *The Book of Margery Kempe.* Edited by Sanford Brown Meech and Hope Emily Allen. London, 1940.

Ker, James. "Roman Repraesentatio." *American Journal of Philology* 128.3 (2007): 341–65.

Krieger, Murray. "*Ekphrasis* and the Still Movement of Poetry; or *Laokoön* Revisited." In *Ekphrasis: The Illusion of the Natural Sign*, 263–88. Baltimore, Md., 1992. First published in Frederick P. W. McDowell, ed., *The Poet as Critic*, 3–26. Evanston, Ill., 1967.

———. *Ekphrasis: The Illusion of the Natural Sign.* Baltimore, Md., 1992.

Lacan, Jacques. "The Mirror Stage as Formative of the Function of the I as Revealed in Psychoanalytic Experience." In *Ecrits: A Selection*, translated by Alan Sheridan. New York, 1977.

Lachmann, Karl. *In T. Lucretii Cari De rerum natura libros Commentarius.* Berlin, 1850.

Lalou, Elisabeth, ed. *Les tablettes à écrire de l'Antiquité à l'Epoque Moderne.* Actes du colloque international du Centre National de la Recherche Scientifique, Paris, Institut de France, 10–11 octobre 1990. *Bibliologia* 12. Brepols, 1992.

La Penna, Antonio. "Lettura del nono libro dell'*Eneide.*" In Marcello Gigante, ed., *Lecturae Vergilianae.* Vol. 3, *L'Eneide.* Naples, 1983.

La Rocca, Eugenio. "The Newly Discovered City Fresco from Trajan's Baths, Rome." *Imago Mundi* 53 (2001): 121–24.

Lausberg, Heinrich. *Handbook of Literary Rhetoric: A Foundation for Literary Study.* Translated by Matthew Bliss, Annemiek Jansen, and David E. Orton. Leiden, 1998.

Leach, Eleanor Winsor. *The Rhetoric of Space: Literary and Artistic Representations of Landscape in Republican and Augustan Rome.* Princeton, N.J., 1988.

Lessing, G. E. *Laokoon, oder, Über die Grenzen der Mahlerey und Poesie.* Berlin, 1766.

Litchfield, Henry Wheatland. "Cicero's Judgment on Lucretius." *Harvard Studies in Classical Philology* 24 (1913): 147–59.

Littlewood, C. A. J. *Self-Representation and Illusion in Senecan Tragedy.* Oxford, 2004.

Ljungquist, Kent. "Poe's Nubian Geographer." *American Literature* 48.1 (1976): 73–75.

Lloyd, G. E. R. *In the Grip of Disease: Studies in the Greek Imagination.* Oxford, 2003.

Löfstedt, Bengt. "Zu Dhuodas Liber manualis." *Arctos: Acta Philologica Fennica* 15 (1981): 67–83.

Long, A. A. *Hellenistic Philosophy: Stoics, Epicureans, Sceptics.* 2nd ed. Berkeley, Calif., 1986.

Loraux, Nicole. "Thucydide a écrit la guerre du Péloponnèse." *Metis* 1 (1986): 139–61.

Lowe, E. A. *Codices Latini Antiquiores.* Oxford, 1934–66.

———. "Some Facts about Our Oldest Latin Manuscripts." In *Palaeographical Papers, 1907–1965.* Oxford, 1972. Originally published in *Classical Quarterly* 19 (1925): 197–208.

Lucretius, *De rerum natura libri sex.* Edited by Cyril Bailey. Oxford, 1947.

———. *De rerum natura libri sex.* 4th ed. Edited by H. A. J. Munro. Cambridge, 1893.

Malcovati, Enrica. *Cicerone e la poesia.* Pavia, 1943.

Manieri, Alessandra. *L'immagine poetica nella teoria degli antichi:* Phantasia *ed* enargeia. Pisa, 1998.

Marichal, Robert. "Les tablettes à écrire dans le monde romain." In Elisabeth Lalou, *Les tablettes à écrire de l'Antiquité à l'Epoque Moderne, Bibliologia* 12, 165–85. Brepols, 1992.

Marincola, John. *Authority and Tradition in Ancient Historiography.* Cambridge, 1997.

Marinone, Nino. *Cronologia Ciceroniana.* Rome, 1997.

Marshall, Morrison. "Pericles and the Plague." In E. M. Craik, *"Owls to Athens": Essays on Classical Subjects Presented to Sir Kenneth Dover,* 163–70. Oxford, 1990.

Masson, John. *Lucretius: Epicurean and Poet.* London, 1907.

McCarthy, Kathleen. "*Servitium Amoris: Amor Servitii.*" In Sandra R. Joshel and Sheila Murnaghan, eds., *Women and Slaves in Greco-Roman Culture: Differential Equations,* 174–92. London and New York, 1998.

McGann, Jerome J. *Radiant Textuality: Literature after the World Wide Web.* New York, 2001.

———. *The Textual Condition.* Princeton, N.J., 1991.

Meiggs, Russell. *Trees and Timber in the Ancient Mediterranean World.* Oxford, 1982.

Merrill, William A. "Lucretius and Cicero's Verse." *University of California Publications in Classical Philology* 5.9 (1921): 143–54.

———. "The Metrical Technique of Lucretius and Cicero." *University of California Publications in Classical Philology* 7.10 (1924): 293–307.

Meyboom, P. G. P. *The Nile Mosaic of Palestrina: Early Evidence of Egyptian Religion in Italy.* Leiden, 1995.

Mitchell-Boyask, Robin. *Plague and the Athenian Imagination: Drama, History and the Cult of Asclepius.* Cambridge, 2008.

Montevecchi, Orsolina. *La papirologia.* Rev. ed. Milan, 1988.

Morgan, Thomas E. "Plague or Poetry? Thucydides on the Epidemic at Athens." *Transactions of the American Philological Association* 124 (1994): 197–209.

Müller, Gerhard. "The Conclusions of the Six Books of Lucretius." In Monica R. Gale, ed., *Lucretius,* 234–53. Oxford, 2007.

Nepos, Cornelius. *A Selection, Including the Lives of Cato and Atticus.* Edited by Nicholas Horsfall. Oxford, 1989.

O'Donnell, James. *Avatars of the Word from Papyrus to Cyberspace.* Cambridge, Mass., 1998.

Padel, Ruth. *In and Out of the Mind: Greek Images of the Tragic Self.* Princeton, N.J., 1992.

Page, D. L. "Thucydides' Description of the Great Plague at Athens." *Classical Quarterly* n.s. 3 (1953): 97-119.

Parry, Adam. "The Language of Thucydides' Description of the Plague." *Bulletin of the Institute of Classical Studies* 16 (1969): 106-18.

Parry, Milman. *The Making of Homeric Verse: The Collected Papers of Milman Parry.* Edited by Adam Parry. Oxford, 1971.

Pauly, August Friedrich von, Georg Wissowa et al. *Realencyclopädie der classischen Altertumswissenschaft.* Stuttgart, 1894-1980.

Pennacini, Adriano. "L'arte della parola." In Guglielmo Cavallo, Paolo Fedeli, and Andrea Giardina, eds., *Lo spazio letterario di Roma antica.* Vol. 2, 254-67. Rome, 1989.

Pintaudi, R., and P. J. Sijpesteija, eds. *Tavolette lignee e cerate da varie collezioni.* Florence, 1989.

Persius. *A. Persi Flacci et D. Iuni Iuvenalis Saturae.* Edited by W. V. Clausen. Oxford, 1959.

Poe, Edgar Allan. *The Complete Works of Edgar Allan Poe.* Edited by James A. Harrison. New York, 1965.

Pontanus (Spanmuller), Jacobus. *Symbolarum libri xvii quibus P. Virgilii Maronis Bucolica, Georgica, Aeneis, ex probatissimis auctoribus declarantur, comparantur, illustrantur.* Augsburg, 1599. Reprint, New York, 1976.

Porphyry. *Sullo Stige.* Edited and translated by Cristiano Castelletti. Milan, 2006.

Porter, James I. "The Disgrace of Matter in Ancient Aesthetics." In Ralph Rosen and Ineke Sluiter, eds., *Kakos: Badness and Anti-Values in Classical Antiquity*, 283-314. Leiden, 2008.

———. "Lucretius and the Poetics of Void." In Annick Monet, ed., *Le jardin romain: Epicurisme et poésie à Rome: Mélanges offerts à Mayotte Bollack*, 197-226. Villeneuve d'Ascq, 2003.

Purcell, Nicholas. "Town in Country and Country in Town." In Elisabeth Blair MacDougall, ed., *Ancient Roman Villa Gardens*, 185-203. Washington, D.C., 1987.

Putnam, Michael C. J. *The Poetry of the Aeneid: Four Studies in Imaginative Unity and Design.* Cambridge, Mass., 1965.

———. *Virgil's Poem of the Earth: Studies in the Georgics.* Princeton, N.J., 1979.

Quintilian. *The Orator's Education.* Edited by Donald A. Russell. Cambridge, Mass., 2001.

Rapp, Claudia. "Holy Texts, Holy Men, and Holy Scribes: Aspects of Scriptural Holiness in Late Antiquity." In William E. Klingshirn and Linda Safran, eds., *The Early Christian Book*, 194-222. Washington, D.C., 2007.

Ricardou, Jean. "'Le Caractère singulier de cette eau.'" *Critique* (1967): 718-33. Translated by Frank Towne as "'The Singular Character of the Water.'" *Poe Studies* 9.1 (1976): 1-6.

Richlin, Amy. "Cicero's Head." In James I. Porter, ed., *Constructions of the Classical Body*, 190-211. Ann Arbor, Mich., 1999.

———. *The Garden of Priapus.* Rev. ed. New York, 1992.

Rilke, Rainer Maria. *Sonnets to Orpheus.* Translated by M. D. Herter Norton. New York, 2006.

Roman, L. "A History of Lost Tablets." *Classical Antiquity* 25.2 (2006): 351-88.

Rood, Tim. *Thucydides: Narrative and Explanation.* Oxford, 1998.

Rosati, Gianpiero. *Narciso e Pigmalione: Illusione e spettacolo nelle "Metamorfosi" di Ovidio.* Florence, 1983.

Rosenmeyer, Thomas G. *The Green Cabinet: Theocritus and the European Pastoral Lyric.* Berkeley, Calif., 1969.

Rouse, Richard H., and Mary Rouse. "The Vocabulary of Wax Tablets." In Olga Weijers, ed., *Vocabulaire du livre et de l'écriture au moyen âge: Actes de la table ronde, Paris 24-26 septembre 1987,* 220-30. Brepols, 1989.

Russell, D. A. "De imitatione." In David West and Tony Woodman, eds., *Creative Imitation and Latin Literature,* 1-16. Cambridge, 1979.

Rutherford, R. B. *Homer. Greece and Rome: New Surveys in the Classics* 26. Oxford, 1996.

Salzman-Mitchell, Patricia B. *A Web of Fantasies: Gaze, Image, and Gender in Ovid's Metamorphoses.* Columbus, Ohio, 2005.

Scaliger, J. C. *Poetices libri septem.* Lyon, 1561. Reprint, Stuttgart, 1964.

Schiesaro, Alessandro. *The Passions in Play: "Thyestes" and the Dynamics of Senecan Drama.* Cambridge, 2003.

Sedley, David, *Lucretius and the Transformation of Greek Wisdom.* Cambridge, 1998.

Segal, Charles. *Orpheus: The Myth of the Poet.* Baltimore, Md., 1989.

Seneca. *Thyestes.* Edited by R. J. Tarrant. Atlanta, Ga., 1985.

Shanske, Darien. *Thucydides and the Philosophical Origins of History.* Cambridge, 2006.

Skeat, T. C. "Roll Versus Codex—A New Approach." *Zeitschrift für Papyrologie und Epigraphik* 84 (1990): 297-98.

———. "The Origins of the Christian Codex." *Zeitschrift für Papyrologie und Epigraphik* 102 (1994): 263-68.

Small, Jocelyn Penny. *Wax Tablets of the Mind: Cognitive Studies of Memory and Literacy in Classical Antiquity.* London and New York, 1997.

Solaro, Giuseppe, ed. *Lucrezio: Biografie umanistiche.* Bari, 2000.

Sontag, Susan. *AIDS and Its Metaphors.* New York, 1989.

———. *Illness as Metaphor.* New York, 1978.

Spaeth, John W., Jr. "Cicero the Poet." *Classical Journal* 26.7 (1931): 500-512.

Sparrow, John. *Half-Lines and Repetitions in Virgil.* Oxford, 1931.

Spitzer, Leo. "*Pageant* = Lat. *Pagina.*" *American Journal of Philology* 64.3 (1943): 327-30.

Spivak, Gayatri Chakravorty. "Echo." *New Literary History* 24 (1995): 17-43.

———. "*Glas*-Piece: A *Compte Rendu.*" *Diacritics* 7.3 (1977): 22-43.

Stallybrass, Peter. "Books and Scrolls: Navigating the Bible." In Jennifer Andersen and Elizabeth Sauer, eds., *Books and Readers in Early Modern England,* 42-79. Philadelphia, 2002.

Stein, Gertrude. *Look at Me Now and Here I Am: Writings and Lectures, 1909-45.* Edited by Patricia Meyerowitz. London, 1971.

Stoddard, Roger. "Morphology and the Book from an American Perspective." *Printing History* 9.1 = 17 (1987): 2-14.

Stofferahn, Steven A. "The Many Faces in Dhuoda's Mirror: The *Liber Manualis* and a Century of Scholarship." *Magistra: A Journal of Women's Spirituality in History* 4.2 (1998): 89-134.

Stroud, Helen. *Engendering Inspiration: Visionary Strategies in Rilke, Lawrence, and H. D.* Ann Arbor, Mich., 1995.

Swain, Simon. "Man and Medicine in Thucydides." *Arethusa* 27.3 (1994): 303-27.

Tennyson, Alfred. *The Holy Grail and Other Poems.* Boston, 1870.

Thomas, Richard F. *Reading Virgil and His Texts: Studies in Intertextuality*. Ann Arbor, Mich., 1999.

Thucydides. *La guerra del Peloponneso, Libro II*. Edited and translated by Ugo Fantasia. Pisa, 2003.

———. *The Peloponnesian War, Book II*. Edited by Jeffrey S. Rusten. Cambridge, 1989.

———. *History of the Peloponnesian War*. Translated by Rex Warner. New York, 1972.

Traglia, Antonio. *La lingua di Cicerone poeta*. Bari, 1950.

Turner, Eric G. *The Terms Recto and Verso: The Anatomy of the Papyrus Roll. Papyrologica Bruxellensia* 16.1. Bruxelles, 1978.

Van Hook, Larue. *The Metaphorical Terminology of Greek Rhetoric and Literary Criticism*. Chicago, 1905.

Vasaly, Ann. *Representations: Images of the World in Ciceronian Oratory*. Berkeley, 1993.

Vinge, Louise. *The Narcissus Theme in Western European Literature up to the Early 19th Century*. Lund, 1967.

Virgil. *Aeneid Book IX*. Edited by Philip Hardie. Cambridge, 1994.

Walker, Andrew D. "*Enargeia* and the Spectator in Greek Historiography." *Transactions of the American Philological Association* 123 (1993): 353–77.

Warmington, E. H., ed. and trans. *Remnants of Old Latin*. Cambridge, Mass., 1938.

Webb, Ruth. "*Ekphrasis* Ancient and Modern: The Invention of a Genre." *Word and Image* 15 (1999): 7–18.

———. "Imagination and the Arousal of the Emotions in Greco-Roman Rhetoric." In Susanna Morton Braund and Christopher Gill, eds., *The Passions in Roman Thought and Literature*, 112–27. Cambridge, 1997.

West, David. "Two Plagues: Virgil, Georgics 3.478–566 and Lucretius 6.1090–1286." In David West and Tony Woodman, eds., *Creative Imitation and Latin Literature*, 71–88. Cambridge, 1979.

Wimsatt, William K., and Monroe C. Beardsley. "The Intentional Fallacy." *Sewanee Review* 54 (1946): 468–88. Revised in William K. Wimsatt, *The Verbal Icon: Studies in the Meaning of Poetry*, 3–18. Lexington, Ky., 1954.

Woltjer, J. "Studia Lucretiana." *Mnemosyne* 23 (1895): 221–33, 321–28.

Yates, Frances A. *The Art of Memory*. Chicago, 1966.

Zanker, Graham. "Enargeia in the Ancient Criticism of Poetry." *Rheinisches Museum für Philologie* 124 (1981): 298–311.

———. *Modes of Viewing in Hellenistic Poetry and Art*. Madison, Wis., 2004.

———. "Pictorial Description as a Supplement for Narrative: The Labour of Augeas' Stables in *Heracles Leontophonos*." *American Journal of Philology* 117.3 (1996): 411–23.

———. *Realism in Alexandrian Poetry: A Literature and Its Audience*. London, 1987.

INDEX

INDEX LOCORUM

153

WISCONSIN STUDIES IN CLASSICS

General Editors

William Aylward, Nicholas D. Cahill, and Patricia A. Rosenmeyer

---

E. A. THOMPSON
Romans and Barbarians: The Decline of the Western Empire

H. I. MARROU
A History of Education in Antiquity
Histoire de l'Education dans l'Antiquité, translated by George Lamb

JENNIFER TOLBERT ROBERTS
Accountability in Athenian Government

ERIKA SIMON
Festivals of Attica: An Archaeological Commentary

WARREN G. MOON, editor
Ancient Greek Art and Iconography

G. MICHAEL WOLOCH
Roman Cities: Les villes romaines by Pierre Grimal, translated and edited by
G. Michael Woloch, together with A Descriptive Catalogue of Roman
Cities by G. Michael Woloch

KATHERINE DOHAN MORROW
Greek Footwear and the Dating of Sculpture

JOHN KEVIN NEWMAN
The Classical Epic Tradition

JEANNY VORYS CANBY, EDITH PORADA, BRUNILDE SISMONDO
RIDGWAY, and TAMARA STECH, editors
Ancient Anatolia: Aspects of Change and Cultural Development

PAT GETZ-GENTLE
Personal Styles in Early Cycladic Sculpture

CATULLUS
DAVID MULROY, translator and commentator
The Complete Poetry of Catullus

BRUNILDE SISMONDO RIDGWAY
Hellenistic Sculpture III: The Styles of ca. 100–31 B.C.

ANGELIKI KOSMOPOULOU
The Iconography of Sculptured Statue Bases in the Archaic and Classical Periods

SARA H. LINDHEIM
Mail and Female: Epistolary Narrative and Desire in Ovid's Heroides

GRAHAM ZANKER
Modes of Viewing in Hellenistic Poetry and Art

ALEXANDRA ANN CARPINO
Discs of Splendor: The Relief Mirrors of the Etruscans

TIMOTHY S. JOHNSON
A Symposion of Praise: Horace Returns to Lyric in Odes *IV*

JEAN-RENÉ JANNOT
Religion in Ancient Etruria
Devins, Dieux et Démons: Regards sur la religion de l'Etrurie antique, translated
by Jane K. Whitehead

CATHERINE SCHLEGEL
Satire and the Threat of Speech: Horace's Satires, *Book 1*

CHRISTOPHER A. FARAONE and LAURA K. MCCLURE, editors
Prostitutes and Courtesans in the Ancient World

PLAUTUS
JOHN HENDERSON, translator and commentator
Asinaria: The One about the Asses

PATRICE D. RANKINE
Ulysses in Black: Ralph Ellison, Classicism, and African American Literature

PAUL REHAK
JOHN G. YOUNGER, editor
Imperium and Cosmos: Augustus and the Northern Campus Martius

PATRICIA J. JOHNSON
Ovid before Exile: Art and Punishment in the Metamorphoses

VERED LEV KENAAN
Pandora's Senses: The Feminine Character of the Ancient Text

ERIK GUNDERSON
Nox Philologiae: Aulus Gellius and the Fantasy of the Roman Library

SINCLAIR BELL and HELEN NAGY, editors
New Perspectives on Etruria and Early Rome

BARBARA PAVLOCK
The Image of the Poet in Ovid's Metamorphoses

PAUL CARTLEDGE and FIONA ROSE GREENLAND, editors
Responses to Oliver Stone's Alexander*: Film, History, and Cultural Studies*

AMALIA AVRAMIDOU
*The Codrus Painter: Iconography and Reception of Athenian Vases
in the Age of Pericles*

SHANE BUTLER
The Matter of the Page: Essays in Search of Ancient and Medieval Authors

ALLISON GLAZEBROOK and MADELEINE HENRY, editors
Greek Prostitutes in the Ancient Mediterranean, 800 BCE–200 CE